The Man from U.N.C.L.E. Book

The Man from U.N.C.L.E. Book

The Behind-the-Scenes Story of a Television Classic

Jon Heitland

Special Introduction by Robert Vaughn

ST. MARTIN'S PRESS

New York

Library of Congress Cataloging-in-Publication Data

Heitland, Jon.
The Man from U.N.C.L.E. book.

1. Man from U.N.C.L.E. (Television program)
I. Title.
PN1992.77.M2653H45   1987   791.43'72   87—16279
ISBN 0-312-00052-9 (pbk.)

10 9 8 7 6 5 4 3 2

This book is dedicated
with appreciation
to my late father,
Elwood B. Heitland,
and to my mother,
Neva Heitland

Contents

Contents

Special Introduction by Robert Vaughn

Phone calls take many forms. General communication, requests, orders, gossip, teenage marathons, reminders, chats, etc. And there are the phone calls that change one's life.

In the fall of 1963, I was filming at Camp Pendleton, California, on a segment of Gene Roddenberry's television series, *The Lieutenant.* Roddenberry would later create the enduring *Star Trek* series and films.

Norman Felton of Arena Productions at MGM studio phoned and asked me if, when I returned to the studio that evening, I would be kind enough to pick up a copy of a pilot film script to be shot for NBC, Arena, and MGM. Its working title was *Solo,* and it was to be, as Norman described it, "James Bond on television."

I tooled up to the MGM auto gate around midnight, picked up the script, went on to Gary Lockwood's home (he had the title role in *The Lieutenant),* and proceeded to stay up most of the night, retiring near dawn. I was due in Norman Felton's office at nine A.M. to discuss "Solo," which at that point I had not read.

At each intersection between my home on Mulholland Drive and MGM in Culver City, I read a few pages; I finished the material in time for my meeting with Norman. He explained that the genesis for the project came from his friendship with Ian Fleming, the creator of the James Bond character.

I said I was definitely interested, and he said before he could make a deal with my agent, he would have to get NBC to okay me for the role. This was done, and we commenced shooting the pilot November 20, 1963—two days before my thirty-first birthday and the assassination of President John F. Kennedy.

The show first aired in the fall of 1964 on Tuesday evenings on NBC. The initial critical reaction was a mixed bag, due largely to reviewers' inability to get a fix on the style of escapist fare being served up. Was it action-adventure? Was it spoof? Was it serious? Was it funny? Was it tongue-in-cheek? What was it?

By the end of the year, although it was not making any great dent in the Nielsen ratings, the show was beginning to show up on many newspaper polls as one of the favorite new shows of the season, and David McCallum and I were beginning to be inundated with requests for personal appearances throughout the country. These requests we duly honored, and by the 1965–66 season, the show had become a kind of national craze, with David and myself being treated more like rock stars than television actors in a series.

Airport mobs in America, Asia, England, and Europe awaited us every time we journeyed from Culver City. Fraternities changed meeting nights to avoid missing the show. The usual run of dolls, guns, games, etc. followed. Napoleon and Illya were wanted on every network special, every variety and talk show. Our weekends were spent at parades, carnivals, etc. There were more requests for personal appearances than either of us could possibly accept. Fan letters by the hundreds of thousands came from throughout the world. The Hollywood Foreign Press Association presented its 1966 Golden Globe to *The Man from U.N.C.L.E.*, selected as the favorite television show in the world.

The show gave me the opportunity to meet, work with, respect, and have great affection for two fine actors and gentlemen, David McCallum and our venerable *U.N.C.L.E.* boss, "Mr. Waverly," played by the real class of the show, Leo G. Carroll. It was a wonderful time and I shall treasure each year of *The Man from U.N.C.L.E.* all of my days.

—Robert Vaughn
August 30, 1986

Acknowledgments

Although thank-yous in books are not generally read, these should be because this book is the result of the contributions of a great many people who agreed that it was high time someone wrote a book about *The Man from U.N.C.L.E.* Thus, I would like to thank Jimmy Britton, whose questions showed me the need for this study; Robert McCown of the University of Iowa Library (Norman Felton papers), Gene Gressley of the University of Wyoming Library (Sam Rolfe papers), and Herbert Nusbaum of the MGM legal department (photo releases), for their assistance; to Albert Tonik, for sharing his research on the *U.N.C.L.E.* magazines and books; to Mike Wetherell, the world's foremost expert on the *U.N.C.L.E.* guns; and to Bob Short, for sharing his extensive expertise on the series and giving so generously of his time.

I would also like to thank all of those who submitted to my interviews, the exceptionally creative team that made *The Man from U.N.C.L.E.*: Actors Robert Vaughn, David McCallum, and Noel Harrison; executive producer Norman Felton; developer and producer Sam Rolfe; associate producer George Lehr; supervising producer David Victor; writers Alan Caillou, Harlan Ellison, Les Roberts, Yale Udoff, Dean Hargrove, and Peter Alan Fields; directors Richard Donner and E. Darrell Hallenbeck; director of photography Fred Koenekamp and camera operator Til Gabbani; producer Mort Abrahams; *Girl from U.N.C.L.E.* producer Douglas Benton; guest stars Mary Ann Mobley and Patricia Crowley; publicist Chuck Painter; dialogue coach John Hackett; property masters Arnold Goode and Bob Murdock; film editor Ray Williford; actress Leigh Chapman; director Bill Finnegan; production manager Robin Clark of *Return of the Man from U.N.C.L.E.* and screenwriter Danny Biederman.

Thanks also to Lynda Mendoza and *The McCallum Observer* for biographical information as well as moral support; to Bill Parisho for guest-star and producer bios; to Bruce Button for technical information; to Jim Rondeau for help with obtaining scripts; to George Zivic and Eldon Rahmuller for photographic assistance; to Deanne Keller, Connie Knospe, and Mary Heitland for research assistance; to Jim Mishler for sharing his James Bond and Walther P-38 expertise; to Wolcott Wheeler for literary advice; to Jean Graham and Barb Fister-Litz for creating interview opportunities; to Deb Coyne and Ray of Jerry Ohlinger's Movie Material Store, New York City, for still photos; to Jim Beres for encouragement, and to Bob Miller and Stuart Moore, my editors, for having enough faith in this book to publish it.

Also, thanks to a host of *U.N.C.L.E.* fans for keeping the show alive—Linda Brevelle, Sue Cole, Dave Heilman, Jayna Peters, Jerry Singer, Susan Wyllie, Linda Volp, Joe Bell, Lee Pfeiffer, Ron Plesniarski, Paula Smith, Bob Sidis, Donna Sapp, Art Lozano, Charlene Kirby, Joy Ashenfelder, Darlene Kepner, Lamont Hamilton, Denetia Arellanes, Matt Powers, Stan Warpechowski, Rhonda Bertsch, Sandra Williams, and D. J. Driscoll, along with British *U.N.C.L.E.* fans Jay Felton, Mark Rogers, Bill Sheehan, and Mary Whitta, as well as many others.

And, although they are mentioned last, thanks first and foremost to my wife Mary, my mother, and Jason, Melissa, and Molly—the children from D.A.D.D.Y., who tolerated my absence for a great many weekends and evenings for the benefit of "the book."

—Jon E. Heitland
Iowa Falls, Iowa
January, 1987

Introduction

September 22, 1964, was a Tuesday. On that day, news events typical of that era were giving the decade its image of turmoil, strife, rebellion, and change. In a place called Vietnam, government forces reported that on that day they had "inflicted heavy casualties" on Communist forces invading South Vietnam. The Warren Commission was on the verge of releasing the conclusion that Lee Harvey Oswald had acted alone. In the South, the Heart of Atlanta Hotel was asking the U.S. Supreme Court to overturn the 1964 Civil Rights Act. In Mississippi, a grand jury continued to hear testimony concerning the slaying of three civil rights workers.

Other news that day was more pleasant. Astronaut L. Gordon Cooper received an award for his Mercury space flight the year before. The World's Fair began to wind down in New York, and the Beatles left the city that day to return to England after completing a record-breaking U.S. tour. The song most heard on the radio was "The House of the Rising Sun."

That evening, Americans came home from work to relax. If they decided to go out to a movie, they could choose Dick Van Dyke in *Mary Poppins,* or see Peter Sellers in *Dr. Strangelove.* But, as it was a weeknight, the most favored mode of relaxation among Americans was television. Since September was the start of a new television season, several new shows were debuting. The week before, *Shindig* had appeared, seeking the teen music audience, and *Peyton Place* had gone to a twice-a-week format.

On this Tuesday night, a viewer in the United States turning the dial would come across a strange scene: a man racing through a series of steel corridors as alarms sound and doors slide automatically shut. The man suddenly faces a figure in the shadows, and shoots at him. But the bullets only splinter a sheet of bulletproof glass in front of the man, and as the lights come up, so do the credits for this new show: *The Man from U.N.C.L.E.*

What was this show about? Who was that man behind the splintered glass? What did "U.N.C.L.E." stand for, anyway? It was obvious that this was something new and different for TV.

In the months that followed, that series would be slated for cancellation only thirteen weeks after it debuted. Just five months later, it would create a national fad, the stars getting mobbed at all of their public appearances and receiving more fan mail than Clark Gable ever did. Every national magazine would run an article on this show, hundreds of toy items based on the show would sell like hotcakes, and no less than eight successful movies would be created from the series. But only twenty months later, the same show would suffer such low ratings—due to drastic changes in approach—that it would be canceled in midseason.

The amazing roller-coaster history of *The Man from U.N.C.L.E.* is interesting in several respects. It is interesting to millions of people who recall the show as a thrilling diversion in the turbulent 1960s. It is interesting, also, to students of television and Hollywood, as an example of how a series becomes popular, and how it can quickly become unpopular through unwise decisions. It is interesting as a bit of American culture, as the story of a national fad that rivaled the popularity and the impact of other fads of the sixties, such as the Beatles.

Of course, the story is of interest to the fans of the show as well. Not just those who remember it fondly as part of their teenage or college-age years, although there are literally thousands of them. By *fans,* I refer to those who have made this show their hobby even into adulthood.

When it was on prime-time TV, *The Man from U.N.C.L.E.* was more popular than *Star Trek,* which always hovered on the verge of cancellation. But *U.N.C.L.E.,* after it went off prime-time TV in 1968, was the victim of a smear campaign by various parents' groups. These groups lumped it in with such shows as *The Untouchables* as being too violent, thereby killing syndication rerun values for the series. Yet *U.N.C.L.E.* was extraordinarily nonviolent—after all, how many other heroes of the sixties actually used sleep darts in their guns instead of bullets?

While *Star Trek* was constantly rerun through the 1970s, *U.N.C.L.E.* lay virtually dormant in an MGM vault. While new generations of *Trek* fans emerged who had never seen the show on prime time, the *U.N.C.L.E.* torch was kept ablaze only by hard-core fans such as Bob Short, Bill Mills, Don Simpson, and David McDaniel, who ran *Inner Circle II,* an *U.N.C.L.E.* newsletter for a few years after the show was canceled, or Craig Henderson and Jon Burlingame, who put out *File Forty,* another *U.N.C.L.E.* newsletter, in the early seventies. In the latter half of that decade, a new fan club, "U.N.C.L.E. Headquarters," emerged. This club is run by Sue Cole and is based in Rolling Meadows, Illinois. Although the show remained off the air for years, slowly and inexorably *U.N.C.L.E.* fans from the sixties joined this club and adopted the show as their hobby. These fans are now in their twenties and thirties, with careers and families; their ranks include lawyers, college professors, newspaper editors, and many others with "normal" occupations. Today more than five hundred members hold an annual convention in Chicago to share and celebrate their appreciation of a show that many will tell you, with all seriousness, changed their lives. And their faith is being vindicated: as the cable Christian Broadcast Network (ironically in light of the earlier condemnation of the show as violent) has brought the show back to a national audience, the number of *U.N.C.L.E.* fans is increasing geometrically. Along with a revival movie in 1983, the reruns are reminding the nation that, yes, there once was quality television, with shows that you hated to miss and left you breathless, and here is one of the finest examples. This book is the story of that phenomenal TV series.

Creating a Television Series: From Conception to Prospectus to Pilot

Chapter 1

Norman Felton and Ian Fleming

It cannot be said that one person alone created *The Man from U.N.C.L.E.* television series. It was a team of professionals consisting of directors, actors, writers, and technical crew members who produced the finely polished finished product. But it is clear that, early on, two men—Norman Felton and Sam Rolfe—formulated the central concepts of the series, and fine-tuned the flavor and approach that would guide the show to phenomenal success.

The original idea for *The Man from U.N.C.L.E.* was conceived by Norman Felton. He was born in London, England, on April 29, 1913, the son of John Felton, a lithographer, and Gertrude Anne (Francis) Felton. In 1929, his family emigrated to Cleveland, Ohio. Felton dropped out of school and worked as a truck driver until he happened to meet a man by the name of Clancy Cooper in a tavern in 1936. Cooper had his own amateur theater and, intrigued by Felton's English accent, invited Felton to participate. Felton wrote plays for the amateur group on an old typewriter, with the two-finger method he still uses today. He showed talent, and Cooper encouraged him to try for a Rockefeller Fellowship at the drama department of the University of Iowa in Iowa City, Iowa. Felton traveled by bus to Iowa City, but soon learned that the fellowship was for graduate students only. But he was able to "test out" of many courses and shorten his education, gaining his bachelor's degree in 1940 and his Master's in 1941. Felton also met Aline Stotts while at the university, and they were married on September 15, 1940.

After graduation, Felton worked as a director of community theaters and developed a new type of stage presentation, which he called "arena theater." This caught the attention of the radio industry, and from 1943 to 1948 he directed or produced several radio shows for NBC, including *Author's Playhouse, Guiding Light,* and *The Lucky Strike Theater.* He then moved into the fledgling television industry, and was made director of *Robert Montgomery Presents,* which won him an Emmy in 1952 as well as two Sylvania Awards, a Christopher Award, and the *TV Guide* Gold Medal and Silver Bowl awards. He was later appointed executive producer for CBS West Coast from 1959 to 1960, and produced both *Studio One* and *Playhouse*

90. In 1961, he became director of television films for Metro-Goldwyn-Mayer, and received Emmy nominations for *The Eleventh Hour, The Lieutenant,* and the highly successful *Dr. Kildare* series.

In television, producers are usually juggling at least two tasks: keeping existing programs popular, and scouting for new concepts that can be developed into the hit series of next season. Thus, Norman Felton, in the midst of the popularity of *Dr. Kildare,* began to give consideration to a new series he could present to the television networks. He decided it was time for a wholly new direction in television.

In casting around for inspiration, Felton took note of the Alfred Hitchcock spy features that had been prevalent in the thirties and forties. He noticed that in films like Hitchcock's *The Man Who Knew Too Much, Saboteur,* and *The Thirty-nine Steps,* an innocent person was caught up in a spy plot through a series of happenstances. But undoubtedly the Hitchcock movie that had the most influence on *The Man from U.N.C.L.E.* was MGM's 1959 *North by Northwest.* The lead character, played by Cary Grant, was suave, witty, cool, and quick-thinking. Early in the film, Grant is mistaken for a spy by foreign agents, and spends the remainder of the movie trying to elude them and expose their plot.

The most striking similarity between *North by Northwest* and *The Man from U.N.C.L.E.* is the presence of Leo G. Carroll. In the Hitchcock film, Carroll plays the role of a U.S. intelligence agency head known only as "the Professor," and displays many of the same mannerisms and idiosyncrasies he would later bring to the role of Mr. Waverly on the *U.N.C.L.E.* series, such as wearing suspenders, using eyeglasses when reading, and smoking a pipe.

It can be argued that the Alfred Hitchcock spy films were the direct inspiration for *The Man from U.N.C.L.E.* Robert Vaughn is of the same general appearance type as Cary Grant, and he displays the same cool, smooth mannerisms. Sam Rolfe was later quoted as saying that he had had a "Cary Grant type" in mind when he wrote the prospectus for the series.

Felton recalls that "the very beginning of *The Man from U.N.C.L.E.*, you might say, was when I went to England in 1961 to a meeting of British broadcast executives to try to sell *The Eleventh Hour* to British TV. There was a lady comptroller there, and she asked me why it was that most American TV shows, such as all the Westerns that were on then, all had American heroes that were six-four and strong and husky, when there were other types of people in the world besides that kind of man. I said, 'You've got a point.'"

The woman's comments stuck in Felton's mind. "I got to thinking," he says, "we were selling a lot of things around the world, and maybe we should have a series that is international, and not all big husky people, but maybe people who are smart. So I put that in the back of my mind."

In 1963, Felton recalled these things when it came time to develop a new series idea. He concluded that American TV audiences were tired of doctors, attorneys, psychiatrists, and other professionals, all of which he himself had brought to the screen at one time or another, and that they would welcome a different kind of hero.

Courtesy of the Norman Felton collection.

...arching for the right format for ... series, Felton was eventually ... away from the Hitchcock concept ... ward the spy novels of English ... Ian Fleming. But initially, it was ... of Fleming's James Bond novels ... as considered. Fleming had also ... *Thrilling Cities,* a travel book on ... places to wine and dine around ... ld, based on Fleming's own expe- ... as an intelligence agent in World ... and as a journalist afterward. ... *g Cities* was the direct connection ... *The Man from U.N.C.L.E.* and ... Bond. Felton and Arena Produc- ... ere represented by the Ashley- ... talent agency in October of 1962. Alden Schwimmer, one of the partners of the firm, forwarded a copy of the Fleming book to Ted Ashley. Ashley set up a breakfast meeting at the Beverly Hilton Hotel with Felton and Jack Ball of the J. Walter Thompson advertising agency, who attended on behalf of Ford Motor Company. Ashley suggested that Felton read the Fleming book prior to the meeting and see if it would be an appropriate basis for a television series, which Ford would then sponsor.

Felton read the book, but saw no inspiration for a series. The first James Bond movie had just been released. The James Bond books themselves were known chiefly because President John F. Kennedy had mentioned *From Russia with Love* as one of his ten favorite books. Felton knew nothing more of Ian Fleming or James Bond in October of 1962.

Felton remembers "Driving down to the breakfast meeting the next morning, I thought, I've got to think of something. And I started thinking of this idea of doing something that was adventurous,

and would go to many places like *Thrilling Cities."* At the meeting, Felton told Ashley and Ball that although *Thrilling Cities* was a good travel book, he did not see it as a television series. But Felton had decided to try a mischievous prank on the two men. He looked around the dining suite, then lowered his voice ominously. He asked his companions if they knew who was in the next booth; he said he had heard that the man was an agent who worked for the Secretary General of the United Nations in solving secret international problems. Jack Ball expressed further interest, and Felton extemporaneously made up a detailed story of how the man operated, traveling in disguise and eluding those who pursued him. Felton provided incredible detail, stating that the man was Canadian, that his father was an American electrician at the Hotel Frontenac and his mother was a cook. Felton described the man as slight, witty, and intelligent, having attended Oxford on a Rhodes scholarship. Following college, he had been assigned to undercover intelligence work.

Ball and Ashley soon caught on that Felton was describing his idea for a new series, and both were intrigued. Felton's tongue-in-cheek introduction to his series idea set the tone for the eventual series itself. Ball mentioned Fleming's Bond novels, which seemed to have the same flavor, and suggested that Felton meet Fleming and try to develop a series.

A week later, Ashley made the necessary arrangements and Felton flew to meet with Fleming from October 29 to 31, 1962, in New York, to try and work out a series. Felton found Fleming to be a charming man. Fleming had already been diagnosed as having a heart condition at that point, so much of the time the two men had together was spent walking around Manhattan at night for exercise. Although Felton enjoyed Fleming's reminiscences, he found it difficult to get Fleming to concentrate on the task at hand. Instead, Fleming would talk about his family, his Bond books, anything but the prospective TV series.

As their time together in New York drew to an end, Felton decided that something had to be put on paper for the series. The day before Fleming was to go back to England, Felton went to the New York office of NBC and wrote further character development for the hero and some notes on an initial plot circumstance, working into the night amid the noise of the office cleaning staff. When Felton told Fleming that he had made some notes, Fleming seemed surprised and protested that that was his task. At brunch in Fleming's room on October 30, 1962, the morning he was to leave, Fleming looked Felton's notes over and expressed agreement. Fleming then suggested that the hero be given the name Napoleon Solo.

Fleming then had a surprise for Felton. He produced a series of eleven Western Union handwritten telegram blanks on which he had made his own notes on the proposed series, complaining that there was no stationery in his room, although Felton suspected Fleming just enjoyed the novelty of creating a television series on telegram blanks. The notes contained plot ideas for the series such as drug smuggling in Istanbul, intercepting a gangland murderer in Soho, hijacking a payoff at the Bonanza Hotel in Las Vegas, arms smuggling from East Germany to an African state, etc.

The other pages gave additional detail on Napoleon Solo, the hero. Fleming's Solo was to be a collector of U.S. gold coins and bandanna handkerchiefs, who smoked cigarillos and dressed in dark blue suits with white shirts and black ties. His Solo was "not a superman, but suffers from normal human frailties—hangovers, colds, corns, fibrositis." He did not take pills for these ailments, but instead exercised occasionally, and got plenty of fresh air. He kept proficient at shooting, judo, and boxing, which Fleming suggested would make useful story lead-ins. He ate and drank carefully, made conversations with all kinds of people about their jobs, and had a "gramophone" (and a particular taste in

13400 Maxella Avenue
Marina Del Rey, CA 90292
(310) 306-3213
Fax (310) 306-2904

records) and a book-lined bedroom with a view of the river, where he was often found watching ships go in and out.

Fleming's Napoleon Solo was known to his neighbors as a writer. He never wore a hat, and he owned a pet bird that he talked to, which Fleming felt would be "useful in getting over plot problems." His Solo had served in a Canadian Highland regiment (adopting Felton's original designation of Solo as Canadian) and kept prints of his unit on his wall, along with a display showing the evolution of the Colt revolver. Solo was a bachelor who cooked his own meals in a "rather coppery kitchen" in an apartment kept up by a Scottish, Irish, or German daily woman whom he joked with, a device "useful for eliciting scraps of his background." Fleming's Solo, like his Bond, drove a good souped-up vintage car, possibly a Cord, which Fleming noted was cared for by a friend of his at a neighborhood garage. This Solo had contacts with the FBI and Pinkerton's, as well as with the editor of the *Clarion* and the local librarian with an encyclopedic knowledge, recurring characters who would help him in his assignments. None of these items made it into the series.

Solo displayed stoicism and an "inner citadel of reserve which intrigues women," qualities Fleming felt were perhaps gained from the death of Solo's wife and child in an accident. Solo was to be human, yet slightly superhuman. He would answer to a mysterious "He" at his headquarters. It was also stated that "He" had a secretary whom Solo would flirt with outside the superior's office, a concept that closely resembled the role of Miss Moneypenny in Fleming's Bond novels. The secretary was named April,

and Solo's daily woman would constantly urge him to settle down and marry her. At the top of the first telegram page, Fleming has noted "April Dancer . . . intercom in her office." Thus, Fleming not only coined the name Napoleon Solo but also April Dancer, the name given to the lead character in the *Girl from U.N.C.L.E.* spinoff series much later.

Felton and Fleming came up with additional details of Solo's character and habits, such as his preference for cherry-stone clams and blue polka-dot bow ties. They discussed how their Solo would be hard-hitting, fearless, and imperturbable. The series would be "designed for those who like straightforward action laced with humor, color, and pretty girls." The plots would be filled with "derring-do . . . the stuff of adventure," with the characters "somewhat larger than life, and the stakes as large as the world."

Prior to leaving New York, Fleming slipped out of the hotel to a haberdashery next door and purchased a pair of cufflinks shaped like a pair of Colt .45 handguns—one of the guns used by James Bond, and planned as the gun in the display on Napoleon Solo's apartment wall—and presented them to Felton as a memento of their visit.

After he and Ian Fleming concluded their meeting with a handshake on a Manhattan street at midnight, Norman Felton returned to California and set to work further developing the Solo project. He made notes on the secret organization Solo was to work for, specifying that his office was to be near the United Nations buildings in New York City. He envisioned that Solo's assignments would involve threats to the entire world, not just one country. At about this time the tentative title of the series was *Solo—Cities Around the World.*

In March of 1963, Ian Fleming was in New York again, and the Ashley-Steiner agency began negotiations with Fleming for his continued involvement as advisor to the proposed series, now called *Mr. Solo.* Fleming requested a $25,000-per-production-year consultation fee for script material, format, and direction, including two trips by Fleming each production year to California, where he would be available from two to four weeks. This constituted an exclusive option on Fleming's services; he would do no other television work while the agreement was in force, and he would not sell any of his books to television or let his

Norman Felton, executive producer. *Courtesy of the Norman Felton collection.*

name be used on any other series—an important item, since the James Bond movies were then becoming popular.

Meanwhile, Felton decided he needed someone to develop a prospectus for the series, a detailed outline establishing the characters and the format. He brought in Sam Rolfe, whom Felton considered one of the top producers and writers in television. Rolfe set to work, using almost none of Fleming's original ideas. Rolfe was even reluctant to use the name Napoleon Solo, fearing it would be reduced to "Nappy" (which it was in the second-season episode "The Deadly Toys Affair" and the third-season episode "The Sort-of-Do-It-Yourself-Dreadful Affair"). Felton insisted the name be used "for now."

Felton contacted Fleming by personal letter on June 7, 1963, enclosing a copy of Rolfe's prospectus, pointing out that the idea of Solo working out of a two-room office had been enlarged to a more elaborate organization, as this would offer more story opportunities down the road in what he felt would be a long-running series. Solo was now seen as an American.

Felton also mentioned in his letter the element of an "innocent" person becoming involved in each of the adventures of *Mr. Solo.* This concept, a hallmark of *The Man from U.N.C.L.E.,* had been only superficially discussed by the two men in New York, although Fleming was especially intrigued by the idea, feeling it would separate the series from his Bond stories (which seldom involved everyday people). Felton, recalling the Hitchcock thrillers, felt the innocent's involvement was crucial to audience empathy, providing a vicarious involvement in the action, and remarked to Fleming in his letter how "a young mother living in Dubuque, Iowa, or Epsom Downs, England . . . who has two children to pack off to school in the morning will be visited by Solo. She will be the only one who can assist him on a venture . . . in a few hours . . . she will be swept away from her humdrum surroundings into an adventure that she'll always remember." Those lines later formed the basic plot of the pilot episode script by Sam Rolfe, "The Vulcan Affair."

After mischievously inviting Fleming to submit his comments on Rolfe's prospectus "on the paper margins, on a telegraph blank or a paper towel," Felton set up another meeting with Fleming, this time in England. But trouble began brewing, as word of Fleming's involvement with the new series spread. Since late May 1963, Fleming had been receiving pressure from Albert Broccoli, the producer of the James Bond movies, not to participate further in the *Solo* project. Broccoli and Harry Saltzman had bought the movie rights to all but one of the Bond novels. Eon Productions, the company making the Bond movies, was already suing Fleming over the rights to *Thunderball,* which was co-written by Fleming with Kevin McClory and Jack Whittingham for the screen but later published by Fleming as a novel. In addition, Fleming experienced a heart attack about this time and was not feeling well. Although the *Thunderball* case was settled out of court, Fleming's lawyers advised him to steer clear of the *Solo* project. They felt that since Broccoli had already objected to Fleming's dealings with Felton, further involvement was sure to drag Fleming into a suit by Broccoli against Felton and Arena.

In June 1963, Felton flew to England

Originally, Napoleon Solo was to be the sole star of the series. *Courtesy of the Norman Felton collection.*

to again meet with Fleming. He found Fleming in ill health and unwilling to go along with the series. Fleming was willing to sign over any interest he had in the project, and executed a release to that effect on June 26, 1963. To make the release binding under both English and American common law, Fleming acknowledged being paid the token sum of one pound as consideration for the release, witnessed by his secretary, Miss Griffiths. Fleming gave Felton an autographed copy of his latest book, *On Her Majesty's Secret Service,* and wished him luck with the series.

NBC, which had authorized the series on the strength of Fleming's name, began to have second thoughts. Felton remembers telling the network executives,

"You liked the project at the beginning. One man, Fleming, is not necessary for our project." After seeing Rolfe's prospectus, the network decided to go ahead.

When press references to Fleming's involvement in the series continued in September of 1963, Sir Leslie Farrer, attorney for Fleming and later for his estate, contacted Felton. Gunther Schiff, Arena's attorney, and Felton both assured Farrer that since the series was still in development, no publicity of any kind had gone out that could have contained Fleming's name. Press items mentioning Fleming continued to appear as late as January of 1964, however.

Felton next heard from Eon Productions in February of 1964. Although Fleming's release meant that Felton was free to proceed with the project and use Fleming's names and ideas without fear of legal action from Fleming, it did not eliminate legal action from those Fleming had assigned his rights to. Eon Productions felt that the use of the names *Solo, Napoleon Solo,* and *Mr. Solo* by Arena violated their interests in the *Goldfinger* property, purchased from Fleming along with the other Bond novels, since Solo was the name of a minor villain in that novel. (Fleming had apparently forgotten he had used the name.) Eon also objected to such proposed *Solo* items as the use of a vintage car, felt to be too close to Bond's use of a Bentley, and references to "He" as being too close to Bond's "M."

Felton brought in MGM's legal staff, and they sent Felton to obtain an affidavit from Fleming himself on February 24, 1964. The affidavit pointed out how the *Solo* project differed from James Bond, in terms of the central character, story backgrounds, and the viewpoint and philosophy of both the main character and the series itself. He cited as examples the fact that Rolfe's Solo was American, whereas Bond was English; that Solo worked for a private organization, as opposed to Bond's governmental Secret Service; and that Solo combated threats to the entire world, while Bond was concerned with enemies of Her Majesty's government. Fleming acknowledged that he had read the pilot script by Sam Rolfe and viewed the pilot film as well, and found nothing in either that he felt he had contributed. Fleming died shortly after this.

Eon agreed to forego any suit if the name of the series was changed—one of the reasons why the title became *The Man from U.N.C.L.E.* Rolfe's prospectus had established "U.N.C.L.E." as the name of the international crime-fighting organization Solo worked for, although at this point no one had yet assigned words to the letters. The name Solo could be used in the series itself, but MGM would have to issue a news release disclaiming any involvement by Fleming.

In response to these legal actions, Felton decided in May of 1964 that all scripts would need to be reviewed by the legal department to be sure that no storyline too closely resembled any of the Bond novels. Even as late as July 1965, when the show was a big hit, Felton was advised not to discuss his meetings with Fleming with a writer doing a biography of the English author.

Although Fleming had bowed out of the project and had left behind only the name Napoleon Solo, his influence was still felt. The movie version of *Goldfinger* was one of the top ten money-making films for 1964, the year *The Man from U.N.C.L.E.* premiered. The next Bond film, *Thunderball,* was *the* top money-maker for 1965, the year the *U.N.C.L.E.* series was to catch on with the public. The fad the James Bond movies created gave an impetus to *The Man from U.N.C.L.E.* far beyond anything contributed by Fleming in his meetings with Felton.

Chapter 2

Sam Rolfe and the Pilot

When Ian Fleming dropped out of the *Solo* project, Norman Felton needed someone to develop the pilot script for the proposed series. At first, Felton himself tried to flesh out the character and the series. At one point he changed Solo's first name to Edgar, and had him work for a CIA-type organization where he answered only to the president of the United States; at another point the organization was to be a mystery, with strong suggestions that it was tied to the United Nations. Felton did much to enlarge Fleming's idea, but his responsibilities as executive producer of the series, which required him to put the whole package together and sell it to the network, did not allow him time to write a pilot script and prospectus that would outline the main character and secondary characters.

To write a basic concept for the *Solo* series, Felton drew on the talents of Sam Rolfe. Samuel Harris Rolfe was born in New York City, the son of a bookbinder, on February 18, 1924. He served in the army in World War II, where he was a boxing champion, and later studied engineering at Princeton and advertising at New York University. In 1954, he married his wife Hilda, and in 1955 they had a son, David, and in 1958, a daughter, Elizabeth. He moved to Los Angeles and worked as a dance instructor and as a laborer unloading freight cars. On a whim, he wrote a script for a radio program called *Suspense,* and sold it for the equivalent of two months' regular salary. In 1950, he began writing for such radio shows as *Hollywood Star Playhouse, Sam Spade, Philco Playhouse,* and *Richard Diamond.* He then moved from radio to writing for movies, and his 1952 screenplay for MGM's *The Naked Spur* was nominated for an Academy Award for Best Screenplay. *The McConnell Story* won him *Motion Picture Herald*'s Box Office Champion Award.

But his greatest claim to fame lay in television. Prior to *The Man from U.N.C.L.E.,* Rolfe had created, written, or produced several television series, including three series that Norman Felton was also involved with: *Studio One, The Eleventh Hour,* and *Playhouse 90.* He was also the cocreator and producer of the classic Western series *Have Gun Will Travel,* which was nominated for an Emmy.

When Felton asked Rolfe to write a prospectus for *The Man from U.N.C.L.E.,* Rolfe was producing *The Eleventh Hour* for Arena Productions. Rolfe welcomed the invitation, thinking the series had great promise and would be fun to work on. He himself had proposed a similar series, to be called *The Dragons and St. George,* some years earlier, but was unable to convince the networks to buy it since it did not fall easily into any existing television category.

Rolfe was hired by Arena Productions on May 20, 1963. Felton had a commitment from the network for a series, but no series. Rolfe took his old *St. George* story and used many concepts from it for the *Solo* pilot. He created an organization he named "U.N.C.L.E.," developing it in minute detail, making sure it was an international organization so the series would not be seen as an allegory for the Cold War. He stated at the time that he thought audiences did not want to tune in just to see the same things that scared them on the news earlier in the day. But Rolfe confesses that one reason he chose "U.N.C.L.E." was because it was provocative—it could be mistaken for the United Nations, or Uncle Sam. U.N.C.L.E. was to be opposed by an international criminal group, later called THRUSH, that would be used when the series could not come up with an individual villain of interest.

Rolfe breathed life into the character of Napoleon Solo, in the process giving him a far different character than Fleming had. He also invented the characters of Illya Kuryakin and Mr. Allison, later to become Mr. Waverly, the head of U.N.C.L.E. and Solo's boss. Rolfe threw in thirty story ideas for scripts for the series, some general and some detailed. The completed prospectus ran to over eighty pages.

Felton was pleased with the prospectus, and took it with him to England for his second meeting with Fleming. Felton later told Rolfe that not only did Fleming like it, he even offered to buy some of

Developer and pilot scriptwriter Sam Rolfe. © *1964–1967 Metro-Goldwyn-Mayer, Inc.*

Rolfe's story ideas for his Bond novels.

NBC liked Rolfe's prospectus and continued to back the series even without Fleming. Rolfe was to be listed as the person who "developed" the series as opposed to "created" it. Rolfe agreed to this, although in the long run it deprived him of income from the series since he was not listed as creator. Another potential sore point was that at one point Rolfe's completed prospectus was labeled "Ian Fleming's SOLO," although Rolfe had created the series format from scratch. Regardless of labels, however, it is certain that Sam Rolfe took an original series idea from Norman Felton and a name coined by Ian Fleming and created what came to be *The Man from U.N.C.L.E.*

Both Rolfe's prospectus and his pilot script would undergo changes. The prospectus introduced the audience to U.N.C.L.E. itself first. In the very first paragraph, he points out that although "U.N.C.L.E." is not defined, it does *not* stand for "United Nations Committee for Law and Enforcement," even though he does place the headquarters for the organization a block from the United Nations complex in New York City. Rolfe described a city block made up of a large public parking ramp on the south end, followed by four brownstones and an apartment building on the north side of the block. But these buildings constitute a façade only, as behind the exterior is one large, three-story modern office building that constitutes U.N.C.L.E. headquarters.

Agents for the secret organization entered through one of four hidden entrances. The first, used by clerical staff, was through the public garage where they entered as employees and passed through a hinged wall in the shower room of the locker area. Two of the other entrances were not described in the original prospectus, but were later described as a secret underground tunnel to the river and a nightspot called the Mask Club.

Rolfe spent the most time detailing the entrance used by enforcement agents, and this eventually became the only one seen on the series. Enforcement agents like Napoleon Solo entered headquarters through a tailor shop at the base of the first brownstone. In the original prospectus, the tailor's name was Giovanni; it was later changed to Del Floria. He was described as a sixty-year-old immigrant with a sour disposition. Solo would enter the below-street-level shop and enter a dressing cubicle, whereupon Del Floria would activate a button under his presser allowing the agent to turn a clothes hook in the cubicle. The rear wall would then swing in to reveal a stainless-steel reception area for the headquarters.

Rolfe described the reception area in detail also, since it would eventually play an important role in his pilot script. The receptionist watched a close-circuit TV screen on her desk, which monitored all visitors to the tailor shop by a camera hidden in a normal-looking TV set next to the tailor's press. If she recognized the person entering, she would affix a badge to his lapel that would allow him to pass through the building without setting off the security alarms. A chemical on her fingers was necessary to pass the sensors; this was an important part of the pilot.

Rolfe also wrote an opening sequence for the pilot episode designed to set the tone of the series in the first few minutes and also introduce the audience to Napoleon Solo and U.N.C.L.E. A peddler enters the tailor shop and lays his coat over the TV set. He brings out of the box he was carrying a toy robot, which is designed to walk and throw small plastic balls in the air. Unable to sell the toy to the tailor, the man exits but leaves a robot behind. When Giovanni (Del Floria) goes to remove the coat that is blocking the hidden camera in his TV set, the robot fires a glass ball at him that releases a knockout gas. (In the final version, the robot aspect was removed. It was later used in "The Double Affair" instead.)

The peddler reenters with five other

men, and they proceed to enter U.N.C.L.E. headquarters through the changing booth, where they surprise the receptionist and knock her out also. The leader of the group grabs triangular badges and distributes them. They pass along the steel-lined corridors until the sensors detect that a chemical from the receptionist's fingers is not on the badges. A two-tone gong alarm sounds, and steel doors start to slide shut along the corridors. A Nigerian and a Japanese agent capture all but the leader and an accomplice, who slip into an elevator. The leader is then confronted by a man—Solo. He fires several shots, but the bullets only splinter a bulletproof shield. Solo steps out and shoots the THRUSH agent.

As "an armed Slavic man" (the first reference to the character that would become Illya Kuryakin) joins him, Solo is chastised by "a fifty-five-year-old pedantic-looking man," Mr. Allison, his boss, for killing the leader instead of keeping him alive for questioning. The older man acknowledges that the intruders were trying to kill him, and that they must have had quite a bit of information on U.N.C.L.E.'s defenses in order to get as far as they did. Solo and his boss realize that they must have gotten their information from an inside informer from THRUSH. Since the intruders knew about the tailor shop entrance but did not know of the chemical on the badges, the U.N.C.L.E. agents are able to deduce which section the traitor is in. The surviving intruders later die from poison capsules they had taken before the raid,

Del Floria's tailor shop "somewhere in the east 40s"—the secret entrance to U.N.C.L.E. headquarters, New York. *Courtesy of the Norman Felton collection.*

15

designed to kill them whether they succeeded or failed.

The badge security system that played such an important role in this sequence was fully developed by Rolfe. For example, a red badge allowed access only to the ground floor, containing routine personnel and equipment. A blue badge, changed to a yellow badge in the rewrite, permitted entry to the second floor as well, where the communications and code devices were located. A white badge allowed entry to all three floors; on the third floor were the armory, interrogation rooms, offices of the Enforcement agents, and offices of Policy and Operations.

These referred to the top two sections of an elaborate organizational scheme Rolfe provided for U.N.C.L.E. He divided the personnel into six sections, each assigned a Roman numeral and each divided into two "departments" with overlapping jurisdiction. These consisted of: Section I, Policy and Operation; Section II, Operations and Enforcement; Section III, Enforcement and Intelligence; Section IV, Intelligence and Communications; Section V, Communications and Security; and Section VI, Security and Personnel. Rolfe assigned Solo to Section II.

After detailing the organizational structure of U.N.C.L.E. and its novel headquarters, Rolfe set to fleshing out Napoleon Solo, describing him as a tall, dark man, athletic and easygoing. Solo had been a member of the Royal Canadian Navy, where he had served as the commander of a corvette, and so Rolfe, like Fleming, gave him a small apartment overlooking the East River decorated with nautical mementos. Rolfe also gave Solo a thirty-foot sloop of his own

to sail, as well as hobbies of scuba diving and downhill skiing. But he added that when not working or enjoying these pursuits, Solo exhibited a lazy streak.

He described Solo as a bachelor but definitely interested in women. Rolfe picked up Fleming's idea of a tragedy in Solo's background, stating that he had been married at nineteen and his wife had died in an automobile accident a year later. Solo was changed to American instead of Canadian. Rolfe's Solo had served in Korea and later attended a University where he majored in philosophy, minored in languages, abstained from a fraternity, and played on the lacrosse and swim teams. Solo's neighbors thought he was accident-prone since he often returned from his trips injured.

Along with Solo, Rolfe suggested some recurring characters for the series as well. The head of U.N.C.L.E., referred to in the original break-in sequence as "the pedantic-looking man," was to be Mr. Allison, no first name given. Mr. Allison was described as one of the five men of differing nationalities who made up Section I, Policy and Operations. Allison occupied the only office in U.N.C.L.E. headquarters with a window, which provided a view of the UN. Rolfe added a note of mystery, suggesting that a fifth entrance to the complex existed, since no one knew how Allison entered the building. This entrance was shown later in "The Mad, *Mad* Tea Party Affair." Allison was described as being in his fifties, a professorial type with little or no sense of humor.

To establish an international flavor, Rolfe also suggested in his second prospectus that a Nigerian agent and a Japanese agent be developed for the series, and he gave Solo a partner, whom he designated a Russian and gave the name of Illya Nickovetch Kuryakin. Illya was to be of equal rank with Solo, and an aid to him in times of trouble. But unlike Solo, Illya was to be a loner, quiet in manner and totally dedicated to the job. The fact that Illya was to be Russian undoubtedly helped Rolfe's concept of U.N.C.L.E. as an international organization that had no Cold War philosophical differences to contend with. Illya was seen as living in a small apartment, where he kept his clothes but nothing else tidy and where he secreted a collection of jazz records under his bed.

Rolfe envisioned a secretary for Mr. Allison. Miss Marsidan was to be fat and fiftyish, possessing a photographic memory, the ability to speak eleven languages, and a genuine motherly concern for her two favorite agents, Solo and Kuryakin. She would constantly urge Solo to settle down and get married.

Rolfe also provided for a female U.N.C.L.E. agent. Doris Franklyn, who in one draft is named Mary Smith, was to be an agent whose alternative occupation was as a starving actress in Greenwich Village. She was to speak several languages and in one version would be employed by Berlitz school of languages. She longed to be on Broadway, and used her talents of mimicry and impersonation in her role as an agent. This character was later dropped from the prospectus, as was Miss Marsidan.

Rolfe decided that since U.N.C.L.E. was going to be such an elaborate organization, it needed an elaborate and sophisticated opponent. He saw U.N.C.L.E. being called in by countries when they were unable to handle situations on their own, as the UN is called upon on many occasions. For examples,

he cited an attempt by a nation to break up an alliance by causing a foreign missile to "accidentally" fire; a deadly germ bacilli becoming lost; and also more conventional types of international crime such as smuggling, narcotics, and assassination. But Rolfe also realized that U.N.C.L.E. could not encounter individual villains of such scope each week without straining credibility. He therefore created a sort of international Mafia whose resources and power would be a match for, and sometimes more than a match for, U.N.C.L.E. In Rolfe's original conception, the organization was headed by an individual referred to only as Thrush, presumed to be a male individual but, since no one actually ever saw him, possibly by a woman or even a committee. Thrush would operate for its own profit or power, or hire itself out to any nation. Thrush later evolved into THRUSH, and was clearly an organization headed by a committee.

But Rolfe also kept in mind Felton's basic concept for the series—the involvement of an ordinary person in these adventures, to provide a vicarious experience for the viewer. He therefore set forth a series of one-paragraph story ideas for these "innocents"—a teacher on vacation who visits her brother's grave in Italy and runs into Solo; a honeymooning couple on a pleasure cruise whose ship disappears in the Sargasso Sea; a Siberian farmer who orders a new tractor and finds instead a moon-walking craft diverted there by THRUSH; and so on.

Rolfe envisioned most *Solo* stories starting with an interest-provoking event at a location somewhere in the world, followed by a scene at headquarters where Solo would get his assignment and go off to solve the problem. The headquarters would serve only as a springboard for the later action and as a means of establishing information crucial to the plot.

For the rewrite of the prospectus, Rolfe also provided several two- and three-page plot synopses, which later were used as "The Bow Wow Affair," "The King of Knaves Affair," "The Iowa Scuba Affair," and "The Mad, *Mad* Tea Party Affair." One of the more fully developed stories, "The Cold, Cold Affair," was never produced.

MGM was committed to finance one pilot for Arena Productions, Felton's company, per year. In 1961, Arena had created *Dr. Kildare*; in 1962, *The Eleventh Hour*; and in 1963, *The Lieutenant*. *Solo* was designated as the pilot for the 1964 television season. NBC committed itself to considering the pilot and the series on July 25, 1963. On July 16, 1963, a profit-splitting agreement was reached, giving one-third to MGM, one-third to NBC, and one-third to Arena.

On August 7, 1963, Rolfe signed an agreement with Arena to also develop the pilot script for the series. Although Norman Felton preferred a two-hour pilot, Ross McDonald of NBC informed Felton on September 24, 1963, that the pilot would be one hour only. Felton at that point began to formulate ideas for two-part episodes for the series itself.

Rolfe had actually begun work on the pilot script in April 1963. In a memo dated July 16, 1963, Felton informed Rolfe of what he wanted in the pilot script, stating that the first episode should not only introduce Solo, but show as many aspects of his life as possible. In addition, although only a portion of U.N.C.L.E. headquarters would be fea-

tured, the entire headquarters should be established at least briefly. Solo's boss should be introduced, but other secondary characters could be developed later. Also, the story should be indicative of the series itself so viewers could decide whether they would tune in again. He suggested this be done with a story that would immediately grab the audience's attention and hold it throughout.

Felton also reminded Rolfe that the basic premise of the series—involvement of an ordinary person—had to be established in the first episode. Felton specifically suggested the use of a young married woman with a couple of children, who "lived a normal humdrum life." Solo would involve her in a "glamorous situation fraught with danger, and then return her to her home at the conclusion of the story." Felton recommended the use of glamorous women in the script, and suggested that Solo make an appearance in evening clothes. All these elements were used in Rolfe's script.

Felton stressed two important additional points. First, that the episode have a teaser and three acts, with Solo appearing at the close of the teaser in such a way "that he can come on in a strong fashion." Second, U.N.C.L.E. must be portrayed as an international organization, but at the same time be kept cloaked in mystery. Felton suggested that both these aims could be accomplished by using the break-in sequence Rolfe had already written as the teaser.

Felton suggested that additional information on the headquarters could be established by showing a diagram of headquarters, which had been prepared for a presentation to the network to help sell the series. He also recommended a line by Solo's boss commenting that the intruders had used the most difficult entrance, through Del Floria's, to establish that there were other entrances. Both of these details did appear in the final version.

Rolfe first compiled a fifty-page synopsis of the story in June 1963. The teaser—the portion of the story designed to catch the audience's interest so that they would watch the full program—basically adopted the headquarters break-in sequence from the prospectus, with only a few changes. The story itself incorporated all the elements requested by Felton. An innocent housewife and mother, Elaine May Donaldson, is the only person who can help Solo get near a THRUSH official, Andrew Vulcan, who plans to assassinate a visiting African premier. Solo gets Elaine to pose as a rich widow, who "accidentally" reunites with Vulcan. She eventually takes a tour of Vulcan's chemical plant, which Solo infiltrates. Solo discovers that a reactor at the plant is set to explode during a tour by the premier the next day. Solo is discovered, and after a wild chase through the plant he and Elaine are captured by the premier, who, they learn, is not the target of the assassination plan but a part of it. The premier is in the employ of THRUSH, and the explosion will kill his two top ministers, allowing him to turn the country over to THRUSH. Solo and Elaine are left to die chained to a steam pipe. Solo works his way free, and escapes in time to warn the visiting dignitaries. The reactor explodes, killing Vulcan and the premier.

Rolfe's original script ran 101 pages, and was completed on September 16, 1963. This was later shortened to an 86-page script by October 11, 1963, and revised again on October 29, 1963. Titled "The Vulcan Files" in June 1963, it was changed to "The Vulcan Affair" in October 1963. The word *Affair* would be used for every episode of the series. The script had undergone three drafts, with the first two drafts being revised once each. By November 11, 1963, a final revised shooting script was done—just nine days before shooting was to begin.

On February 10, 1964 Rolfe signed a contract with Arena to serve as producer for the first season of the series. On February 20, 1964, he signed an agreement to write additional scenes for his "Vulcan Affair" pilot script so that a feature-length film could be made from it for theater distribution. And on March 20, 1964, MGM Studio head Robert M. Weitman issued a news release that Rolfe had been hired to produce the new hour-long adventure series, formerly known as *Solo* but now titled *U.N.C.L.E.*

Chapter 3

Casting and Filming the Pilot

After the pilot script was completed by Rolfe, Felton set to work on setting up the production of the pilot itself. His goal was to have a final print, or film copy, of the pilot available for the network by January 10, 1964. Felton contacted Don Medford, a veteran director who had worked on such series as *The Twilight Zone, The Dick Powell Show, Alfred Hitchcock Presents, Wagon Train, Playhouse 90, General Electric Theater, Climax,* and *Suspicion.* He had worked with Felton before on *Dr. Kildare* and *The Eleventh Hour.* Although "The Vulcan Affair" would be Medford's only involvement with the series, he is given credit for the fine production values of the pilot.

Since Rolfe was in England at the time, Norman Felton produced the pilot himself. The biggest problem remaining, since Felton now had a producer, director, and a script, was choosing a cast. The guest stars, who would only appear in the pilot, presented less of a problem than the continuing characters. Since Felton's basic premise for the series was the involvement of an innocent person, he wanted the first "innocent" to convey the flavor of the series to come. Felton chose Patricia Crowley to play the role of the housewife in "The Vulcan Affair."

Patricia Crowley had already appeared in several films by 1963, and had guest-starred on television in *The Twilight Zone, The Fugitive,* and *Bonanza.* She had also appeared in the Norman Felton productions, *Dr. Kildare, The Eleventh Hour,* and, more importantly, *The Lieutenant,* where she had become friends with Robert Vaughn.

For the villains in the pilot, Felton turned to two accomplished actors. For the part of Andrew Vulcan, the THRUSH industrialist, Felton hired Fritz Weaver. A tall, serious-looking actor, Weaver had appeared on Broadway and on television. Like Crowley, he too had previously guest-starred in Felton productions, such as *Dr. Kildare.* Well respected by his peers, he made a perfect cold-blooded villain for the first episode. Patricia Crowley shared that respect: "I adored him. He's just such a good actor and a delightful man. I was very impressed with him on this show."

For the part of Premier Ashumen, Felton chose William Marshall. His perfect diction made him a logical choice for the modern leader of an emerging nation.

The camera crew dons protective clothing during a fiery scene from the filming of the pilot. © 1964–1967 Metro-Goldwyn-Mayer, Inc.

Unlike Crowley and Weaver, who would not appear on the series again, Marshall was brought back as a guest star later on.

Once the three main guest stars were cast, several secondary guest roles were filled. Soumarin and Nobuk, the two aides to Ashumen, were played by Ivan Dixon and Rupert Crosse, who would also guest-star again on the series.

The role of the head of U.N.C.L.E. was given to Will Kuluva. For television, Kuluva had appeared in *The Defenders, The Fugitive, Bonanza, Alfred Hitchcock Presents,* and *Ben Casey.* Kuluva was to play a rather gruff, very serious Mr. Allison, Solo's boss.

Of course, the biggest task lay in casting the lead role of Napoleon Solo. Felton had considered Harry Guardino, a good friend of his, for the role. Robert Brown was also reported to have been considered at one time. Felton recalls, "I was looking for someone who would give the character a certain visual sense of sophistication, which I thought Robert Culp had, and which, later, I thought Robert Vaughn had." Felton decided to offer the role to Robert Culp, but Culp was committed to another project.

Felton continued his search for a Napoleon Solo, and eventually offered the role to Robert Vaughn, who was costarring with Gary Lockwood in another Felton series at the time. He says, "One day I was pondering over several people for the role, and I had a call from Gene Roddenberry, who was down in San Diego at the time at Camp Pendleton shooting *The Lieutenant*. And when I hung up the phone after settling the problem he had called about, I thought to myself, 'Robert Vaughn! Why not?' So I got in touch with him, since *The Lieutenant* was not going to be renewed, and asked him to stop by MGM when he got back that night and pick up a script from the night watchman and read it right away and then talk to me about it. So he did come up that night, late, and

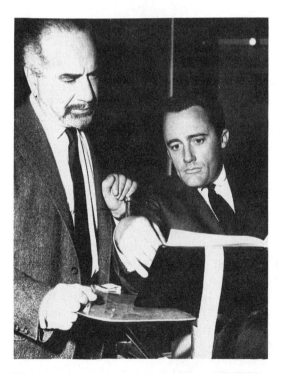

The original head of U.N.C.L.E., Will Kuluva, studies the pilot script with Robert Vaughn. *Courtesy of the Norman Felton collection.*

picked it up and we talked and he got the role. That's how it occurred."

Robert Francis Vaughn was born at Charity Hospital in New York City on November 22, 1932. His father, Gerald Walter Vaughn, was a radio actor who performed in such broadcasts as *Gangbusters* and *Crime Doctor*. His mother, Marcella Gaudell Vaughn, was a stage actress, with several appearances on Broadway. Robert was an only child. Six months after his birth they were divorced and Robert was sent to live with his maternal grandparents in Minneapolis, Minnesota, as his mother's occupation as an actress could not accommodate raising the youngster.

At the age of twelve, he traveled with "Sweet's Famous Players," an Iowa tent show, for the summer. He made his radio acting debut as Billy on the *Jack Armstrong, All American Boy* radio show. He appeared in various theatrical productions during high school, and also participated in basketball and track. During his seventeenth year, he suffered the loss of his father, stepfather, and both grandparents.

After graduating from high school in 1950, he decided to attend the University of Minnesota and majored in journalism, where he covered sports for the *Minneapolis Star-Journal,* and was an A student. He continued his theatrical appearances, appearing in his favorite role as Shakespeare's Hamlet. In 1951, he won the Philip Morris Intercollegiate Acting Contest, and decided to give up journalism and devote himself to acting.

He moved to Los Angeles. Shortly after this his mother passed away. In 1952, he enrolled in Los Angeles City College, then transferred to Los Angeles State College. There he appeared in var-

Robert Vaughn. *Courtesy of the Norman Felton collection.*

alcoholic earned him a nomination for an Oscar as best supporting actor. In 1960, he completed his master's degree from the University of Southern California, and played one of the title roles in the classic Western, *The Magnificent Seven.* But most of his time was spent as a guest star in various television dramas. From 1956 to 1963, he appeared in over 250 guest-starring roles, on such shows as *The Millionaire, Father Knows Best, Tales of Wells Fargo, Wagon Train, The Rifleman, Cheyenne, Thriller,* and *Bonanza.* In 1962, he appeared in the Felton series *The Eleventh Hour.*

In 1963 he received his first major television role in MGM-TV's *The Lieutenant.* Vaughn took the role with the specific purpose of making the transition from guest-starring actor to costarring actor. Vaughn played Captain Ram-

ious stage productions, including *Mister Roberts.* In the summer of 1953, he was the resident director and leading man in the Albuquerque, New Mexico, summer theater. He performed his first leading role on network television while still in college, appearing on *Medic.* After winning the Director's Award for *View from the Bridge,* he graduated with a degree in theater in 1956. He then signed a contract for a film, but was drafted into the army instead.

Upon his discharge in 1957, he started his first film, *No Time to Be Young.* He also appeared in *Hell's Crossroads, Teenage Caveman* and *Unwed Mother.* In 1959 he appeared in *Good Day for a Hanging,* and in *The Young Philadelphians* with Paul Newman. It was in this film that his role as a young, one-armed

© 1964–1967 Metro-Goldwyn-Mayer, Inc.

bridge in the NBC series based on the peacetime Marine Corps, which starred Gary Lockwood, who would later marry Stefanie Powers, the Girl from U.N.C.L.E. The series was created by Gene Roddenberry, who went on to create *Star Trek.*

Vaughn asked Felton years later what it was that prompted him as the choice for the Solo role: "I asked Norman why he had thought of me in this role, which was basically tongue-in-cheek and quite humorous, a romantic figure. I had not played that kind of role very often on television, and certainly not on *The Lieutenant.* He said he liked the things I used to say on the end of takes, when they said 'cut.' I would generally say something semi-humorous."

After Vaughn indicated his interest, Felton talked to NBC and got the network's approval. Felton offered him the role the next day.

Only one role remained for Norman Felton to cast for the pilot episode, that of Solo's fellow agent, Illya Kuryakin. This role was almost a throwaway in Rolfe's pilot script, at first only referred to as "the Slav" since his function as a Russian assistant to Solo was to provide an international flavor to the series and at the same time make a statement that the Cold War of the real world had nothing to do with the series. He was not even given a name until later.

Not much thought or concern went into who was to play the role of Solo's occasional partner, since no one dreamed at this point how important the role would become. Illya was to be a seldom-seen Tonto to Solo's Lone Ranger, a sometime Dr. Watson to Solo's Sherlock Holmes.

Felton at one point gave thought to casting Martin Landau in the role. Although he would later play a guest villain in the series, he was not seriously considered for the role of Illya for long.

Eventually, the role was assigned to a young actor who was virtually unknown in America at the time, but who would in a little more than a year become the proverbial household word—David McCallum.

David McCallum was born on September 19, 1933, in Glasgow, Scotland. Unlike Vaughn, he was not born into a theatrical family but a musical one. His father, David McCallum, Sr., was a concertmaster violinist and played for the Royal Philharmonic Orchestra, the London Philharmonic Orchestra, Sir Thomas Beecham's Symphony Orchestra, and the Scottish National Orchestra. His mother, Dorothy Dorman, would later become a concert cellist for the London Philharmonic Orchestra. She met David McCallum, Sr., while the two of them were playing in the same orchestra pit for a silent movie house.

The McCallums moved to London at the start of World War II. After two brushes with death from German bombs, young David was sent with older brother Iain to live with relatives in the country. At age four he began receiving violin and piano lessons. He gradually mastered the oboe and French horn as well. His parents then enrolled him in the Royal Academy of Music. But at age ten, he became involved in various children's radio programs in London, and by 1946 had his first professional appearance on a BBC radio repertory company. At the age of fourteen, he took work at a Glasgow theater as an electrician's helper.

He did not neglect his education. He

attended the University College School in Hampstead, London, and eventually enrolled in 1949 in the Royal Academy of Dramatic Arts in London. In 1950, he made his movie debut at age seventeen in *Prelude to Fame*. But, like Robert Vaughn's, his movie career was interrupted early on by military service. For ten months, David McCallum served as a lieutenant in the Royal West African Frontier Force in Ghana.

After his discharge in 1953, he again returned to the English stage, appearing in various plays. In 1956 his talents earned him the notice of the J. Arthur Rank talent organization, which signed him to a film contract at the age of twenty-four. In that same year he appeared in *Dangerous Years,* and then in 1957 came the first film in which he played a major role, *The Secret Place.*

It was also in 1956 that he changed his hairstyle to the long blond cut that would later catch so much notice in his *U.N.C.L.E.* role. In 1957, McCallum starred in *Robbery Under Arms* with British actress Jill Dorothy Ireland. One week after they met, they were married. He also appeared in such British films as *A Night to Remember, Billy Budd,* and *Freud.*

During an actor's strike in 1962, he moved to America to appear in *The Greatest Story Ever Told,* the Biblical epic in which he played Judas. He recalls, "When I look back, I was very surprised that I was chosen for the part. We decided to move lock, stock, and barrel to Los Angeles and take a house. I did as much as I could to get some work. I was well known in England from television and theater and films, but in the United States nobody knew me, so I had to get some sort of film."

David McCallum. © *1964–1967 Metro-Goldwyn-Mayer, Inc.*

In 1963 he appeared in *The Great Escape*. While doing this film he met Charles Bronson, who would later become a good friend of the McCallums. McCallum then moved into guest roles on TV, including *Outer Limits, Perry Mason, The Travels of Jaimie McPheeters,* and *Profiles in Courage.* To McCallum, it was necessary to get as much exposure as possible in America so his career would not suffer by the move to the States: "You needed to try and get together as much footage of film as possible, so you could show people," he says. "And then, things were pretty rough. But one day Charles Bronson said, 'Why don't I take you around to the studios?' And he took me to MGM, and we had lunch with a man named Don Medford." Medford mentioned the Illya role to McCallum in the course of their lunch conversation, but very little detail was given. "The only thing I remember," says McCallum, "was that it was mentioned that he was a Russian and that he had a box of jazz gramophone records under his bed."

McCallum didn't hesitate long in expressing an interest in the role: "I was pretty desperate at that point. Because actors, when they are out of work and they've moved from one country to another, are desperate. I remember I bounced one check in my life. In England, you don't bounce checks; they call you and tell you before they do it. The Bank of America bounced one of my checks. And it was such a horrific moment. At that point I was very worried about what was going to happen to me."

Medford apparently liked the young actor, and discussed him with Norman Felton. They contacted McCallum's agent, Paul Kohner, and offered the role of Illya Kuryakin. But fate plays strange tricks: *Solo* was not the only series interested in David McCallum's services at that point. When it rains, it pours, and McCallum suddenly found himself offered three series roles at the same time. "The same day that I received the notification from Paul Kohner," he remembers, "there were two other series that he had come up with. One was on Alexander the Great, and the other was a religious series based on Judas Iscariot. So the three came at the same time. My logic was that Alexander the Great was not the way to go, since period pieces had never really gone well. I couldn't see a series being played on Judas Iscariot in the United States. So I thought, if I do

this *Mr. Solo*, I'll be able to get film together and after three or four episodes, if it runs for a year or something and I do thirteen shows, then I would have a good reel of film to show people, and I would be able to get back in playing character parts in pictures. So I accepted the role on the premise that I was going to get some film, nothing more devastating than that."

Both Felton and Rolfe were pleased with the choice of McCallum to play Illya, and he was signed for seven of

Courtesy of the Norman Felton collection.

the first thirteen episodes. Both Mc-Callum, at five-nine and 140 pounds, and Vaughn, at five-ten and 165 pounds, fit the original requirement of heroes of average size.

But Felton had misgivings about the role of Illya itself, wondering if the network would approve of a Russian character on an American television series, a daring idea for 1963, with the Cuban missile crisis only a year past and the Berlin wall and Vietnam in the headlines. Rolfe, however, recalls that "The original concept of *U.N.C.L.E.* was very one-worldish. I said, wouldn't it be great if we were all together in one organization. Now, whether I really believed all this or not, it sounded good. So I said, okay, every nation will have to throw agents into this pot, like you would money into a central pot. They will all work for that organization, but underneath it all they are all really spies for their own countries. So Illya Kuryakin—and this was really my concept—worked with the American agent, and they'd be great pals until somebody in Moscow pushed a button and said okay, now you've got to go knock him off and go on to the next job. Or vice versa; the CIA might say that Solo should go take care of him and go on to something else. Of course, that never arose. That was just one of my own little concepts in the back of my head."

With the casting completed, the actual shooting of the pilot for *Solo* began on November 20, 1963, and continued until December 9. A major portion of the shooting took place at Lever Brothers company, a large manufacturing plant in Los Angeles adjacent to the Santa Ana Freeway, that made, among other things, soap. This location would double

as Vulcan's factory, called Vulcan Chemical Company in the script but changed to Global Chemical Company in the final version.

Most of the scenes shot at Lever Brothers, with it's multitude of catwalks, steam boilers, and pipes, were done at night. George Lehr, associate producer, went to the plant before shooting began to see the pipes and other fixtures to make sure they would fit the script. There was concern over whether there would be sufficient light to film at the plant at night. Felton says "George Lehr came forward and he felt that we could shoot the latest available Eastman Kodak film at night using available light, and that's when we found the soap factory, which I can still smell to this day. George went there himself with a camera and took color film at night of various things in this plant with available light, which was not much. And he came back and it was developed, and it was decided we could do it, although we had been told by the lads in the MGM camera department that it wouldn't work. It did work."

This was the first location used. Prior to actual shooting, one day was spent on lining up the crew, equipment, etc., and another day was spent on rehearsals. Other location work would use three more days, nine days would be filmed on sound stages at MGM, and exterior shots would be done on Lots 2 and 3 on MGM's backlot on one more day. A day of holiday, for Thanksgiving, was also scheduled, giving a total of sixteen actual days of filming. A second unit was assigned one day to do some additional location filming.

But just two days into filming the pilot at Lever Brothers, an event that touched the lives of all Americans brought filming to a halt. Patricia Crowley, who was at Lever Brothers to film her scene in the steam-pipe room with Vaughn, recalls that "A most devastating event occurred when we were shooting at Lever Brothers for those several all-night shootings, and that was when President Kennedy was killed. It was an enormous shock to everybody, of course, and we were just devastated on the set. It was a difficult time for everybody."

The Kennedy assassination was especially shocking to Robert Vaughn, who was a great admirer of the president. The assassination occurred on Vaughn's birthday. He recalls, "We received word that Friday, while on location at Lever Brothers. By the end of Friday, I was forgetting my lines. I went up to Don Medford, the director, and said this isn't going to work. And he agreed, and we stopped shooting. Of course, we had the national day of mourning on Monday, and on Tuesday we resumed shooting."

When shooting did resume, the action called for the many chase scenes at the factory to be shot in a very short period of time in order to maintain the schedule as much as possible. "We were running all over that factory out there, inside and out," Pat Crowley remembered, "and shooting from every possible angle. I think it was kind of cool as the night wore on, and you do get that funny tiredness when you are up all night. You try to sleep the day before, but of course you can't. So you're working on that nervous energy level that happens when you are up for days at a time like that."

In the early days of the series, the actors were given considerable latitude to interpret their characters. Even Robert Vaughn was not given explicit instructions on how to play the most important role, Napoleon Solo. He recalls, "I tried to develop those aspects of the character that were attractive to myself. His relationships with women, a detached, devil-may-care aura, these were at the time more my nature. Now I'm married and have more responsibilities. I tried to use things in my personal life that I felt were effective."

David McCallum and Robert Vaughn first met when McCallum's two brief scenes in the pilot were shot. Vaughn was familiar with McCallum from his appearance in *Freud,* and was impressed with him because "virtually every young man in town was trying for the role of Judas Iscariot in *The Greatest Story Ever Told,* and David got it."

The version of the pilot that emerged from all this, however, was not what was seen by the television audience later. For one thing, when the pilot was done filming, it was still titled *Solo.* But several aspects of the script itself were also changed for various legal reasons.

When MGM's legal staff discovered that Rolfe had used "Elaine May Van Essen" as the name Patricia Crowley's character would use in the party scene, and that she would play the widow of Carl Van Essen, a recently deceased oilman, they immediately objected because there was a real Mrs. Karl Van Hoessen, who was related to a C. R. Van Hoessen, an oil producer. Eventually the name was changed to Van Every. Similarly, the Vulcan Chemical Company was dangerous because of the real-life Vulcan Materials Company, and the name was changed to Global Chemical Company. Even the reference to the PTA in the script was altered to National Parent's Conference.

Perhaps even more noteworthy than what was said in the pilot is what was not said. For example, although U.N.C.L.E. is referred to, the letters those initials stand for are never mentioned. The reason, quite simply, is that at that point no one had decided what they should stand for. Similarly, Robert Vaughn is referred to only as Mr. Solo throughout the pilot. The character's first name of Napoleon is not used.

After 172 hours of shooting, the sixty-eight-minute rough print of the pilot episode of *Solo* was completed on December 16, 1963.

After the pilot was "in the can," Felton and Rolfe were able to turn their attention to the series itself. On January 22, 1964, Norman Felton suggested in a memo that the series should be filmed in color, even though color television was relatively new and expensive in 1964. Felton's reasoning was based on foresight. If the episodes were filmed in color, which was clearly going to be the norm on television in the near future, the residual value of reruns of the series would be enhanced. But this advice was rejected and the first season was filmed in black-and-white.

Felton was to encounter this prejudice against color yet again when he tried to screen the completed pilot for the network. "When it was time for the network to decide if they would air the series," he says, "they had a lot of pilots to choose from. Bob Weitman moved up to be the head of the studio, and he agreed with me that they ought to see our pilot in color. So I took the pilot, in a number of cans, because the picture and sound-tracks were separate, and got on a plane for New York. Someone called from MGM in New York and said that New York was snowbound, but I didn't get the message in time. So we took off, and halfway there they said we had to land at Louisville because of the weather. I managed to get a small plane from there to Washington, but couldn't get out of there. So I got on the train at two A.M., and tipped right and left to get the porters to load all the film cans."

The intrepid Felton continued on his mission: "When I got into Penn Station, I went to where the taxis were, and the snow was still falling. Arrangements had been made to show the film at NBC at ten A.M. It was then about nine thirty. I went up to a policeman who was directing traffic, and said I've got this film, it's got to get to the National Broadcasting Company before ten o'clock, help me! And he did. He flagged down a taxi that was leaving, stopped it, and told the people to get out with their baggage, and it took me to NBC with five minutes to spare. But when I arrived, there was no one there, because they assumed I wouldn't make it. But eventually they started to come in."

Seemingly home free, Felton was to have his hopes dashed. "The executives brought the chairman of the company in, and they had long faces. They had told him that I was going to run the color version, and he refused to see it, he wanted to see the black-and-white. So I had to scramble around to find a black-and-white print."

Reactions varied, but were generally enthusiastic. The series was considered novel and unique. The pilot script was well thought-out and written. However, NBC in New York was not completely happy with the casting. Felton received a call from an NBC executive in New York, saying that they wanted to replace

A production scene from the pilot episode break-in sequence. *Courtesy Norman Felton collection.*

one of the secondary players, but the executive could not think of the name. As Felton recalls the conversation, "I was fighting all the time with the network. I was younger then. Nobody at NBC liked to talk to me. So he called, and he said he wanted me to drop someone. He kept saying 'K . . . K . . .' and I said Kuluva? And he said, 'That's it.'"

To the executives' surprise, Felton did not argue and agreed to recast Kuluva's part. In fact, Felton and Rolfe had already discussed replacing him. "Sam Rolfe had the idea," Felton remembers,

"that since we had very few things going for us, with Vaughn and McCallum still relatively unknown, maybe we could get an older actor who has name value to play the head of U.N.C.L.E. He felt that now that we had a deal for a series we could afford a name actor even though we couldn't in the pilot."

So Felton told the executive he was filling the role with Leo G. Carroll. The executive responded with surprise, and asked if Carroll wasn't a little old for the role. Felton was puzzled by this response, but the reason became clear some time later. Felton recalls that the executive called again and said, "'Norman, what was the name of the guy who was replaced by Leo G. Carroll?' And I told him Will Kuluva. And he said, 'We actually meant David McCallum—Kuryakin.' He wanted to get rid of that Russian with the long hair, and he thought Leo G. Carroll was a little old to play Solo's sidekick. I told him it was too late, we had already picked up a deal on McCallum for seven of the first thirteen episodes. I also told him that if I had realized that, I would have fought him on it, because we felt he was important. He said to just forget he ever made this call; he was very embarrassed about it. Several years later, I saw him at a party and he said it was the best mistake he'd ever made."

After surviving this near miss, McCallum's presence on the series was again jeopardized. The producers of the movie *The Greatest Story Ever Told* had a "first call" in their contract for his services, and they objected when he signed on for *U.N.C.L.E.* "We were faced with a serious problem," Felton says. "We were already in production, and we had never been told of this by McCallum's agent.

But we were able to work out a severance."

When the decision to drop Will Kuluva was made, not only did Felton and Rolfe begin to look for another actor to play the role, but a new addendum to the prospectus was written, giving the character a new name and background. The new head of U.N.C.L.E. was to be called Mr. Waverly. He was described as being seedy and old-fashioned, in sharp contrast to the ultramodern organization he headed. He dressed in tweed jackets with patches on the sleeves, and handled a pipe but never smoked it. He tolerated Solo's girlfriends, but not too well. He tended to forget names, and liked to spot-check his agents. To Rolfe and Felton, Leo G. Carroll seemed to offer just the right touch of bureaucratic authority.

Leo Grattan Carroll was born in 1892, the son of Irish parents, in Weedon, Northamptonshire, England. He was named Leo for Pope Leo XIII, and Grattan for Henry Grattan, an Irish member of Parliament. His father was an army man, Captain William Carroll. He and Leo's mother, Catherine, raised Leo in York, England, where he attended school until the age of fifteen when he became an apprentice wine merchant.

In 1911 he made his professional debut on the London stage in *The Prisoner of Zenda*. In 1912 he traveled to New York City to appear on Broadway in *Rutherford and Son*. But like both Vaughn and McCallum, his acting career was interrupted by military service. Leo Carroll served in the infantry in World War I as a member of the Artist's Rifles in France, Greece, and in Palestine, where he was wounded and hospitalized for two years.

During the next few years, he would make more than sixty transatlantic crossings to appear on both the New York and London stages. In 1927 he married Nancy DeSylva, an actress. In 1934, the Carrolls moved to Hollywood, and he began his film career with *The Barrets of Wimpole Street,* followed by *Clive of India* in 1935, *London by Night* in 1937, and *Wuthering Heights* in 1939.

Throughout the 1940s and 1950s, he continued to appear in films, including

Leo G. Carroll brought both authority and compassion to the role of U.N.C.L.E.'s chief, Alexander Waverly. © *1964–1967 Metro-Goldwyn-Mayer, Inc.*

31

Suspicion, The Desert Fox, and *North by Northwest.* He appeared in over thirty movies and over three hundred stage plays in this period. By the time he was chosen for the Waverly role, he was already well known to American television audiences from his regular roles on *Topper* and *Going My Way.* Leo G. Carroll was in London when his agent arranged for the role, and when he returned to start filming, he grew ill after the first two weeks of the series and had to be hospitalized for operations. Thus, some first-season episodes, such as "The King of Knaves Affair" have no Waverly scenes in them.

The addition of Leo G. Carroll was well received by the cast and crew. George Lehr recalled that Leo quickly became accepted on the set: "Chuck Painter and the casting people and Sam Rolfe had a list of three or four people, and I think Norman was also very involved in that. Norman, being British by birth, kind of favored Leo, and I think everybody did after a while. Sam initially, I think, wanted to go with Will Kuluva, but after a while he felt [Kuluva] was too much on the heavy side. It was kind of a committee decision on Leo."

Lehr feels that Leo G. Carroll brought to the role of Waverly a warmth that was missing in Kuluva's portrayal of Allison. "There was something about Leo. He was an authority figure and at the same time he had a certain impish pixie quality that had a certain sense of humor."

But the change in actors for the head of U.N.C.L.E. did entail problems for the already-filmed pilot. It would be confusing to the audience to tune in the pilot and see Will Kuluva as Mr. Allison, the head of U.N.C.L.E., one week, and see Leo G. Carroll as Alexander Waverly the

next. So Kuluva's scenes in the pilot were cut, refilmed with Leo G. Carroll, and then spliced into the final version. Kuluva as Allison did remain in the movie version, however.

But the problems with the pilot were not yet over. At the same time Will Kuluva was being dropped, a controversy developed over the name of the evil organization U.N.C.L.E. was to oppose. Sam Rolfe had designated the organization THRUSH, and this was the term used in filming the pilot. But NBC objected to THRUSH, saying that it presented legal problems because it sounded too much like SMERSH, the real-life Soviet spy organization referred to in the Bond novels.

On May 5, 1964, NBC offered a long list of possible replacements, many of which, like THRUSH, conveyed the image of an animal or bird, including SCORPION, VIRGO, ADDER, TARANTULA, RAVEN, SHARK, SMEAR, CRUSH, CONDOR, LUCRE, ASP, and MEDUSA. Sam Rolfe offered alternatives to his own THRUSH: STIGMA, HAZARD, HARM, and SCOURGE. An executive of NBC suggested SNIPE, VERSUS, RAVEN, THRUST, THREAT, VULTURE, SPHINX, THOR, SCORPION, PHANTOM, SPIDER, NOOSE, SQUID, BRUTE, and ZEUS, and had even worked out words for each letter, such as "the Society for Quiet Unification through International Destruction."

Many of the suggested names were, of course, ludicrous. SMEAR would have been dangerously close to SMERSH, which was the very problem to be avoided. CRUSH and THRUST were so similar to THRUSH a change would hardly have been justified. VERSUS, suggested by NBC's Marcy Tinkle, was rejected as looking good on paper but being hard to pronounce. The only favorite to emerge was MAGGOTT, which no one was really satisfied with either. But for a considerable amount of time this distasteful name was used, and even appeared in the first drafts of some scripts for first-season episodes, such as "The Four Steps Affair." When the pilot was being converted into a feature-length film for theater distribution, it was decided to use WASP as the name of the organization. Thus, in the feature film version of "The Vulcan Affair," called *To Trap a Spy,* every time Robert Vaughn, Will Kuluva, or Fritz Weaver mentions THRUSH, the word WASP was dubbed in, but with Robert Vaughn's voice doing the dubbing not only for his character but the others as well.

Felton and Rolfe continued to push for reinstatement of THRUSH. It was discovered that WASP could not continue to be used, since there was a pilot for a children's program called *Stingray* that had an organization in it called W.A.S.P.—World Aquanauts Security Patrol. Felton finally convinced Fred Houghton of NBC on May 20, 1964, that they would be retaining THRUSH because it seemed unique, conveyed the proper note of a quiet threat, and had a sinister ring.

But the problems with THRUSH were minuscule when compared to the problems Felton and Rolfe ran into with the title of the series itself. At various times it had been called *Solo—Adventures in Thrilling Cities, Solo, Napoleon Solo,* and *Mr. Solo;* now, the legal problems with the Bond producers dictated that "Solo" not appear in the title. In the early

stages, there was consideration given to changing the character's name to Just or Banner. The series could thus be called *Just's World* or *Banner's World,* or *The Affairs of Banner.* If "Solo" could be retained, *The Affairs of Solo* or *Solo's World* were considered. But NBC suggested that the series be titled *The Man from U.N.C.L.E.* Felton's immediate reaction was that the title was trite and too unwieldy. In April 1964 Felton pleaded with the network to at least shorten the title to *U.N.C.L.E.* But NBC had done some audience testing and had concluded that *The Man from U.N.C.L.E.* was a better title.

Just when Felton thought all the legal problems had been solved, he received another panic call from the legal department. Apparently someone had thought that the "U.N." in "U.N.C.L.E." stood for United Nations, and sent them a copy of the script for their approval. The UN objected to a television show using their name. In addition, the State of New York had a criminal statute, Paragraph 974(a) of the New York Penal Code, that made it illegal to use the name of the United Nations for commercial gain. Felton stated he could live with spelling out the initials so no one would mistake U.N.C.L.E. for the United Nations, but he refused to come out and say it was not the UN—if people really thought U.N.C.L.E. existed, he said, "then I fear for the sanity of us all." But NBC's legal department told Felton that the name of the organization would have to be changed completely, not just spelled out.

Felton and Rolfe had hoped to add an air of mystery to the show by not assigning a meaning to the name. They toyed with some words to go with the letters, at one point using "Unilateral Network of Combined Leaders against Evil." Eventually, "United Network Command for Law and Enforcement" was decided upon by Rolfe.

Felton eventually resolved the legal problem by using a device he had previously used on *Dr. Kildare.* NBC had asked Felton to obtain the approval of the American Medical Association for the *Kildare* series, and this was shown by a tag card at the end of each episode saying "We thank the American Medical Association without whose help this series could not have been made." Felton had used a similar thank you to the United States Marine Corps on *The Lieutenant.* So on May 21, 1964, Felton proposed using the tag "This film could not have been made without the cooperation of the Unified Network Command for Law and Enforcement," which was later changed to "We wish to thank the United Network Command for Law and Enforcement, without whose assistance this program would not have been possible." This tongue-in-cheek tag more than satisfied the legal department, but Felton would later learn that it had an unusual effect on some viewers.

Because the total final cost for the pilot was $445,859, and since the final film ran sixty-eight minutes, Norman Felton renewed his request to NBC to make the pilot a two-part episode on January 22, 1964. Felton proposed filming thirty more minutes rather than cutting the sixty-eight minutes. Back in September of 1963, Felton had made the same request, proposing that perhaps the entire season could consist of two-part episodes, thereby ensuring audience return and better production quality. Felton had pointed out that two-parters would result in good showmanship, and would attract better writers, actors, and directors because of the enhanced production time. Also, Felton pointed out, the only way the high production costs of the series could be offset was by amortizing the sets over two episodes instead of just one. Not only would cost of sets be reduced, but the hundred-minute two-part episodes could be released as feature films and generate additional revenue. The idea had been tabled at that time.

NBC tested the pilot in small theaters in the Los Angeles area to gauge audience reaction. Each audience of about two hundred was monitored for their interest level. Some theaters used a sensor device placed on the finger of the viewer to gauge his or her pulse and skin reactions, like a lie detector. From this, a line graph resembling a polygraph or lie detector readout was obtained. The chart ranged from a rating of zero for "very dull" to 250 for "dull" to 500 for "normal." The chart then progressed to 750 for "good," and up to 1,000 for "very good." At the behest of the MGM Research Department, the pilot was shown to an audience that was studied in this fashion by Audience Studies Incorporated on January 31, 1964, at the Screen Director's Theater in Hollywood. During the headquarters break-in sequence, audience interest rose steadily from the 500 range; it reached a peak of 750 by the end of the sequence, when the title came on the screen, and generally stayed at this level.

The audience was given a questionnaire as well. In response to the question "How did you enjoy the program you have just seen?" 34 percent rated the pilot "excellent," with females showing the highest interest. Robert Vaughn as Solo was rated excellent by 60.8 percent of the audience, with females and the over-thirty-five age group rating him highest. The story itself received a 32-percent excellence rating.

When asked if they would watch *Solo* over *The Red Skelton Hour* and *McHale's Navy* (the likely competition), 29 percent said they would. With three shows competing for the prime-time audience, each would want twenty-nine to thirty percent of the audience to stay on the air (slightly less than one-third because of public television). This was a very respectable result for a new series pitted against two established shows. *Solo* was also preferred by the test audience in direct comparisons to other popular shows of the time, such as *The Fugitive* (67 percent preferred *Solo*), *Ben Casey* (77 percent), and *The Beverly Hillbillies* (57 percent). A full 59 percent of the audience thought *Solo* could become their favorite TV show. Written comments ranged from the negative—"corny," "unreal," "improbable"—to the enthusiastic—"exciting," "suspenseful," "different." Based on these high scores, actual production of the series began on June 1, 1964.

From the Brink of Cancellation to National Fad, in Six Easy Lessons

Chapter 4

The First Season

The first season of *The Man from U.N.C.L.E.* was broadcast in black-and-white. A normal season at that time was twenty-nine episodes. "The Vulcan Affair" premiered the series on Tuesday, September 22, 1964. The rest of the season presented a collection of stories that established the trademarks of the series. Among fans of the series, the first season is generally considered to be the best of the four. The stories were better constructed, and under producer Sam Rolfe's guidance all the elements of the production team coordinated beautifully to present a slick finished product.

The episodes of the first season established the elements of the series: Solo, often accompanied by Illya, would be sent by Waverly to deal with a problem somewhere in the world. He would be helped by an ordinary person who would play a crucial role in the resolution of the problem. The plots were bold, modern, and imaginative, and the villains unique.

Each episode took time to allow the audience to develop empathy with the innocent. Herbert Anderson played a long-suffering husband who was just as glad to be away from his wife when he was kidnapped in "The Shark Affair." Zohra Lampert played a woman who really wasn't sure she wanted to get married and thought her entire life could be carved on the head of a pin until her day at U.N.C.L.E. headquarters made her decide the quiet life was not so bad after all in "The Mad, *Mad* Tea Party Affair." June Lockhart's portrayal of the teacher in "The Dove Affair" took the same approach, as she bemoaned the fact that her life was a disappointment to her.

The U.N.C.L.E. cast—Robert Vaughn, David McCallum, and Leo G. Carroll. *© 1964–1967 Metro-Goldwyn-Mayer, Inc.*

Barbara Feldon got her chance to live the life of a spy instead of a clerk in "The Never Never Affair," but was happy to go back to her desk after coming so close to death at the hands of THRUSH. Katherine Crawford in "The Iowa Scuba Affair" complained of her humdrum existence on the farm, not realizing what was going on in the underground tunnel below her feet or what lay in store for her.

In each case, not only was the "innocent" an ordinary person, but often an ordinary person who was bored or dissatisfied with his or her life and craved a change, some excitement. And many times, having found that excitement, he or she gladly returned to his or her former life with a sigh of relief. But whether the episode ended with regrets or relief, the innocent was always a wiser person having escaped, if only temporarily, into the fast-paced world inhabited by Solo and Illya. The audience vicariously felt the same.

The first season achieved what Felton and Rolfe had strived for—the proper blend of adventure and light humor in a sophisticated setting. The stories involved high stakes, often with the very fate of the world hanging in the balance. Almost certainly each story involved a physical threat to Solo or Illya, including being steamed to death ("The Vulcan Affair"), burning up in a fire ("The Deadly Games Affair"), suffocating ("The Neptune Affair"), baking to death under sunlamps ("The Double Affair"), being electrocuted ("The Fiddlesticks Affair"), being bitten by a poisonous snake ("The Yellow Scarf Affair"), being bitten to death by a Doberman pinscher ("The Bow Wow Affair"), drowning while strapped to a mattress floating in a swimming pool until it sinks from the water it has soaked up ("The Girls of Nazarone Affair") or having one's brain turned to mush by a machine ("The Brain Killer Affair"). With all of these and many more, in addition to the more mundane threats of being shot or beaten, present in virtually every episode, one could legitimately question whether there would be any dangers left for a second season.

But of course the predicaments were an important part of the formula. This was a carryover from the Bond movies, where Bond was called upon to use his wits or an outlandish gadget to escape peril. In the first season of *The Man from*

Parade Grand Marshall David McCallum, protected by black-turtleneck-clad Boy Scout bodyguards armed with plastic U.N.C.L.E. guns. *Courtesy of Chuck Painter.*

U.N.C.L.E., for example, Solo must exercise his wits in "The Iowa Scuba Affair." Solo turns on his shower and instead of water, a deadly gas is emitted. Finding the door locked, he quickly improvises a makeshift bomb to blow the door open by lighting an aerosol shaving cream can with his cigarette lighter.

Unfortunately, after Sam Rolfe left the show at the end of the first season the writers turned to rely on gadgets more than ingenuity. The gadgets became a staple of the series, and one of its most popular elements. But each time they were used, they robbed the heroes of an opportunity to use their brains instead.

The first season established a repartee between Solo and Illya that undoubtedly also helped the series achieve success. There was obviously an unspoken rivalry between the two men, and it was also clear that Illya disapproved of many facets of Solo's personality—most importantly his preoccupation with women. In "The Double Affair," when Solo borrows money from Illya to keep a date, Illya does not hide his disgust, but nevertheless makes the loan and even works late in Solo's place. Solo was the flip, suave American while Illya remained the serious, intellectual, and somewhat mysterious Russian.

But at the same time there was an unspoken respect between the two. As a

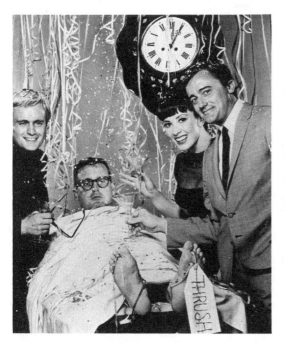

Publicist Chuck Painter helps Vaughn and McCallum celebrate the coming of an important year for the series—1965. *Courtesy of Chuck Painter.*

Sam Rolfe and Robert Vaughn. *Courtesy of the Sam Rolfe collection.*

team, they swung into action without need of a word or signal being exchanged. Although their behavior was always strictly professional, each had a concern for the other's well-being. In "The Secret Sceptre Affair," for instance, when Illya is left behind, Solo is willing to risk his own life to go back for him.

The first season was, however, a floundering process. There was still some ambiguity as to whether NBC wanted a straight adventure series, or a series with humor. Thus, some episodes, such as "The Double Affair," and "The Green Opal Affair," are played very straight, while others, like "The Mad, *Mad* Tea Party Affair" and "The Never Never Affair," have a great deal of humor.

Norman Felton recalls, "We really didn't know quite what we had on our hands. Nor did the network. The network saw our black-and-white shows before they went on the air, and they came in and said they felt it would be a total disaster, because a lot of the things were funny. And they said you can't do humor with suspense, because then people will laugh and break the suspense. Sam Rolfe and I sat and thought, and we weren't sure ourselves, so we thought maybe they were right. So Sam began cutting out some of the humor, and trying to build the suspense. When we went on the air, we went with shows that didn't have much humor. But eventually there comes a time late in the year when you have to use the one you shot earlier. And it surprised everyone—people liked them better."

Thus, after two years of effort, *The Man from U.N.C.L.E.* was on the air. It was, for the times, a unique show—a spy series with sophisticated plots, ultramodern technology, unusual heroes, and a blend of humor and adventure. Now all that remained was the audience reaction. Then, as now, the barometer of that reaction, and the determining factor as to whether the show stayed on the air or was canceled, was the Nielsen ratings.

Chapter 5

Finding the Formula for Success

Besides the obvious factors that influence a show's ratings—the stars, the production values, the writing, the premise, etc.—perhaps the most important factor is the time slot assigned to the show. *The Man from U.N.C.L.E.* has often been cited as an example of just how crucial a time slot can be to a show's success. The show was on its last legs until a change in time slot gave it a shot in the arm and a chance to find a wider audience.

Part of the dynamics of a time slot is the opposition on the other two networks. Among the U.S. commercial television networks, there is a three-way contest for audiences in each prime-time (evening) slot. The Nielsen company gauges the size of a show's audience by extrapolating from the results of tiny electronic boxes attached to the TV sets of a theoretically representative sample of the potential audience. A prime-time series generally must pull a 20 rating, meaning 20 percent of the total homes with TVs, and a 30 share, or 30 percent of the TVs turned on during that time slot, to stay on the air and avoid cancellation. In 1964, there were 52,800,000 homes with TV sets in the U.S., or 92

percent of all homes. A 20 rating meant that over 10 million sets were tuned to a particular show.

When *The Man from U.N.C.L.E.* pre-

McCallum is greeted at an airport by U.N.C.L.E. fans. © *1964–1967 Metro-Goldwyn-Mayer, Inc.*

miered on September 22, 1964, it was aired by NBC on Tuesday nights at 8:30 P.M. eastern standard time. This was opposite *The Red Skelton Hour* on CBS, considered a powerhouse show with high ratings and strong audience loyalty. For the 1964–65 television season, *The Red Skelton Hour* placed number six in the top ten shows for the year. It enjoyed a Nielsen rating of 29.8. ABC offered *McHale's Navy. The Man from U.N.C.L.E.* gathered an 8.3 rating and only 13 percent of the audience in this time slot. Although it would eventually rise to a rating of 19.5 in this slot, that was still well below the success level.

By the end of 1964, *U.N.C.L.E.* ranked fiftieth in Nielsen's ranking of shows, and it was clearly a case of "move or die." *U.N.C.L.E.* would have to gain greater ratings or be canceled. At this point, the network did not have the show in its tentative 1965–66 schedule. A decision was made in December 1964 to move the show to Monday night, in the eight P.M. slot, in January, pitting it against *No Time for Sergeants* and the new show *Voyage to the Bottom of the Sea* on ABC and *I've Got a Secret* and *The Andy Griffith Show* on CBS. Thus, the audience would already be involved in the hour-long *U.N.C.L.E.* when Andy Griffith came on, and therefore be less likely to switch over. But even in the new slot, the ratings, now at 14.1, spelled doom for the series.

The task of avoiding the predicted early extinction fell most heavily on Chuck Painter, who had replaced Al Rylander as publicist for the show. Painter's success in promoting *Dr. Kildare* for Felton led directly to his *U.N.C.L.E.* assignment. Painter states that his job of publicity man for the se-

McCallum and Vaughn signal the all-important first-season time change. *Courtesy of the Norman Felton collection.*

ries involved "acting as a liaison between the various media and print press, television, radio, and so forth, in promoting the show, handling interviews, and scheduling personal appearances." For the *U.N.C.L.E.* job, Painter came on board when the ratings showed his new position might be shortlived. "The first seven or eight weeks on the air were very precarious. We didn't think it was going to survive. It did not get off to a good start."

Felton did give Painter instructions on how to approach publicity for *The Man from U.N.C.L.E.*: "We were to publicize the show as if it were to really happen," Painter recalls. "To take it seriously. Because if we approached it that way, the public could see the tongue-in-cheek by watching the show. Every time we talked about the U.N.C.L.E. show, or the organization of U.N.C.L.E., it was in a serious manner, with slightly bulging cheek."

Painter's answer to the show's problems was a novel one for the times, and, as it turned out, an extremely effective one. It was decided that the best way to improve the Nielsen ratings was to go directly to the source. The decision was a joint one: "It was sort of let's get together and think about it, and what can we do to improve the ratings. So what we did, we went around and hit all the Nielsen cities for those six or eight weeks and lived out of motels and ate the rubber chicken and became honorary sheriffs of various towns and did press and radio and television." Each weekend, after a five-day, twelve-hour-per-day shooting schedule, Vaughn, McCallum, and Painter would fly off to a Nielsen city and make promotional appearances for the show. "Vaughn and McCallum and I volunteered, gratuitously, to get in a studio car at six o'clock on a Friday and go to the airport and hit three cities in two days."

Those Nielsen cities where the ratings seemed to be lowest were targeted. Painter, Vaughn, and McCallum were to visit the local NBC affiliate station and film promotional scenes using local landmarks to catch the attention of the local audience. McCallum recalls, "What I would do is check up on the local political scene, with anything that was current in the local paper. And then I would write a promo for the series, based on the fact that the mayor was running against so and so. And then I would hang from the roof of the studio, over the news set, or something quite ludi-crous. And they would zoom up to me hanging precariously and I would say 'If you want to solve the problem of Mayor so-and-so and so-and-so, watch *The Man from U.N.C.L.E.*'"

Robert Vaughn also recalls those whirlwind tours: "We went out to different cities, and would usually wind up in New York on Sunday night together and fly back on the late-night flight. We would tape promos for the show for the particular channel that was airing the show. And slowly the show began to crop up on local surveys in each town as one of the top two shows on the air."

Painter recalls that the U.N.C.L.E. gun went on the tours also: "In those days, it was remarkable because we carried the U.N.C.L.E. gun, which was a real gun, in my briefcase, which you could never do now, of course. I'd carry the U.N.C.L.E. gun, broken down, in my briefcase so that when we arrived in any particular town (they loved it in Texas, by the way), we'd go to a television station, and especially David loved to put on his black sweater and his black pants and would put the gun together and we'd move the television camera from the studio, we'd have them put extension cables on them, and we'd run the television cameras out on the street and we'd do promos. We'd wing these things. We'd have David come, for a whole minute he'd come running toward the camera, no sound except heavy breathing. He'd come racing up to the camera, slam his back against the wall, look in both directions, then into the camera, say something like, '*The Man from U.N.C.L.E.*, tonight, eight o'clock, WMAQ,' and race on by."

Chuck Painter remembers these weekend excursions with mixed emotions. "It was a lot of physical and mental labor," he remembered. "But it was more fun than that, it wasn't anything negative. There were all sorts of jokes and things like that we played on each other. I look back on it with great affection."

The first sign that the tours were paying off came from an unexpected segment of society. Painter noticed, when driving by college dormitories and sorority houses, that he could hear the U.N.C.L.E. soundtrack coming from the television rooms. The Nielsen system did not gauge college dormitories, only residential homes. It was at that time that the show's ratings began to pick up, as the college crowd adopted the show and, when they went home for Christmas break, 1964, spread the word. *Life* magazine's TV reviewer Scot Leavit credited this word-of-mouth promotion with saving the series from cancellation. These people in turn encouraged their friends to watch the show, and the ratings began to climb.

Norman Felton felt that the tours were instrumental in keeping the show alive. Looking back, Robert Vaughn also feels that the tours were very helpful to the survival of the series. "One never knows what helps a show," he says. "If the show had been on in the 1980s instead of the 1960s it would have gone off before it had a chance to get an audience."

There is no doubt in Chuck Painter's mind that the tours to the Nielsen cities saved *The Man from U.N.C.L.E.* from cancellation in the first season: "I think it was instrumental in goosing the show in the Nielsens to the point where NBC wasn't going to drop it. The ratings leaped up from then on, it was a hit show." When the tours began, the show was gathering a rating of 17.6. After

tours in New Orleans, Dallas, St. Louis, Houston, San Francisco, Milwaukee, Chicago, and Cleveland—twenty-four cities and 23,000 miles in all—the show's rating rose to 20, the magic threshold of survival.

But the grinding schedule took its toll, especially on Painter himself, who was also still serving as publicist on *Dr. Kildare*. "That's what put me in the hospital," he says. "I had a complete physical breakdown in 1965. *Kildare* actually made me as far as reputation goes, and then I had *U.N.C.L.E.* and I was so greedy that I didn't want to give up *Kildare*. So I kept both shows, and I was going twenty-four hours a day." But that pace proved to be the straw that broke the camel's back for Painter: "One day I walked into MGM Vice President Howard Strickling's office, and started to say something, and the next thing I remember I was at Culver City Hospital. I had been under sedation for two days, and had just keeled over backward. And my doctor told Strickling, well, he's either going to have to be a certified public accountant or a Franciscan monk, he can't continue at this pace." So Strickling took Painter off the *U.N.C.L.E.* staff and assigned him to do publicity work on an MGM picture in Europe instead. But Painter found he liked the European lifestyle, and being the only American-trained publicist who spoke Italian, he decided to make his home in Rome and remains there to this day. Painter was replaced on the show by John Rothwell.

The third factor in the phenomenal turnaround in ratings, besides the change in time slot and the promotional tours, was the evolution of David McCallum's portrayal of Illya Kuryakin from secondary character to costar. In the pilot episode, McCallum's total appearance on the screen lasted less than a minute in two brief scenes. In the pilot credits, his name came far down the list. By the end of the first season, however, he would not only be an equal costar with Robert Vaughn but a teen idol and national "sex symbol" as well. This change was both sudden and unexpected, but crucial to the show's success.

Sam Rolfe confirms that Illya was not intended to be a costar originally: "The thought was that he would be a secondary figure. Not the major secondary figure, even. I thought there would be other agents before too long, but [Illya] at least would start us out. The focal point of it all was Bob Vaughn." At the same time, however, Rolfe told McCallum his character would not be "standing around waiting for someone to send him out for sandwiches," but would have important things to do in the story.

But that concept of Illya as seldom seen soon changed. Rolfe recalls "In 'The Neptune Affair,' for example, in the scene where he's in the Russian uniform, your eyes never left him. He just sort of grabbed you. What happened, of course, was that he grabbed everybody. There's something about David in that part, something intangible that makes a star. It isn't that they are the best actor, or the most handsome or most attractive. But there is something that draws your eye to them on the screen. And David had that in this part." Rolfe compares the Illya role to the role of Kookie in *77 Sunset Strip,* or the Fonz on *Happy Days*: "There's something about these secondary characters. If the right person is in the part, they'll take the series and steal it. David did that."

However, Rolfe does not diminish the role played by Robert Vaughn: "Every-body always focuses on the energy of Illya, the nice character of Waverly, etc. If you ever pulled Bob Vaughn out of that series, you would have no series. He was really the spy, the solid central character, the urbane guy who walked through it all. David was the adornment, and the Christmas tree was Bob."

The person most surprised by the meteoric rise in Illya's appeal may have been David McCallum himself. When given the role of Illya, McCallum was not told much about the role he was to play. "I went to Norman Felton one day," McCallum says, "and we had lunch. And I said, 'Norman, I'm a character actor and I would like to have more facts about my character, and shouldn't he be this and shouldn't he be that.' And we discussed a whole lot of ideas. And Norman very simply gave me some very succinct advice: 'Don't make any assumptions. Don't make up your mind about anything. Let it happen from the script.'" McCallum was at first dissatisfied with this vagueness, preferring to have something to go on before going before the camera. "But then what happened was," he now recalls, "after about five or six scripts, there was nothing specific about the character. And I began to realize that there was something wonderfully enigmatic about not knowing what the character was. And so, from then on, whenever something specific arose, such as he was married, or had a family, or lived somewhere, or was educated, or whatever—whenever those arose, I took them out, with the permission of the writers. So in fact in the entire series there's nothing specific about the character of Illya Kuryakin."

One example of these script changes occurred in "The Bow Wow Affair." Illya goes to visit an older lady in the hospital after she has been attacked by her own dog. She asks him if he has ever been married. The script originally called for Illya to say he had been married a long time ago, but McCallum changed the line to an ambiguous literary quote to maintain the mystery. This mystery was further enhanced when, in one session of publicity photos, McCallum forgot to remove his wedding ring. The pictures appeared in several magazines, and immediately letters started to come in asking about Illya's wife and family. Felton and Rolfe decided to just leave these questions unanswered.

McCallum's unique hairstyle predated the Beatles, although the press was fond of calling his a "Beatle cut." "If you go back and look at movies that I'd done earlier, in England," he says, "if you look

David McCallum's overlooked wedding ring in this publicity photo generated much fan mail. © *1964–1967 Metro-Goldwyn-Mayer, Inc.*

at the length, it was outrageously long, but looked like a crewcut compared to what we came into a few years later."

McCallum also sported a distinctive wardrobe for his character. In the first season, Illya was most often seen clad in a black turtleneck sweater, in stark contrast to Solo's tuxedo or business suit. "Robert Vaughn, on the other hand," he says, "had a sartorial wardrobe. He was very elegant at all times. He spent his whole time changing clothes and I never did."

The black color offset his blond hair even more, and added an air of continental mystery. But contrary to reports at the time, the black wardrobe, was not McCallum's idea. "Whose idea it was, I have no idea," he recalls. "I imagine that that would have evolved from a shoot where we were supposed to be wearing clothes in order not to be seen in a night situation. And because it had happened once, we wore them again. My basic premise was I didn't want to change a lot of clothes, so I wore a black suit, a white shirt and a black tie. And then in order to hide the white shirt, I put a black turtleneck over it."

To round out the portrayal, McCallum of course had to emulate the accent of a Russian speaking English. His work with dialects in the British theater came into play here. He remembers, though, that it was not always necessary to use the accent. "In the beginning, I had a quite definite Russian accent. Then it softened. I figured if that guy was living in the States for the number of years we were doing the series, it would soften. When we played *The Return of the Man from U.N.C.L.E.,* I figured by then it would have disappeared so I didn't use it very much."

As written by the scriptwriters and portrayed by McCallum, Illya was a character displaying several traits, but rarely overt emotion. He was a loner, a serious man who did not waste time with women as Solo did. A note of friction between them supplemented their mutual respect and affection for each other. As a character, Illya appealed to the adolescent audience on one level, and to the female audience on another level.

For the former, Illya was the epitome of a word very much in vogue in the 1960s—*cool*. He handled danger and stress with the greatest of ease, and seldom showed fear, anxiety, or other human shortcomings. Just as Felton had predicted, Illya's brains and intellectualism were welcomed as a long-needed change from the brawny heroes television had offered up until then. He had an air of being slightly above all that was going on around him, and his unorthodox appearance and mysterious background made him a natural hero for an emerging generation that venerated nonconformity.

On another level, Illya's character grew in stature and importance because of a very old, tried and true element— sex appeal. Most of the fanatic followers of McCallum/Illya were female. And not just teens, but housewives and teachers and most women of childbearing age. His good looks, combined with a role that put him in a hero's position in a totally new and different show, readily led to his emergence as a new sex symbol, a role and a term he professed both to fail to understand and to hate. Illya, not being a woman-chaser like Solo, represented a nonthreatening male who offered a challenge to his female guest stars—and vicariously his female viewers. As Felton put it, "Illya does not kiss girls—girls kiss Illya."

Felton and Sam Rolfe experimented with what was obviously a new and unexpected element in their show's success. In "The Bow Wow Affair," a first-season episode that featured McCallum almost to the exclusion of Vaughn, Illya ends up kissing guest star Susan Oliver. A flood of angry fan mail came in protesting the scene. It seemed that Illya's female fans wanted him all to themselves, and his apparently celibate background was an essential part of his appeal. For similar reasons, Jill Ireland's character of Marian Raven, once considered as a continuing love interest for Illya, was dropped. By the second season of the show, Felton sent a memo, on October 11, 1965, to Mort Abrahams on "The Adriatic Express Affair" saying that the blond girl chasing Illya through the train in the script must be kept from actually catching him, as it was necessary to preserve the "Illya mystique."

The fourth major factor in the change in the ratings came when the network, which had earlier insisted on more serious scripts with less humor, now stated that audience testing showed that those episodes with humor as well as adventure produced better audience scores.

About this time, Dean Hargrove was hired as a free-lance writer to write an episode for the series. His first story for *The Man from U.N.C.L.E.* was "The Never Never Affair." As he recalls, "During the first year, they were going through a lot of writers. And I came in, I think fairly deep into the season, and I wrote 'The Never Never Affair,' starring Barbara Feldon and directed by Joe Sargent. And up until that point the show had not done overwhelmingly, and they were still casting about to see if the show was going to be an eight-o'clock action adventure thing or have a little more humor or what. In any event, it was that particular episode that NBC felt was the way they wanted the show to be stylistically, in terms of the tone and the use of humor."

The proper blend of humor and adventure having been divined, the episodes began to take on the tone that would make *The Man from U.N.C.L.E.* unique. The stories still dealt with world-threatening situations, and Solo and Illya would still be found in dangerous predicaments. But humor was also present, and this acted as a counterbalance to the suspense.

As the show began to catch on, national magazines noted the reaction, with articles on the show in *Time, Newsweek, The Saturday Evening Post,* and others appearing in a short span of time. *Look* magazine reported in an article on McCallum that in some big cities *U.N.C.L.E.* was in the top five shows. *TV Guide* ran an article on the fan reaction, calling the show's followers "The Mystic Cult of Millions."

The personal appearances of the stars started to take on mob proportions. At Baton Rouge, Louisiana, Louisiana State University's *Man from U.N.C.L.E.* Day found McCallum and Chuck Painter surrounded by a crowd of two thousand college students. McCallum recalls that the squad of fourteen police "saved me by locking me in the ladies' toilet and guarding the door. Unfortunately, they all came in through the windows and I was trying to get out of the ladies' toilet, with four or five state troopers leaning against the door. I was bleeding, and it

was very dangerous. It was just ludicrous."

McCallum soon had a police escort for all his appearances. His arrival at the Springfield, Illinois, airport was met by a crowd carrying placards saying ALL THE WAY WITH ILLYA K. and FLUSH THRUSH. In Dallas, a crowd of girls flattened McCallum and his wife against a wall, with several of the girls asking Jill if they could kiss him.

The *U.N.C.L.E.* producers began to sense the magnitude of McCallum's appeal when he was scheduled to appear at Macy's department store in New York City. Expecting three thousand to five thousand fans to attend McCallum's fifth-floor appearance, security guards and clerks were overwhelmed when over fifteen thousand fans showed up. The crowd was so overpowering that people began to pass out. Amid fears that McCallum would be injured by the human crush, it was decided that the crowd was too large and the event was called off. The disappointed fans stampeded. "They did a colossal amount of damage at Macy's," McCallum says. "They closed off the traffic to get me out of there, and the policeman who drove me out, one of New York's finest, stalled his car in the middle of Herald Square, with screaming sirens and all of these people rushing down. I finally suggested that if he turned off the siren and all the flashing lights he might be able to start the car, which he did and we drove away."

Not all the mob scenes were destructive, however. Later, when McCallum visited Japan on a promotional tour for the show, he was met at the airport by a similarly large crowd, equally enthusiastic but better behaved. "The nicest one was the mob scene in Tokyo," he recalls, "where hundreds of fans came rushing out toward us and stopped six feet away and all bowed. Even in their frenzy they were polite."

McCallum's personal life was affected; he found that he and his family could not go out in public any more without generating a crowd. On one occasion, he awoke to find a woman and her daughter going through his garbage for souvenirs.

The popularity of the show meant mob scenes for Vaughn's appearances as well. As Vaughn recalls those events, "I think it was absolutely the most extraordinary thing at the time. We were in the heyday of the dramatic actor, and I was very much influenced by people like James Dean. And to wind up being treated more like rock stars—it was especially surprising when it happened to me, because it was David who appealed to the teen and preteenage sets."

On one occasion the two actors were both to do promotional work in London, but not at exactly the same time. Vaughn says, "When I was in Virginia with Robert Kennedy's family, on my way to London to appear with David, I saw a picture of David's arrival at Heathrow airport in London and the mob scene there in *The Washington Post*. I called him in Scotland and had the Kennedy children speak to him. I flew over the next day and experienced the same thing. I arrived at two A.M. to find a tremendous crowd at the airport. In fact, I have a sequence of pictures of me getting off the plane in suit and tie and by the time I got to the terminal, they didn't have those chute things then, just steps, I was literally torn apart. My tie was gone, my collar ripped open, my hair a mess." British bobbies had to hide Vaughn in the men's room until the crowd dispersed, but not before he was pinned to the floor and his face scratched. On McCallum's arrival, fans tried not only to grab souvenir bits of clothing but even to snip locks of his hair. At a London press conference, McCallum made the mistake of leaning over to let one girl kiss him, with the result that the entire crowd pushed forward for the same treatment.

The popularity of the show made Vaughn and McCallum heroes all over the world. Vaughn recalls, "I was on a train from Helsinki to Leningrad. Along the way children stood next to the tracks all the way to the Russian border, waving and offering presents. They hadn't even shown the series there yet, only one of the two-hour movies. It was a most extraordinary time." John Hackett, Vaughn's friend and the *U.N.C.L.E.* dialogue coach, accompanied him on the same trip: "At every little Finnish town, these rosy-cheeked children would all come out to meet the train. And when they saw Vaughn, they all asked for autographs. It seemed a far-flung place in the world to find *U.N.C.L.E.* fans."

Although the two stars made separate personal appearances, publicist Chuck Painter made every effort to make sure that for all photo sessions they were together. "I always did that," he says. "You'd never show Stan Laurel without Oliver Hardy in a major publicity story. They were a team."

In spite of the often dangerous nature of the fan adoration, both McCallum and Vaughn exhibited great patience with their fans. On one occasion, McCallum was called to the phone on the *U.N.C.L.E.* set and ended up speaking with twenty-two members of a fan club

Napoleon Solo and Illya Kuryakin, with initialed pistols in their shoulder holsters, comprised the U.N.C.L.E. team. © *1964–1967 Metro-Goldwyn-Mayer, Inc.*

calling from a phone booth in New Jersey.

Even though the series' ratings had jumped and there was little doubt that a second season would be authorized, Felton continually pushed promotions to keep the series in the public eye. In March 1965 he suggested to Chuck Painter that *U.N.C.L.E.* bumper stickers be developed and sent out in response to fan letters, especially in those cities where the Nielsen ratings were still soft to boost the ratings in the fall.

Another promotional device favored by Felton was the use of U.N.C.L.E. identification cards. These started out as

a gimmick to promote the show to television columnists and advertisers, and were given out as placecards at an outdoor dinner meeting on the "New York street" on MGM's backlot. But the printer used different colors for the cards, and Felton later received a call from a Chevrolet executive, one of the sponsors at the dinner, complaining that he only got a blue card while someone else got a gold one. A messenger was sent to obtain a quantity of gold cards for Chevrolet.

The cards were eventually mailed out as a response to fan mail. Celebrities such as Phyllis Diller were card-carrying

U.N.C.L.E. agents; even the star of a rival TV show, *Lost in Space,* requested two cards—one for himself and one for "the robot." The cards became so popular that when the show premiered in England, MGM in Great Britain had to hire eight people full-time to fill orders for them, eventually sending out more than 200,000 in England alone.

The cards produced some unusual tales of fantasy crossing over into reality. Felton recalls how fans wrote and told of using the cards to cash checks, supplement their passports, etc. Felton himself was asked for a supply of them by the president of a bank he did business at. Robert Vaughn claimed that a member of the vice president's Secret Service entourage asked for a supply of them.

Chuck Painter feels that the U.N.C.L.E. cards were one of the all-time great promotional devices of television. "You could become an U.N.C.L.E. agent by sending your name and you would get an U.N.C.L.E. membership card. I still have my gold U.N.C.L.E. card, and I've used it as an ID card on numerous occasions to get past police lines in Italy. They take one look at it, and of course it's all in English, and it's on gold. They just look at it and, rather than admit ignorance, they just wave me through."

The idea was expanded to the production of THRUSH cards as well, for the cast and crew as a joke. But some of the cards were sent to MGM in England, and they began sending out hundreds of them. The front had the slogan "What evil thing have you done today?" and the THRUSH symbol of an enraged bird. Several newspaper articles appeared concerning parents' protests, with one English mother even writing to her member of Parliament about their bad influence on children. Felton called MGM in England and stopped the distribution.

But in spite of this, the THRUSH cards were quite popular. Chuck Painter recalls that "More people started to ask for THRUSH cards than for U.N.C.L.E. cards. Norman Felton got worried, he said these are the bad guys. We must be very careful and not push this THRUSH card past the little joke stage."

The popularity of the show was also evidenced by the numerous TV guest appearances by the stars. Vaughn was asked to appear on a Jimmy Durante special, on former competitor *The Red Skelton Hour,* and on *Art Linkletter's Talent Scouts,* and he and Leo G. Carroll made a joint appearance on the *Today* show. McCallum did a guest spot on *The Andy Williams Show,* where he demonstrated some of the U.N.C.L.E. gadgets, and guested on *The Tonight Show,* on a Carol Channing special, and on a Roger Miller special as well. His popularity even prompted an invitation from President and Mrs. Johnson to have dinner at the White House, but the shooting schedule did not allow this.

McCallum was also asked to host *Hullabaloo,* a teen music variety show, in the fall—a role normally performed by rock stars. This appearance underscored the extent to which the show had caught the public's imagination, especially the teenage audience. *The Man from U.N.C.L.E.* and the character of Illya Kuryakin were so well known by this time that McCallum could host the entire show as Illya, complete with black turtleneck and pen communicator, and never once be referred to by his real name.

Perhaps the biggest indication of the show's popularity was the avalanche of fan mail received. At one point, over ten thousand letters per week—not per month, but per week—were being received at MGM and NBC. The amount of mail addressed to David McCallum was greater than that received by any other male MGM star, including Clark Gable in his prime.

McCallum and Vaughn received the majority of the letters, many of which asked for autographs or pictures. But the fan letters were not limited to the two stars. The producers also received their share of mail, expressing great admiration for the show. Felton made an effort to personally answer each letter sent to him. For the fan letters to the show and the stars, a formal official fan club was set up. The *U.N.C.L.E.* Inner Circle was designated as the official clearinghouse for all *U.N.C.L.E.* letters, and Chuck Painter kept it supplied with news releases, bumper stickers, ID cards, and buttons for all who wrote in.

Some of the letters were sent to an unexpected address. Many people still thought the "U.N." in the title of the series stood for United Nations, and they sent letters to the UN asking for information on U.N.C.L.E. Many believed the end tag when it suggested U.N.C.L.E. was real, and wanted to join up as secret agents. Felton and Rolfe were aghast at this, having assumed that everyone watching would understand the tongue-in-cheek nature of the show and the tag.

Maurice Liu, director of the UN General Services Division at the time, reported an onslaught of *U.N.C.L.E.* mail. Even the official UN newsletter, *The Secretariat News,* in its February 16,

1966, issue, ran a facetious article about a UN visitor who is taken to a secret floor below the basement level where he encounters Napoleon Solo.

Yet another symptom of the show's success was the coverage Vaughn and McCallum received in the teen magazines. Although normally devoted to rock stars, magazines like *16, Teen,* and *Tiger Beat* would run a "David" article (no last name was necessary) nearly every issue in 1965 and 1966.

The adult TV and movie magazines, however, were more prone to promote gossip. These magazines loved to speculate on why Robert Vaughn was still a bachelor, and countless articles prescribed just exactly what it was he was looking for in a wife. McCallum's relationship with his wife Jill Ireland was also a popular topic, as were Vaughn's supposed plans to run for President. It was this type of journalism that led to the prevalent rumor, when the show was reaching its nadir of popularity, that there was a feud between Vaughn and McCallum. These magazines reported that the two actors disliked each other off the set and that Vaughn resented McCallum's popularity.

But there was no feud. Period. Vaughn displayed exceptional professionalism and maturity when confronted with his costar's popularity. Instead of reacting with bitterness, Vaughn said he welcomed the help with the hard work of the series and with the ratings. When McCallum received his Emmy nomination for Best Supporting Actor and Vaughn was not nominated, the crew of the *U.N.C.L.E.* set feared problems. But on the day the nominations were announced, McCallum received a telegram reading "Congratulations. All the way with Illya K.," signed by Robert Vaughn.

McCallum was always quick to point out that Robert Vaughn was the star of the series, and that the original format was a show based on the adventures of Napoleon Solo. McCallum blamed the feud rumor on the fact that Vaughn was a bachelor, and he was a family man. Since the two led completely different lifestyles offstage, they did not socialize much and the fan magazines played this up into a feud.

Chuck Painter confirms the absence of a feud, saying "I'll tell you the absolute truth: absolutely not. Never in any shape, way or form. If there was I would certainly tell you because nobody cares any more, really." Even today, both men still retain their admiration for each other. McCallum says, "Robert and I are close in age, but come from very dissimilar backgrounds. And socially we really have different lives. We have totally mutual respect, and have become good friends."

The reviewers did not know quite what to make of *The Man from U.N.C.L.E.* The reviewer for *TV Guide* had apparently viewed the pilot and "The Double Affair," and hated the show, although he did give credit to the briefcase-switching scene in "The Double Affair." He criticized both the writing and the casting. After this first review, *TV Guide* received many letters stating that he had missed the point, including a letter from a nine-year-old fan of the show stating, "I think you are a THRUSH member trying to kill everyone who works on *U.N.C.L.E.* I also think you are trying to kill me by writing those boring articles in *TV Guide.*" The letter was from David Rolfe, Sam Rolfe's son.

Other reviews were mixed. The *Hollywood Reporter* liked the show, while *Variety* said if the show was supposed to be James Bond for TV, it was "wholly inadequate and inept." Later, when the show became so popular, *Life* magazine's reviewer wrote that when he discovered the show, he wanted to keep it to himself "as I would the discovery of a superb but inexpensive restaurant," but instead he told others, and "I don't think I ever helped save a better show." *Time* magazine said "*The Man from U.N.C.L.E.* is the most popular new hero on the television scene." *McCall's* said the show had its own style of derring-do.

Later reviewers, perhaps acknowledging the fad the show was creating, were generous in their praise. In the July 1, 1967, issue of *TV Guide,* Martin Maloney, a professor of radio and television at Northwestern University, reviewed the show as well. He called the show entertaining, the performances of the regulars "first-rate," and the technical production "smooth and imaginative," and he said the show was overall "immeasurably superior to 75 percent of the films being shown on television." The *TV Guide* reviewer took a rare "second look" at the show, and this time agreed it had great appeal.

The final indicator of the success of the series was the number of times *The Man from U.N.C.L.E.* was parodied. Napoleon Solo, Illya Kuryakin, and U.N.C.L.E. became household words. The title lent itself readily to parody, and thus very early on *Mad* magazine ran its spoof of the show, titled "The Man from A.U.N.T.I.E." In early 1965, one of Bob Hope's TV specials featured a sketch titled "The Woman from A.U.N.T." Even comic books got into the act, with Archie's friend Jughead appearing as "The Man from R.I.V.E.R.D.A.L.E." An MGM Tom and Jerry cartoon was titled "The Mouse from H.U.N.G.E.R.," with agent Jerry Akin (Kuryakin). ABC's *The Addams Family* had a "Feud in the Addams Family" episode with the line "He looks like THRUSH to me." In *I Dream of Jeannie,* when a character is chained to a wall in a dungeon he offers the observation, "The man from U.N.C.L.E. always gets out of these things." An entire episode of *My Favorite Martian,* called "Man from Uncle Martin," revolved around the efforts of an evil organization named CRUSH. *Get Smart* had an episode in which Smart remarks that he thought a certain enemy agent was with THRUSH, but is then told he was transferred. *The Dick Van Dyke Show* spoofed the show's title in its "The Man from My Uncle" episode, as did *The Avengers* in the episode "The Girl from Auntie." Even the movie *The Glass Bottom Boat,* with Doris Day, featured a cameo by Vaughn along with a few bars of the *U.N.C.L.E.* theme

The best *U.N.C.L.E.* parody, however, occurred on the "Say Uncle" episode of *Please Don't Eat the Daises.* The episode featured cameo appearances by both Vaughn and McCallum, and the story concerned the children mistaking their father for a secret agent. The episode featured a tailor shop (although Felton declined to allow the use of Del Floria's, to preserve the mystique—B&C Tailor shop, another set seen in "The Dippy Blonde Affair" was used instead) and the *U.N.C.L.E.* theme music, and the twin children even wore *U.N.C.L.E.* sweatshirts.

None of these parodies would have worked if American audiences did not readily recognize the show they were spoofing. When a rival network uses a reference to a show in its own program, there is no doubt the parodied show is having a nationwide impact.

Certainly all of the above shows a remarkable comeback. The path the show followed from the low ratings of January 1965, to the opening of the second season, which it entered at the crest of it's incredible popularity, is a classic television rags-to-riches tale. The various factors that brought about the turnaround—the switch in time slot to Monday night, the promotional tours, the rise of the Illya character, the evangelism of the college-age crowd, and the finding of the proper recipe for combining humor and adventure—acted together to reverse the virtually certain cancellation that had loomed on the horizon for the show in December 1964.

Another factor in the show's resurgence, the James Bond phenomenon, cannot be overemphasized. Although *The Man from U.N.C.L.E.* was clearly unique and distinct from James Bond, they were also obviously in the same vein. While *U.N.C.L.E.* was creating its own fad, it was fostered by the James Bond fad as well, as the two audiences greatly overlapped. The world was hungry for secret agents and spies in the Bond tradition, and since *The Man from U.N.C.L.E.* was inspired by James Bond, there was a natural carryover.

Almost overnight, the show went from near cancellation to national fad. The ratings shot up. In December 1964, the show was ranked sixty-fourth. By the time of the first summer reruns, just six months later, the Nielsen ratings showed that the first rerun of *The Man from U.N.C.L.E.* drew 50 percent of the New

York audience, a remarkable showing for any episode and especially for a rerun.

Seldom, perhaps never, has a television series improved its standing so much in so short a time. Seldom, perhaps never, has a series created the cultural impact *The Man from U.N.C.L.E.* did in 1965.

Chapter 6

The Second Season

The second season of *The Man from U.N.C.L.E.* began on September 17, 1965. The steadily building crescendo of interest in the series that had begun in January with the college crowd had spread by word of mouth to younger teens, then to their parents, and finally to all groups in American society. News media coverage had exposed everyone to *The Man from U.N.C.L.E.*, and viewers had tuned in to see what all the fuss was about. Since the show had been slow to catch on, many devoted fans had missed some of the early episodes and eagerly awaited seeing them on the reruns over the summer. When the second season finally came, fans were hungry for more of the show.

The advent of color added to the anticipation. NBC touted it's "full color lineup" with 97 percent of it's prime-time schedule for 1965–66 in color. With more and more color TV sets in American homes, the new season was the first opportunity to show off the new technology on a grand scale.

Budget problems, not ratings, would now be the main threat to the show's existence. According to Norman Felton, "When we were developing the pilot film for *The Man from U.N.C.L.E.*, I was very concerned about the cost factor. The network was promised a lot of stars,

and they expected an adventure that went all over the world. Yet the amount of money they were willing to pay for the show was no more than they would pay for a *Dr. Kildare* or *Eleventh Hour,* both of which were principally interiors and very few exteriors." So Felton held a meeting with the staff before the second season even began, where he asked each of them "to use all their ingenuity to keep costs down."

The *U.N.C.L.E.* series was an expensive show to produce, especially in color. "You just can't sell shows and bring them out for what you get from the network," Felton says. "All the departments you work with charge you, and they gradually nibble most of it away."

For the second season, the show underwent another time-slot change. It was moved from Monday night at eight P.M. to Friday nights at ten P.M. eastern time. There had been talk back in January 1965 of making *U.N.C.L.E.* a half-hour show. Norman Felton didn't like the idea, but he told the network he could try and live with it if necessary, and suggested that perhaps two half-hour *U.N.C.L.E.* shows per week would be better, with a cliffhanger ending for the first segment. But when the show became popular, there was no question it would remain in the one-hour format, and it was placed opposite *The Jimmy Dean Show* on ABC and *Slattery's People* on CBS. The decision was based, in part, on a study done in February 1965 showing that the appeal of the show was strongest with teenagers aged twelve to seventeen, and young adults aged eighteen to thirty-four. Friday night was chosen because studies showed that there was more of this audience available during that time period on Friday night than on any other weeknight; the later time would not be a drawback because the next day was not a school day. There were estimated to be more than 24 million viewers aged eighteen to thirty-four during that time period. At the time the study was done, it was anticipated that *The Man from U.N.C.L.E.* would be competing against *Twelve O'Clock High* on ABC and *Coronet Blue* on CBS. Direct comparison studies showed that *U.N.C.L.E.* would draw a larger share than either of those shows.

But not everyone was happy with the time-slot change. Letters were received complaining that the time was too late in the evening, and made housewives choose between watching the show and going out for the evening. Many teens pointed out that Friday was a date night, again prompting a difficult choice for the viewer. A survey by *Newsweek* of college campuses showed that *U.N.C.L.E.* was, for the second year in a row, one of three favorite shows on campus. A petition signed by 138 State University of New York at Buffalo students requested the Monday night slot be retained. Other surveys showed that the show had the largest male audience outside of sports programs.

The stars were of course brought back for another season. Leo G. Carroll's op-

Vaughn, guest star Dorothy Provine, and McCallum in "The Alexander the Greater Affair." *Courtesy of the Norman Felton collection.*

tion was renewed by Arena for another year, although when his health was bad there was thought given to replacing him with Richard Haydn, who had played Waverly's brother-in-law in the first-season episode "The Mad, *Mad* Tea Party Affair."

For the week of October 18, 1965, *The Man from U.N.C.L.E.* attained the number-one Nielsen MNA rating for the first time, edging out *Bonanza, The Dick Van Dyke Show, The Smothers Brothers Show,* and *Bewitched.* The show had climbed from fiftieth place to thirteenth place in the overall Nielsens, with 24 percent of the audience, or twice the viewers it had had at the beginning of the first season—a remarkable comeback unparalleled in TV history.

A major change in the production staff for the second season occurred as well. Sam Rolfe, in keeping with his own policy of not staying with a show after its first season, left the series. "The fun was over for me at that point," he recalls. "From then on, the series was established and it was just what I call bricklaying after that. You just come in and keep laying bricks every week, there's nothing new to develop. I wanted to go on and develop something else, and let someone else take over."

That someone else was David Victor. Before he left, Rolfe dictated a lengthy memo to his successor, to try and leave behind a feel for the series he had developed and guided through its first year. In March 1965 he pointed out that the show should not rely too heavily on the gadgets that had become so popular, that THRUSH should not be used in every episode, and that the innocent in each episode should become involved in the story by believable means, not contrived, unlikely situations. He advocated avoiding Cold War situations in the scripts, and to keep in mind that both U.N.C.L.E. and THRUSH were, after all, "figments of someone's imagination."

He also stressed that *U.N.C.L.E.* was pure escapism, and should not spend much time trying to teach a moral lesson through its stories. He thought that *U.N.C.L.E.* should instead be a "bubbly, frothy romp . . . each story should involve run, hit, kiss, jump, skip, hop, twist and double twist."

After he left the show, Rolfe pursued a claim through the Writers Guild in May of 1965 that he be listed on the show as creator instead of developer, which would have meant more royalties. Rolfe correctly perceived that little, if any, of Fleming's contribution had made it into the series, that he had literally formulated the show himself from scratch. Although his name continued to be listed as "developer," he did win additional compensation.

The Man from U.N.C.L.E. decided to kick off the second season with its first two-part episode, "The Alexander the Greater Affair." A two-part episode would involve more guest stars, spread the story out over two hours instead of one, and leave the audience with a cliffhanger ending at the end of part 1 to entice them to tune in to part 2.

The two-part episodes were Felton's personal pride and joy. He felt that they would allow better production values, because of the extra shooting time, as well as better story and character development. With the possibility of releasing the two-part episodes as feature films, more money could be invested in getting bigger-name guest stars that would in turn increase the "marquee value" of the movie version.

"The Alexander the Greater Affair" featured Rip Torn as the egomaniac Alexander, who planned to conquer the world by breaking each of the ten commandments. Dorothy Provine played Tracy, Alexander's ex-wife, who tagged along with Solo and Illya against their will while they tried to recover a will gas stolen by Alexander to carry out his plan. At the end of Part 1, Solo was left tied to a slab with a scimitar swinging steadily downward to slice him in two, while Illya and Tracy Alexander were tied together swinging over a bottomless pit with a candle burning the rope holding them up. What viewer could help but tune in again the next week to see how they escaped?

The second season of *The Man from U.N.C.L.E.* was destined to be popular, given the impetus the show enjoyed from the first season. But the stories of the second season stand on their own. Though they lacked Sam Rolfe's touch, they nevertheless adhered to the *U.N.C.L.E.* formula of adventure with humor. The plots were not to be taken too seriously, but the villains still exuded menace.

A scene from a rare episode, "The Very Important Zombie Affair." © *1964–1967 Metro-Goldwyn-Mayer, Inc.*

The other networks, wishing to capitalize on the impact of *The Man from U.N.C.L.E.*, deluged the schedule with their own spy shows in the 1965–66 season: *The Wild, Wild West* and *Mission: Impossible* on CBS; *Honey West* on ABC, which also altered the format of it's detective series *Burke's Law* to become *Amos Burke, Secret Agent*; and NBC itself offered *I Spy* and *Get Smart,* the latter a comedy spoof of *U.N.C.L.E.*

The working relationship between Solo and Illya was refined in the second season as well. A touch of jealousy was introduced. Solo, for example, is annoyed when Diana McBain expresses an attraction for Illya instead of him in "The Deadly Toys Affair." There is no question that they are now a team, and no longer is Illya a second fiddle. All the episodes play equally to both characters, and there are no all-Solo episodes in the second season. The show is clearly now *The Men from U.N.C.L.E.* even though the title would always remain singular.

The Man from U.N.C.L.E. ended up with an overall rating of 24.0 for the season, which placed it thirteenth among the sixty-six shows on the air. It beat out such established shows as *The Lawrence Welk Show, Walt Disney's Wonderful World of Color, My Three Sons,* and *The Ed Sullivan Show. Variety* called it a show that was "riding high and rightfully so," and predicted that if "pace and excitement are sustained, Metro will have a top 10-er."

The producers of the show clearly interpreted the success they were enjoying as a sign that what made the show popular was its emphasis on the absurd, that no one took it as a serious adventure but rather almost akin to a comedy where many things could be poked fun at. They often used the phrase "tongue-in-cheek" in describing the show, and reviewers often called the series a "spoof" of the James Bond craze.

Already in the second season, however, the emphasis of the series began to change. The signs were present that a shift to comedy, as opposed to humor, was in the works for the third season. Unfortunately, this was a misreading of the public pulse. The viewers of *The Man from U.N.C.L.E.* liked the show for what it was in the second season: an adventure show with a less-than-serious approach, a series featuring a pair of heroes who, although they were fallible and made mistakes, were nevertheless admirable because of their cool handling of danger and their ability to engage in humor in dangerous situations. The public saw *The Man from U.N.C.L.E.* as a lighter version of James Bond, at the same time that the producers were shifting the show toward the absurd and often slapstick comedy of shows like *Batman*. The third season of the show would prove to be a turning point in several respects.

The Making of a Television Series: Behind the Scenes of *The Man from U.N.C.L.E.*

Chapter 7

Producing *U.N.C.L.E.*

The executive producer throughout the three and a half seasons of *The Man from U.N.C.L.E.* and the single season of *The Girl from U.N.C.L.E.* was Norman Felton. Felton served as the head of Arena Productions. As executive producer, he held the top position in the entire production staff. As president of Arena, his job was to provide a series that the network would buy, and then see that it stayed appealing enough to the public to generate high ratings so that the network would continue to buy it. His job was also to keep the costs of producing the show low enough to generate a profit for the company. The producer, on the other hand, coordinates all aspects of the actual production of the product. These positions, along with the writer, director, and assistant director, are commonly referred to as "above-the-line" positions, referring to the position of their costs on an accounting sheet for the production.

For the pilot episode, "The Vulcan Affair," Norman Felton served both as executive producer and producer. Later, Sam Rolfe was hired by Felton not only to create a format for the series and write the pilot script, but to produce the first season as well. As noted earlier, it is generally agreed among fans of the show that the first season was, from the stand-point of entertainment and quality, the best of the series, and that this is attributable to Sam Rolfe's influence.

It was Rolfe who set the tone and flavor for the series. Rolfe made sure that the series incorporated the right blend of intrigue, adventure, and humor without straining believability. He kept the show light and amusing without sinking into comedy. He seemed to know instinctively that too much humor would destroy any sense of danger or suspense. Having developed the show, Rolfe found himself, as producer, in a position to put his ideas and concepts into each episode. Because of this, the first season was internally consistent, without the distracting lapses in continuity and deviation from the prospectus that marred later seasons.

There is no question that Norman Felton and Sam Rolfe, together, were the creative influences that not only brought the series into being, but guided it in the directions that resulted in its phenomenal success.

Associate Producer George Lehr describes Rolfe's role: "It was his baby. He set it all in motion. He had the ultimate responsibility, along with Norman Felton. He fought very strongly for this concept where you had to walk the line between reality and make-believe, and you could step one direction one second, but you had to step on the other side of the line the next. During the first year, when Sam was there, he very consciously walked that line. That was the key word. And the key decisions were made by Sam Rolfe and Norman Felton. They were the makers of the series."

The associate producer for the first season was Joseph Calvelli. Nicknamed Doc, he was known for his sense of humor. Director Richard Donner called him "One of the most fun guys you'd ever want to work with, one of the wittiest, funniest guys I've ever known." David McCallum recalls Calvelli as "a very funny, lovely man," and David Victor, second-season producer, calls Calvelli a "marvelously funny guy." Al-

Joseph "Doc" Calvelli, associate producer.
© *1964–1967 Metro-Goldwyn-Mayer, Inc.*

though the credits only list him as associate producer, he actually served as story editor as well.

Calvelli served as associate producer for *The Man from U.N.C.L.E.* for roughly two-thirds of the first season. The rest of the season, Robert Foshko fulfilled these duties. Calvelli returned for *The Girl from U.N.C.L.E.* two years later, where he wrote the scripts for "The Mother Muffin Affair" and "The Little John Doe Affair," and also played a small role in the latter episode.

The position of "assistant to the producer" for the pilot episode was held by Joseph Gantman. However, he was not carried over into the series itself. George Lehr served as assistant to the producer for the other twenty-eight episodes of the first season and became, for all intents and purposes, the third member of the Felton-Rolfe team. He undertook a myriad of duties on the show, including all postproduction work. Lehr, who had worked on *The Lieutenant* with Felton and on *The Eleventh Hour* with Rolfe, brought to *U.N.C.L.E.* a wide array of knowledge of the industry, and his flexibility filled in many gaps that otherwise might have existed on the production staff. His initial duties as assistant to the producer were, in his words, to "work on helping Sam get this project off the ground."

David Victor, who replaced Rolfe as producer, guided the first ten episodes of the second season as line producer, then took over the newly created position of supervising producer, which he held for the rest of the series. David Victor does appear to "return" as producer for a later broadcast episode, "The Yukon Affair," but this episode was actually shot in August 1965, before the staff changes.

He also produced "The Moonglow Affair" in the second season, as that was the *Girl from U.N.C.L.E.* pilot episode and he was slated to be supervising producer on both shows for the third season.

This change was part of a general restructuring of responsibilities on the *U.N.C.L.E.* staff that took place in late September 1965. With "The Cherry Blossom Affair," several people on the staff occupied new positions. Victor was promoted from producer to supervising producer; Mort Abrahams from production executive to producer; and Boris Ingster, who later became producer, joined the team as production executive. Because of the staff changes, each "regular" producer only lasted for a third of the second season: David Victor for the first third, Mort Abrahams for the middle third, and Boris Ingster for the final third.

With three producers in the second season, no clear style emerged. The first producer, David Victor, was born in Odessa, a port on the Black Sea in the Ukraine, USSR. He came to the United States at the age of twelve with his widowed mother, and began working for newspapers and magazines. He wrote many radio plays, then moved to television, where he wrote for such series as *Fireside Theatre, Walt Disney Presents, Gunsmoke, Rawhide,* and *Playhouse 90.* His writing for *Gunsmoke* and another series, *The Restless Gun,* won him nominations for Writers Guild awards. Victor then served as producer on *Dr. Kildare* for five years. After Sam Rolfe left *The Man from U.N.C.L.E.* as producer, Norman Felton, who was executive producer of *Dr. Kildare* as well, asked Victor to serve as producer for *U.N.C.L.E.* and at the same time stay on as supervising producer for *Dr. Kildare.*

When Victor took over the reins of *U.N.C.L.E.* production, the series was already well established and enjoying its heyday of popularity. He says, "When we moved to Friday night, it became very, very popular all over the world." But Victor had his own ideas about which way the series should go. "My direction was always to stress the innocent even more than they had before. In other words, there was always somebody the audience could identify with, such as the secretary who goes out to lunch without any knowledge that she holds something very important to THRUSH. We could get emotionally involved with somebody who was less esoteric than the rest of the characters."

Another theme that Victor decided to stress in the second season was believability. "Another rule of mine was my insistence that we never lose some sense of reality, even in the most outlandish situations. So the element of danger would not be lost. In other words, even if we are hanging upside down and a rotating saw is coming to slice them up like a bologna, they should never exchange any light remarks at that time . . . so reality was always stressed."

A third theme that Victor decided to retain concerned the two main characters themselves: "One thing that we actually had a philosophy on was that we would keep those figures very mysterious. You know if you've studied the show, we never gave any information or any indication of their personal life. We didn't know if they were married, single, where they lived, how they felt about things. That was by design . . ."

One of the first things Victor did upon

taking over the show was to get to know his two stars: "Coming in the second year, I had quite a chat with both of them. I told them I wasn't going to guarantee we would have perfect scripts each time, but they would always have me working with them, and my only desire was to see the show succeed. And I told them they would probably get a lot richer from the show than I would."

For the third season, Victor continued to serve as supervising producer for Arena. As Douglas Benton described Victor's duties, "David's job was more of an administrative executive. It was his job to see that the show had a flow of scripts coming in, and that the production schedules were maintained." U.N.C.L.E. writer Peter Allan Fields recalls that David Victor "is a man who loves, and treats with great respect, creative talent. Producers need the creative talent, but sometimes resent that. David Victor was the antithesis of that. He is not only a kind and gentle man, but also a brilliant man and well-read. But he knew what he wanted also."

The second of three second-season producers was Mort Abrahams. As Peter Allan Fields describes his tenure, "Mort Abrahams was there only a short time. Dean Hargrove and I knew the show better than he did, so he had to learn the show. But he was very congenial, and then went on to other things." Abrahams, who had earlier worked on General Electric Theater and Route 66, had been an acquaintance of Felton's when they both worked in New York. Abrahams undertook his U.N.C.L.E. duties without any grand plans for change: "We were a successful series," he recalls, "and we wanted to keep going in the same direction. We were losing writers, however, so we were trying to get other

writers involved. By then the characters were established, so there were no drastic changes that year. There was no indication of falling audiences." But Abrahams himself soon left the series to do feature work.

Boris Ingster, the third second-season producer, would continue as line producer for the third season of The Man from U.N.C.L.E. as well. Prior to becoming producer in the second season, he had served as production executive, and had written "The Very Important Zombie Affair" as well as the first-season episode "The Yellow Scarf Affair." Even after taking over as producer, he continued to write for the series, authoring "The Five Daughters Affair" and, with David Giler, "The Matterhorn Affair," in the third season.

Ingster, like David Victor, was of Russian extraction. Also like Victor, Ingster had his start in writing before becoming a producer. Born in 1913, he began writing screenplays in 1935 with The Last Days of Pompeii, followed by Happy Landing (1938), Paris Underground (1945), and Something for the Birds (1952). He also turned to directing, with Stranger on the Third Floor (1940) and The Judge Steps Out (1949).

U.N.C.L.E. writer Peter Allan Fields had the impression that Boris Ingster "really didn't want to be there. He seemed a little less enthusiastic when it came to the kind of show that had heretofore been produced." Another U.N.C.L.E. writer, Harlan Ellison, recalls Ingster with special fondness. He says "Working on The Man from U.N.C.L.E. was one of my most pleasant television experiences, because I was working with Boris Ingster, who was an amazing, wonderful character. He was an ex-Russian nobleman or something

Second and third season producer Boris Ingster. © 1964–1967 Metro-Goldwyn-Mayer, Inc.

like that. His office was on the ground floor of a little building right next to the Thalberg Building on the MGM lot, right behind the entrance you come in. Ken Hollywood was the guard at the gate, and his office was right behind him. And when his window was open in the summertime, I could literally step into his office through the window, and I often would. And we would have these terrible fights about what was being done to a script, and when I would get annoyed with what Boris was doing to my script, I would jump into his office window and land on his sofa and then bounce off the sofa and run around his desk screaming, 'Ingster, you fucking Cossack, what have you done to my script?'"

Ellison recalls that Ingster would often respond in kind: "We had this friendly adversarial relationship. And he

would start screaming in that thick Russian accent, 'Ellison, you are driving me crazy. Get the hell out of my office.' And I would jump on his desk, and I would go to sleep on his sofa."

Ellison recalls, "Ingster would come into his office, and I would have all of his furniture stacked up in the middle of the room. And I'd tell him, 'You rearranged my script, so I rearranged your furniture.' That went on for months and months. It was great fun, it was serious but it was also great fun. Boris and I were born to fight. And there was never any rancor and never even a moment of bad feelings. Boris was an amazing man."

Ingster served as producer for all of the third season, except for "The Apple A Day Affair," which was produced by Irving Pearlberg, normally an associate producer since George Lehr had been sent over to *The Girl from U.N.C.L.E.* to help get that show off on the right foot.

For *The Man from U.N.C.L.E.*'s fourth and final season, Felton and Victor chose Anthony Spinner as producer. *The Girl from U.N.C.L.E.* had by then been canceled due to low ratings, and there was a feeling that *The Man from U.N.C.L.E.* was in trouble as well. The show needed new blood, and a different approach. Actually, Felton and Victor realized they needed an *old* approach, one more like the elements that had made the first and second seasons a success but that had somehow been lost or forgotten in the third season. Spinner was selected to bring the show back to its roots. Spinner had written for the show in the first season, penning "The Secret Sceptre Affair."

Spinner saw that the show had gotten too silly, too ridiculous even for a series that prided itself on being tongue-in-cheek. He announced a shift back to the old formula, with less spoofing and more straight action adventure.

Spinner was assisted by two associate producers in the fourth season. Since *The Girl from U.N.C.L.E.* had been canceled, George Lehr was again available for that job. But Felton and Victor were satisfied with Pearlberg's work as well, so rather than discharge Pearlberg or deny Lehr his old job they were both put on the payroll as associate producers for the fourth season, without any assistant to the producer. As Lehr explains it, "When *Girl* was canceled and that group disbanded, Norman said, 'Look, we had Irv over on the other show, so we're going to give him a new line and both you and Irv will be associate producers.' Irv was primarily the story editor, and I had been doing what I had been doing all along, which was primarily production liaison—helping prepare, and having meetings with Irv and Tony, to get the directors going, and then liaison between the production office and our production staff to get them prepared for shooting, and then all the post production supervision."

Unfortunately, Spinner's well-laid plans were not given a full chance to work. *The Man from U.N.C.L.E.* was canceled in midseason, an ignominious end for any show but especially for a show which, just two seasons earlier, had been creating a tidal wave of popularity. Spinner went on to serve as story consultant and producer for a series called *Search,* and produced both *Dan August* and *The F.B.I.*

Norman Felton, in looking back on the series, acknowledges that the frequent changes in producers probably hurt the show. "Every series has problems," he says, "but on *The Man from U.N.C.L.E.,* we ate producers up. When you have a serious-based subject matter, it's tough. But when you have something like *The Man from U.N.C.L.E.* with its unique challenges, somehow you could have a laugh along with it and get it solved. In that way, we were able to overcome tremendous production problems."

Chapter 8

Directing *U.N.C.L.E.*

In any film production, whether it is for television or feature films, perhaps the most crucial member of the production team on the set itself is the director. Directors are hired on an episode-by-episode basis, and are not part of the permanent production staff. The director is the person responsible for coordinating the actual shooting of the visual image; the cameramen, actors, script persons, lighting personnel, etc., all take his direction. The director instructs the actors on how to perform their lines, where to stand and move, how to time their actions and dialogue, and how to emote. He decides when retakes are necessary, and when a take is adequate for printing. The director is the primary person responsible for bringing the story in the script to the film negative. Or, as property master Arnold Goode succinctly put it, "the director is God on the set."

A director's authority also extends to

Director Barry Shear (center) oversees a scene from "The Her Master's Voice Affair." © *1964–1967 Metro-Goldwyn-Mayer, Inc.*

Director and cameramen worked closely together to achieve unusual shots for "U.N.C.L.E." *Courtesy of the Norman Felton collection.*

revising the script when necessary. As an example of this, *U.N.C.L.E.* writer Alan Caillou recalled many occasions when he was on the set as an actor in a script he himself had written. Many times, he pointed out, a line of dialogue that looked good on paper proved to be a tongue-twister for an actor or actress to say. When this occurred, Caillou would be called upon by the director to do an on-the-spot rewrite. Since Caillou was trained in classical Shakespearean theater himself, he found it difficult to understand why actors had trouble with the dialogue he had written.

Another duty of the director is to re-view the "dailies," the film shot the previous day, to see if any scenes need to be reshot. George Lehr recalls, "We looked at dailies every day about eleven or twelve o'clock. We'd look at everything we shot the day before. And the director would come up and he'd tell the editor, now here's what I want, I think you could use this here, or that there."

The guest star for the first episode of the series, Patricia Crowley, describes other functions of the director: "As you approach each scene, he has his ideas of how each scene should be played, and his angles for the shots, and how he feels the pace should be, whatever his feelings for

A swimsuited camera crew films the final sequence of "The Neptune Affair."
© *1964–1967 Metro-Goldwyn-Mayer, Inc.*

expressing the role are." Her comments were in regard to her director on the pilot episode, Don Medford, who did not return to the *U.N.C.L.E.* series after that. "He is an amazing director. He's just got this tremendous enthusiasm, and lots of good ideas. He gave the actors the freedom to work as one would like to have, and he was just a delight to work with on *U.N.C.L.E.*"

The Man from U.N.C.L.E. ran for 105 episodes, and *The Girl from U.N.C.L.E.* for 29 episodes; together the shows employed thirty-nine directors. But of those thirty-nine, four accounted for over 40 percent of the shows produced. Another handful of directors made frequent appearances, while several had their services utilized only once. Many directors used on the two *U.N.C.L.E.* shows had directed for Norman Felton or Sam Rolfe before on other shows.

U.N.C.L.E.'s most frequent directors were used throughout the series, and many times crossed over to direct *Girl from U.N.C.L.E.* episodes. Alf Kjellin did ten in all, including two *Girl* episodes. Sherman Marks, who directed six episodes, is the only director to work on all four seasons of *The Man from U.N.C.L.E.* and for *The Girl from U.N.C.L.E.* But three directors handled the most

U.N.C.L.E. episodes: John Brahm, who directed thirteen; E. Darrell Hallenbeck, who directed fifteen; and Barry Shear, with fourteen.

John Brahm began with *The Man from U.N.C.L.E.* in the second season, then moved over to *The Girl from U.N.C.L.E.* Born in Germany, Brahm had begun directing films in 1935, and directed for TV on *Alfred Hitchcock Presents, The Outer Limits, The Twilight Zone,* and *Dr. Kildare.*

E. Darrell Hallenbeck, another frequent director, also began his *U.N.C.L.E.* career in the second season and directed in the third and fourth seasons as well as for *The Girl from U.N.C.L.E.* Hallenbeck first came to *U.N.C.L.E.* as assistant director, by virtue of having worked with Sam Rolfe on *The Eleventh Hour.* He would later work on such films as *All the President's Men* and *About Last Night.* Hallenbeck also did *Hoover* for cable TV, in association with another former *U.N.C.L.E.* director, Bill Finnegan.

Barry Shear is the third member of the *U.N.C.L.E.* directing triumvirate. His fourteen episodes began in the second season, with "The Minus X Affair," and continued into the third and fourth seasons and to *The Girl from U.N.C.L.E.* Shear had a reputation as a director who tended to overshoot so as to have plenty of footage for the editor to choose from for the final cut. Associate producer George Lehr recalled how on one episode, Shear had Stefanie Powers hanging from a trapeze by her knees over what was supposed to be a pit of piranhas for several takes, even though the young actress was starting to show obvious signs of exhaustion. Lehr prompted Douglas Benton to come down to the set and convince Shear that the shot was completed so that Powers could come

down from the trapeze. Shear would also insist on reshooting scenes when others on the set, such as the camera operators, felt that the takes were adequate. Noel Harrison recalls Shear as being "a madman" who had "a kind of manic energy." Shear went on to direct other shows, such as *Night Gallery* and *Starsky and Hutch,* and, with Douglas Benton, *Inside the KKK,* a TV movie.

Another frequent *U.N.C.L.E.* director was Joseph Sargent. Sargent directed ten *U.N.C.L.E.* episodes, and they turned out to be among the ten best of the whole series. A native of Jersey City, New Jersey, Sargent was thirty-nine years old when he began directing for *U.N.C.L.E.* He had already garnered credits for directing on many television series, including *Bonanza, Gunsmoke,* and *Route 66.*

Perhaps the *U.N.C.L.E.* director who had the most successful subsequent career is Richard Donner. Prior to *U.N.C.L.E.,* he had directed for Sam Rolfe on *Have Gun, Will Travel,* and for Norman Felton on *Dr. Kildare.* Donner directed four episodes for *The Man from U.N.C.L.E.,* all in the first season (the most by any director in that season).

Donner was known as a prankster on the set, fond of doing unusual things to get the effect he wanted. When he wanted to simulate commotion and confusion in a scene, the six-foot-tall Donner would grab cameraman Til Gabbani and shake him to jiggle the picture. Donner comments, "I used to do terrible things to Bobby Vaughn. Bobby used to take himself very seriously. His hair had to be perfectly straight. I used to run into the shot just before I yelled 'Action' and mess his hair up. . . . Or I'd have a girl pop up in the middle of a shot holding a sign that says 'Smile.'"

Robert Vaughn and guest stars Jack Palance and Letitia Roman have a script conference with director Joseph Sargent on the set of "The Concrete Overcoat Affair." © *1964–1967 Metro-Goldwyn-Mayer, Inc.*

Donner and Sam Rolfe were prone to playing practical jokes on each other on the set. After Donner played a joke on Rolfe, Rolfe planned to get even. Donner recalled, "I forgot all about it. I had rented a house on Malibu Beach, and when we shot ['The Quadripartite Affair' and 'The Giuoco Piano Affair'] we shot them at Fox ranch, right next door. . . . Since it was five minutes from my house, I didn't have to drive an extra half hour into the city to the studio. One day at the studio, Sam Rolfe told me to come in early because there was a new union rule that required all members of the production staff to be driven by a Teamster from the studio to the location. . . . So I figure this is Sam Rolfe getting even with me, and it's a big setup or put-on. So I walked over to the head of the studio, who was on the lot that day with Sam, and I said, 'I think you're being very unfair to your directors, we break our backs to get these things in on time for you . . . so I think if anything you should have a driver pick me up at my house, don't you, so I don't have to drive.' And he looked at Sam and said, 'Oh, I guess so, alright.' So I figured, you know, it's over with. The next morning, I got up and walked outside and there was a driver and a limousine. I said to him, 'What are you doing here?' He said, 'Mr. Rolfe sent me. You've got to have a driver.' It hadn't been a put-on, and I was talking that way to the head of the studio!"

Donner enjoyed working on *The Man from U.N.C.L.E.*: "It was a lot of fun there. . . . It was wonderful. The cast was great to work with." But although he enjoyed directing for *U.N.C.L.E.*, he only did four episodes for the series. "I never used to like to do more than two or three, three or four at the most of a show . . . you get too familiar with the characters, it's no longer a challenge." Donner went on to direct for other TV shows, such as *The Wild, Wild West*. But his career later shifted to feature movies, such as *Superman, The Omen, Ladyhawke,* and *The Goonies.*

The directors on the *U.N.C.L.E.* set were assisted by three assistant directors. The first assistant director usually works quite closely with the director himself, supervising scene and set changes, preparing daily call sheets (a list of which actors were needed when and where), and acting as a go-between for the director and the members of the crew. The second assistant is responsible for all other paperwork, such as daily shooting schedules, and for coordinating the stuntmen and extras. The third assistant acts as a stand-in for the first assistant when his duties take him elsewhere.

Many of the directors for the show graduated to that position from the assistant director slot. E. Darrell Hallenbeck was assistant director for several early episodes, and was promoted to full director for "The Arabian Affair," halfway through the second season. Director Bill Finnegan, who came to *U.N.C.L.E.* in the first season from *The Twilight Zone,* began as a second assistant director. He described his duties as "giving the actors their calls, doing a lot of paperwork, coordinating the extras, scheduling the crew, all under the direction of the first assistant."

Hallenbeck states that his duties as assistant director entailed "the function of

both a production manager and a unit manager. We did both jobs, which means we helped prepare the budget, helped with locations, set up the extras, and we scheduled the show." As assistant director, Hallenbeck was often charged with doing "pickup shots," which involved situations where "sometimes we would shoot maybe nine-tenths of an episode, and we would leave three or four shots we didn't have time for. We would go back and do them later." The same situation occurred when the schedule required two camera crews to shoot in two places at once, often one crew on the lot and another on location. The assistant director was then referred to as a second-unit director.

For example, for "Alexander the Greater Affair" (parts 1 and 2), E. Darrell Hallenbeck, then assistant director, served as director of a second unit that did pickup and title background shots while the main crew shot the story. Sometimes a second unit was needed for a two-part episode, such as "The Bridge of Lions Affair," because of extra footage that was intended to be shot for the feature version. On other occasions, such as "The Indian Affairs Affair," a second unit was used to film location scenes, such as the climactic outdoor battle between Indians on motorcycles and THRUSH jeeps that appears in that episode.

For larger productions, such as the two-part episodes intended for feature-film release overseas, there was yet another assistant. For "The Concrete Overcoat Affair" (parts 1 and 2), even the second-unit director had an assistant director. For "The Prince of Darkness Affair" (part 1 and 2), Maurice Vaccarino was designated "retake director" in addition to the director, assistant director, and second-unit director.

For the most part, each season had one or two assistant directors that alternated between episodes. Most of the first-season episodes were assisted by Bill Finnegan and E. Darrell Hallenbeck. The pilot episode, "The Vulcan Affair," had Maurice Vaccarino as assistant director. For the second season, Hallenbeck, Finnegan, Tom McCrory, and Wilbur Mosier continued to perform as assistant directors. They were occasionally joined by Robert M. Webb, Eddie Saeta, James Sullivan, and George W. Davis. Finnegan and Saeta alternated as assistant directors for all the episodes of the third season, with the exception of "The Pop Art Affair," on which Richard F. Landry served. For the fourth season, most of the episodes had Maurice Vaccarino, who had not been associated with the series since the pilot, or Glenn N. Cook as assistant director. For *The Girl from U.N.C.L.E.*, assistant director's duties for all the episodes but one were alternated between Ray DeCamp and Dick Bennett, who had served in the same role earlier on *The Man from U.N.C.L.E.*

Beginning with the second season, there was more continuity among directors. Each director left his own mark on the episode. The episodes directed by Barry Shear, for example, reflected the less serious, more satirical approach the series was moving toward in the third season. The work of directors like Hallenbeck and Sargent provided a consistency to the series, maintaining the original flavor Rolfe had in mind. When the director failed to grasp the concept of the series, the show noticeably suffered. But when the director understood the show and its style, the series thrived.

Chapter 9

Filming *U.N.C.L.E.*

For the photography of the series, Felton brought two key people, Fred Koenekamp and Til Gabbani, from *The Lieutenant.* Koenekamp had been working as a camera operator for MGM for twelve years when he was hired by Felton for *The Lieutenant* as first cameraman. Felton recalls, "Fred Koenekamp is one of the brilliant cinematographers today in feature films. About halfway through the making of *The Lieutenant,* I happened to hear from someone that when a man is an operator of a camera, and he wants to become a director of photography, and he gets a position as one, he can take it but at the end of six months he has to make his decision whether he wants to stay a director of photography. If so, he can't go back to being an operator again. And I saw Fred coming out of the camera shop one day, and I said 'Fred, I get the feeling your six months is about up.' And he said, 'Today's the day.' So I said, 'I don't think "The Lieutenant" is going to continue, but I have another series, and we're making the pilot. You can't make the pilot, we have another man doing it. But if it goes to a series, you've got the job.' He thanked me, he did get the series, and he stayed with it."

Fred Koenekamp served as "director of photography" on *U.N.C.L.E.* His duties were to assist the director in the selection of camera setups for each scene; in some cases the director assigned this task completely to him. As director of photography he was also responsible for all camera moves, as well as for lighting. His main concern was the total look of the picture, and because of this he

David McCallum tries the Arriflex camera, which revolutionized television filming. © *1964–1967 Metro-Goldwyn-Mayer, Inc.*

worked closely with the director and the camera operator.

Felton feels that *U.N.C.L.E.* could not have kept to its six-day shooting schedule without Koenekamp's contribution. "Because of the speed with which we could travel," he says, "we never could have made the series without Fred." One of the problems facing Koenekamp was the number of hours available for shooting daylight scenes: "Late in the afternoons," Felton explains, "we would begin to lose the sun. In the summer we had a long day, but as time went on I knew we'd be filming in the fall and winter, and we would have short days if

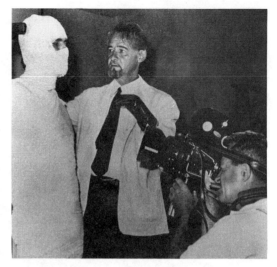

Til Gabbani uses a headband to steady his hand-held camera. *Courtesy of the Norman Felton collection.*

we shot outside. And exteriors were one of the things that the network was excited about."

Koenekamp, according to Felton, met the problem by innovating new film techniques: "He came to me after several weeks of work on the show, and said that he thought that we could work longer each day when it got dark if we were to 'force' the film in development in the labs. He hinted that the labs weren't too happy with this idea, and would tell me that it couldn't be done, but he thought it could. That meant that he could film under less light and the lab could put it in the coat a little longer." The technique worked, and allowed the crew to shoot longer each day.

U.N.C.L.E.'s first season was shot in black-and-white, as the budget did not permit color. But black-and-white presented special problems for Koenekamp: "It was a lot harder to shoot in black-

Til Gabbani manages a camera angle achievable only with the Arriflex in "The My Friend the Gorilla Affair." © *1964–1967 Metro-Goldwyn-Mayer, Inc.*

Use of both the standard BNC camera (right) and the hand-held Arriflex (left) kept filming on schedule. © *1964–1967 Metro-Goldwyn-Mayer, Inc.*

and-white than color. In black-and-white, you have a range of about twenty filters you must really get acquainted with, and you use them all the time in your exterior work. In black and white, that's the only way you get contrast in your film. Whereas in color, there's only a couple of filters involved."

This difference prompted Koenekamp to suggest to George Lehr a change in *U.N.C.L.E.* headquarters itself when the show switched to color in the second season. The interior walls of the hallways in the headquarters scenes consisted of painted plywood panels. "The walls were silver initially," Lehr explains. "And silver was a big problem, because of all the glare and reflection. You could use something to mask your lights, but when it was silver, you saw all the hot spots in the glares from your set

lights. Freddie Koenekamp said 'These walls are killing us,' so we told him we would make them any color he wanted, and we converted them to gray."

The use of the gray walls gave the proper metallic appearance in black and white, but Lehr says, "When they bought the second season in color, we said what are we going to do now. We had these gray walls, and it was kind of dull. So Fred suggested we just spray it with a lacquer, and that will give it a sheen, yet won't present any reflective problems." So the walls were redone again.

Koenekamp was also responsible for the unusual look of the many scenes in the series that took place in caves or caverns, such as "The Bat Cave Affair," "The Tigers Are Coming Affair," and "The Deadly Goddess Affair," among others. The eerie red glow seen in these episodes was accomplished with red lights hidden behind artificial rocks and directed upward.

The *U.N.C.L.E.* camera crew consisted of the director of photography, the camera operator, and generally two assistant cameramen. One of these, designated the first assistant, was in charge of the camera itself. It was his job to set the camera up, and be responsible for its function and the focus. The second assistant was responsible for caring for and loading the 35-mm Eastman Kodak film. After production was completed, both 35-mm and 16-mm prints would be made. The second assistant was also responsible for doing the "slating"—clap-

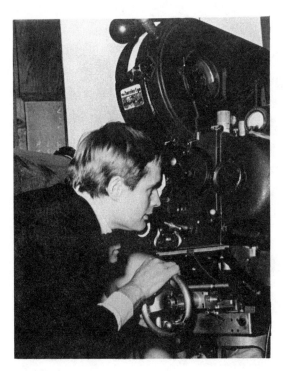

David McCallum peers through the main U.N.C.L.E. camera, a Mitchell BNC. *Courtesy of the Norman Felton collection.*

ping the swing arm of a metal chalkboard showing the production number, scene number, director, and take number. The sound of the clap, when matched with the image frame showing the swing arm hitting the chalkboard, provided the editor with a set starting point for synchronizing the sound track with the film. Assistant cameraman duties were performed by first assistant Chuck Arnold and second assistants Gail Parker, Chuck Short, and Robert Wasserman.

But the actual camera work fell quite literally on the shoulders of the camera operator, Til Gabbani, also a veteran of *The Lieutenant.* Unlike Koenekamp, Gabbani had worked on the pilot as well.

Gabbani was responsible for a major innovation that is credited with making the series a success. The standard camera used on *The Man from U.N.C.L.E.* was a large, bulky Mitchell BNC. But *U.N.C.L.E.* involved a lot of exteriors, and a lot of action footage—fight scenes, car chases, etc. The big, heavy BNC was difficult to move and was limited in the number of available shooting angles, even when mounted on a crab dolly or crane.

Gabbani was in Munich, Germany, doing work on a Marlon Brando film, when he saw a German camera crew using a lightweight, handheld camera called an Arriflex. Gabbani brought one back to 20th Century–Fox, where he was working, and proposed using it in the camera department. The head of the department was not interested, so Gabbani went over his head to the president of the studio, and pointed out to him that the studio was spending sixteen thousand dollars an hour shooting *Adventures in Paradise,* and that the new camera would save an hour of shooting a day. Gabbani, who was then working on *The Diary of Anne Frank,* shot identical scenes with the Arriflex and the Mitchell cameras, and when the "dailies" were viewed, no one could tell the difference. The studio bought the camera.

The chief advantage of the Arriflex was that it was a much smaller camera than the Mitchell, and could be held in the hand. The Arriflex used eight different lenses, and could be used with a battery pack when shooting on location.

Gabbani and Koenekamp had used it on location at Camp Pendleton for *The Lieutenant.* Gabbani had also used the Arriflex to shoot a scene in *Whatever Happened to Baby Jane* at floor level—something that could never be done with a Mitchell BNC.

In George Lehr's opinion, the *U.N.C.L.E.* series could never have kept to it's six-day shooting schedule were it not for the Arriflex camera: "Originally, MGM didn't want to make the show," he recalls, "because of all the action. The

Til Gabbani used a battery pack with the Arriflex for scenes such as this one from "The Sort-of-Do-It-Yourself-Dreadful Affair." *Courtesy of the Norman Felton collection.*

solution was using the handheld Arriflex, MOS, meaning without sound. While the company was moving from one stage to another, Til Gabbani would take photo doubles for the guys, depending on who was in the next shot, and then run off and do a half dozen handheld shots, such as guys running, or chases. We literally shot the seventh day on the run."

The Mitchell was still the main camera, however. The Arriflex was used for scenes not requiring sound, and for action scenes where the sound could be dubbed in later. Both cameras could be used at once in fight scenes to provide different angles on the action.

The use of the Arriflex sometimes made the camera operator a stuntman as well. For one car scene, Til Gabbani rode on the hood of a car to get a shot through the windshield. On another occasion, he was filming a scene of a car coming at him head-on. George Lehr, who was on the set at the time, remembers, "We had a jerk-away where the stunt man had to drive through a set of double gates, and it was a blind drive, that is, the stuntman was on the floor operating the controls of the car and couldn't see. And Tilly Gabbani was outside the wrought-iron gates with the Arriflex, and on a break cord. This was an elastic piece on a harness so that in case of danger the special effects man could pull him out of the way." But, as Lehr and the other members of the crew watched in horror, "The car went through the gate, but instead of stopping short, as it should have, the technical aspects failed and the car kept on going." In using the Arriflex, Gabbani had to keep one eye closed, and when he looked up, the car was coming right at him. As Lehr describes it, "The

car hit Tilly Gabbani head on and knocked him about twenty feet into the air. He hit the ground spreadeagled, flatter than a pancake, still holding the Arriflex in his hand. I thought he was dead." But Gabbani, who was in superb physical shape, survived, and was hospitalized for four months.

Gabbani developed his own equipment to supplement the Arriflex, such as special foam rubber shoes to reduce bouncing when he walked with the camera, and a special harness for the handheld camera that allowed him to carry it without using his hands. He also used a quiltlike fiberglass cocoon to wrap himself and the camera in to muffle sounds, but after a time the fiberglass began to itch and was abandoned.

The handheld Arriflex soon became an industry standard, and Til Gabbani began conducting classes for other cameramen on its use. Fred Koenekamp says, "I'm kind of proud to say that we really started a trend on that series for the type of shows with car chases and shoot-'em-up stuff."

A typical scene for *The Man from U.N.C.L.E.* required a number of people behind the camera. In addition to the four-man camera crew, the set also housed a mike boom operator and sound recordist; a gaffer and his crew, who operated the lighting; the director, assistant director, script supervisor, and several others.

The camera itself would be mounted in one of several fashions. Normally the BNC camera rode on what was called a "crab dolly," mounted with a bicycle horn so that the operator could signal when the camera was ready to film. Other times it was attached to a crane for overhead shots. The operator sat on a padded seat and was held in place by a seatbelt for those times when the camera was moved by the crane or dolly. The Arriflex was usually mounted on a tripod or carried by hand.

Fred Koenekamp stayed with the series through all four seasons. In the last season, he began to receive offers for feature film work, and thus he was replaced in the last few episodes by Ray Flin and Robert Hauser. After *U.N.C.L.E.*, Koenekamp worked on such films as *Patton, Papillon, The Towering Inferno,* and *First Monday in October,* and on TV movies including *Alice in Wonderland* and *Flight 90: Disaster on the Potomac.* Til Gabbani stayed with the entire *U.N.C.L.E.* series.

David McCallum recalls, "The crew was like family, and Big Daddy was Fred Koenekamp. And Tilly Gabbani, with his cigar in his mouth and his camera strapped to his hand with a band. Tilly used to teach me how to work one. One day I did a handheld shot, and I dropped the camera down before I clicked it off. He gave me such a row. He said, when they look at the dailies, they shouldn't know if the shot had been done on a crane, on a dolly, or handheld. Tilly could even walk with the handheld camera rock-steady." Sam Rolfe also had high praise for Gabbani's camerawork. Rolfe would see Gabbani after viewing the dailies and simply say, "You showed off again."

Like most of the crew, Fred Koenekamp recalls working on *The Man from U.N.C.L.E.* fondly: "As long as I had to do television in those days, I really lucked out. I got a show that was different. It wasn't the average love story or the medical story or stuff like that. The show was fun. We had a chance to explore new things that the other shows weren't doing."

Chapter 10

Scoring *U.N.C.L.E.*

Another element of the popularity of *The Man from U.N.C.L.E.* was the music. Television music consists of a theme for the show, and background music for the scenes themselves. As early as October 1963, Norman Felton knew he wanted Jerry Goldsmith to compose the theme for the show. Goldsmith was a well-known TV composer, with a long list of credits even then, including *Perry Mason, Twilight Zone, Have Gun, Will Travel, Gunsmoke,* and *Climax.* Goldsmith had been nominated for an Emmy for his work on *Thriller,* and had worked for Felton on music for *Dr. Kildare.*

Goldsmith composed a rousing, powerful theme for *The Man from U.N.C.L.E.* that was used, in slightly altered forms, throughout the series. His work on *U.N.C.L.E.* earned him a nomination for an Emmy.

The theme song was played during the opening and closing credits of each episode. The theme was extremely popular, and for a time a 45-rpm single version was on the market. Felton later commissioned a THRUSH theme from composer Lalo Schifrin in February of 1965; this was never used on the series, but does appear on the first soundtrack album. The *U.N.C.L.E.* theme was performed by the Gallants, but they received screen credit only in one first-season episode, "The See Paris and Die Affair," in which they played nightclub musicians.

Three other composers contributed music to the first season besides Goldsmith: Morton Stevens, who also composed for *Hawaii Five-O, Gilligan's Island,* and *The Wild, Wild West;* Lalo Schifrin, who later did work for *Mission: Impossible, T.H.E. Cat, Mannix, Blue Light,* and feature films; and Walter Scharf, who also went on to compose for a great many feature films.

For the remainder of the first-season episodes, individual composers were not assigned. Rather, bits and pieces of the compositions of the above four were used where appropriate, and for this reason often two composers' names will be seen in the credits. When previously composed music was utilized, it was necessary to pay the musician's union a penalty, but, according to George Lehr, this was done because often there was not sufficient time or money to compose an original score.

For the second season, the chief composer was Gerald Fried. Fried altered the theme slightly, causing Felton to receive many letters of complaint from fans. NBC received a petition signed by fifty-two people before a Texas notary public requesting that "the original theme music that opened and closed the show in the first season be reutilized."

Fried was the dominant composer for the second season, scoring no less than eleven episodes. Fried would later work on music for *Gilligan's Island, Star Trek,* and *Mission: Impossible.* The other composer for the second season was Robert Drasnin, who scored six episodes. Drasnin later wrote music for *The Wild, Wild West* and *Mission: Impossible,* and most recently has worked on *The New Twilight Zone.*

Fried was retained as the main composer for the third season as well, and scored eleven episodes again. For "The Off-Broadway Affair," he collaborated with writer Jerry McNeely in composing music and lyrics for the musical numbers in that story.

In the third season, there was a conscious effort to appeal to the teen audience by using rock performers on the show. In "The Hot Number Affair," rock stars Sonny and Cher appeared as guest stars. Although they did not perform on the show, two of their hits, "I Got You Babe" and "The Beat Goes On," are heard in the soundtrack. "The Five Daughters Affair" also featured a rock group, Every Mothers' Son, and their hit song "Come On Down to My Boat." A compensation dispute almost kept them from appearing, until it was pointed out that an appearance on *U.N.C.L.E.* would give the group tremendous national exposure, which would be of mutual benefit to the group, the show, and MGM, who had them contracted to the MGM record label. At other times, plans were made to use Peter, Paul and Mary, the Dave Clark Five, and even the Beatles as guest stars.

Robert Drasnin scored two of the

Courtesy of the Norman Felton collection.

third-season episodes, and all the others used prior compositions except "The Concrete Overcoat Affair." Felton hired veteran composer Nelson Riddle for this episode. Riddle had done TV work for *Route 66* and *Batman,* and many features. After hearing his score for this episode, however, Felton sent him a blistering note, informing him that his services would not be used on *U.N.C.L.E.* again—although his music was reused on four other third-season episodes.

David McCallum's musical talents and

his popularity with teens did not go unexploited on the show, either. In "The Take Me to Your Leader Affair," he and Nancy Sinatra sing his song "Trouble." It was later discovered that no one had obtained permission to use the song, so McCallum's agent issued a limited license after the fact. McCallum also performed on the flute, French horn, and drum in "The Off-Broadway Affair." There was even discussion at one time of developing a "new teen dance—the U.N.C.L.E."

For *U.N.C.L.E.*'s final season, Richard Shores did most of the music composition. Some of Jerry Goldsmith's music was brought back from the first season, in keeping with the "get back to the basics" approach of the fourth season.

For the *U.N.C.L.E.* movies, normally the same score as the TV version was used. However, Gerald Fried had to compose new music for *One of Our Spies Is Missing*, since only precomposed music had been used on the TV version ("The Bridge of Lions Affair"). Fried also composed a new score for *The Karate Killers*, based on "The Five Daughters Affair," but was only given a few hours to do so.

The *U.N.C.L.E.* theme itself, the outstanding example of the music of the series, was performed slightly differently each season. For the first season, it featured a trumpet carrying the melody. A flute played the melody in the second season, accompanied by bongos and an electric guitar. For the third season, an organ provided the melody with a saxophone and a trumpet in the background. For the last season of the series, a trumpet again carried the melody.

Chapter 11

Writing *U.N.C.L.E.*

A television series is a collection of stories. If the basic story is not well crafted and well told, outstanding efforts in direction, acting, camerawork, etc., will not rectify the situation. The first season of *The Man from U.N.C.L.E.* was a process of searching for those writers who could produce scripts offering the right blend of adventure, humor, and character interplay.

Peter Allan Fields and Dean Hargrove were the closest thing to a writing "staff" the show had. As Dean Hargrove says, "Peter and I were the main writers for the show. We wrote, in the second year, between fifteen and twenty episodes of the series." Technically, only Hargrove was "on staff," but Fields worked out of an office at MGM every day alongside Hargrove anyway. "I was a free-lancer," Fields says. "I didn't know all the rules, and they just kept me sitting there in the back room writing, paying me for each one I did. Nobody offered to put me under contract, but I didn't offer to go anywhere else, either."

Fields and Hargrove did their writing for *The Man from U.N.C.L.E.* right on the MGM lot. "It was just an empty office in the back," as Fields describes it. "They were old tacky offices. It was like working inside an old tennis shoe. But it was really enjoyable. Dean and I both

had a pretty free hand. We were the only two writers who went in there every day. It was on the lot itself, just inside the gate. The attendant was a cop there by the name of Ken Hollywood, and behind his little kiosk there were our offices."

The time frame for the writing of an *U.N.C.L.E.* episode varied, but generally was a month-long process. Fields states that "Usually, with the adrenaline flowing, and with something I enjoyed doing, we worked very, very quickly, and worked tremendously long hours. But that was the choice. The only time as I recall that we had to rush, was if there was a script that either fell through and there was an open spot on a date when they had to start shooting . . . or if there was a script that needed to be rewritten or completed by a certain time, and they wanted to keep the schedule."

Hargrove recalls, "In the second year, which was when I did the most work on the show, from the time I would sit down with a story idea to the time it was in preproduction or filmed was no more than four weeks. It would take me about a week to write the story, two weeks for a first draft, and a week to make the production changes. Since I was almost the sole surviving member from the first season, I had a considerable amount of autonomy with the writing. I would develop a premise, and go off and write it. There were few changes asked of me on a creative basis. The only changes I recall making as a general rule were production changes."

Another *U.N.C.L.E.* writer, Harlan Ellison, who worked on the show in the third season, recalls that the writing "staff" was a little unique: "There was no staff. There was a number of us who did rewrites. In those days, you didn't have writing staffs the way you do today. There was mostly free-lance talent used. You would have one or two people on the staff, either the producer or the associate producer or the story editor, who would sort of neaten it up in terms of keeping the characters consistent. But beyond that there was no office staff. There were favored sons and daughters, those of us who had a flair and got the ideas right."

Ellison remembers that the writers would often collaborate on the scripts: "You know, the farther out the ideas the better they liked them. And I was one of those, and they had me on the lot working there. We would spend hours sitting around in the lion's den, the MGM commissary, talking of insane ideas. And that was mostly what it was all about, it was mostly fun writing the show. I mean, hell, I would write an entire act for the show in a day. I would sit down at the typewriter with my music blaring in my tiny little office, which had actually been a storage room for janitorial supplies, and type like a loony for five or six hours, and get an entire act done, and they'd take it down to the stage two weeks later and shoot the damn thing."

The atmosphere of creative freedom on the *U.N.C.L.E.* writing "staff" no doubt contributed to the early success of the series. "I had considerable autonomy by today's television standards," Hargrove says. "Norman Felton was very involved in the show, however, and often had comments or suggestions." In addition, unlike writers on other shows, the writers for *U.N.C.L.E.* had little interference from the stars. "It was a very interesting show in as much as the stars never got involved in the script," Hargrove recalls. "They very rarely voiced criticism, they were totally professional. They were both terrific to work with, and they were both excellent in those parts."

Most scripts began with a story conference with the writer and the producer. Various ideas and story lines would be discussed, and the writer would be assigned to develop a particular story. The writer would commonly prepare a narrative story outline, usually from ten to fifty pages in length. If the story outline was approved by the production staff, the writer then put the story into script form, with dialogue, camera angles, scene shifts, etc.

A script would nearly always undergo several changes, each draft being given a different-colored folder to differentiate it: blue, then yellow, and finally buff. Each version would be rewritten and improved until a "revised final version" was ready. Most scripts were about sixty-five pages long, and each episode was assigned a four-digit production number for bookkeeping purposes.

As second-season producer David Victor recalls, "We used mostly new writers, because it was a new form. Very few of the writers came in with well-developed stories. Most of the things evolved at story conferences, because it is very difficult to foresee all these crazy developments. Essentially, what we were looking for were unique characters in the concept, and crazy ideas, such as a whole generation of Hitlers, or something like that. But the idea was for the writers to always have a very tongue-in-cheek approach."

Many scripts were actually collaborative efforts. For example, the second-season opening episode, "The Alexander the Greater Affair" (parts 1 and 2), was written by Dean Hargrove, but the story idea was actually suggested by David Victor. "I didn't take story credit, but essentially it was my story. I thought that was kind of a very valid and exciting extension of the *U.N.C.L.E.* concept—a man who had taken on everyone else, and now was going to take on God, by breaking all the commandments and getting away with it." The idea was one Victor had used in his radio days, for a show called *Let George Do It.* "In searching around for an idea for a two-hour movie, I felt that this would be a good one, because it lent itself to being developed fully. I think it came off very well, one of the outstanding ones."

There was a high turnover of writers, especially in the first season. But three writers stand out among the many, not only because they wrote so many episodes, but also because the episodes they wrote were of high quality and defined the series and made it a success. One is noteworthy because he wrote the episode that turned the series around, helped save it from cancellation, and defined its pristine elements. The other two are unusual in the diverse routes they followed to become *U.N.C.L.E.* scriptwriters—one a real-life spy who used his experiences in his scripts, and the other a lawyer who had never written a script before in his life.

Alan Caillou (actual name Alan Lyle-Smythe) was born in 1914 in England, and had been a spy himself in World War II, where he served with the British Army Intelligence Corps in Africa. His fluency in Arabic enabled him to operate behind enemy lines, but he was captured by the Italian army in Tunisia in 1943 and sentenced to be shot as a spy. He managed to escape and, after the war, he returned to do police work in a remote area among warring African tribes, operating a safari business and a Shakespearean theater company at the same time. From 1952 to 1957, he was a television actor and writer in Canada, then moved to California. He would eventually write over sixty television screenplays, act in over eighty TV episodes, and appear in over twenty-one movies.

Writing for *The Man from U.N.C.L.E.* was, to him, a natural in light of his own background: "The pilot of *U.N.C.L.E.* was straight drama, no tongue-in-cheek," he says. "It was about espionage, about adventure, and this is my field. So I was invited to write for *Man from U.N.C.L.E.*"

One of the first projects he did was a script concerning two people who want to use a gas to gain world power. When he showed it to Sam Rolfe, Caillou recalls, "He looked at it and said, 'Alan, it needs to be a two-parter.' And I said 'Great.'" This was the beginning of "The Quadripartite Affair" and "The Giuoco Piano Affair," which ultimately were not done as a two-part episode but as two separate episodes with the same characters.

In one episode, he recalls, "I wanted a slam-dunk fight scene between the goodies and the heavies. So what I wrote was, with about three or four lines or sentences, 'They all fight, but everything ends happily ever after.' But Norman Felton called me in and said 'Alan, if you ever write another page like that I will never speak to you again.' He wanted it broken down into twenty-five, thirty-five, or fifty shots. A hits B, and B hits C, and X, Y, and Z go down. But we were very good friends. I always thought of Norman Felton as a damn good producer."

Because he was an actor, he also appeared in some of his own episodes, such as his "The Terbuf Affair" as Colonel Morisco, and in his "The Tigers Are Coming Affair" as Colonel Quillon. "The producer would call me from time to time," he recalls, "and say, 'Alan, why don't you play this role?'" He also appeared in some *U.N.C.L.E.* episodes that he didn't write, such as *The Girl from U.N.C.L.E.* episode "The Jewels of Topango Affair."

Many of his appearances paralleled his own life. In "The Tigers Are Coming Affair," he goes on safari just as he did in Africa. In "The Jewels of Topango Affair," he plays a writer on safari. In "The Terbuf Affair," he plays a police captain.

But Caillou stopped writing for the series when it took its change in direction in the third season. "During that time," he says, *"Man from U.N.C.L.E.* passed from straight drama to tongue-in-cheek drama. I'm British, and tongue-in-cheek in my book means very possible situations as to what is happening. They started moving further and further to cartoon characters. And finally, it became farce. And that is when I stopped writing for them. I felt that they were ruining the whole project."

Caillou has also written for *The Six Million Dollar Man, Voyage to the Bottom*

Courtesy of the Norman Felton collection.

of the Sea, Thriller, The Fugitive, Flipper, Daktari, and *77 Sunset Strip,* as well as authoring two adventure novel series featuring characters named Cabot Cain and Ian Quayle.

Another writer in the first season turned out to be the one who set the tone for the series and launched it on its route to success. Dean Hargrove attended the University of Wichita and UCLA, then began his writing career on such shows as *The Bob Newhart Show, Maverick,* and *My Three Sons.* He joined Arena Productions and *The Man from U.N.C.L.E.* as a writer at the age of twenty-seven. As he

91

remembers it, "They were going through a lot of writers that first year. And I came in, I think fairly deep into the season, and I wrote an episode called 'The Never Never Affair.' And up until that point, the show had not done over-whelmingly, and they were still casting about to see if the show was going to be an eight-o'clock action adventure thing or have a little more humor or what. In any event, it was that particular episode, which was slightly tongue-in-cheek, that NBC felt was the way they wanted the show to be stylistically, in terms of the tone and the use of humor."

That script turned out to be the one that set the format of the writing of the show for the rest of the season and beyond. Hargrove had hit upon a blend of adventure and humor where the latter did not detract from the former. It was this unique combination that would, along with other factors, help the show not only to avoid cancellation but to sky-rocket in the ratings. Hargrove himself considers this his best script.

The third prolific writer on *The Man from U.N.C.L.E.* was Peter Allan Fields. Fields was working with the William Morris talent agency as an entertainment lawyer when one day he decided that he would type out an erotic short story about a vampire over his lunch hour. When he finished the story, he tore it up and threw it away. But his secretary retrieved it, pasted it back together, and sent it to a literary agent. It was published, and he soon wrote three more stories. The secretary who retrieved the manuscript was Leigh Chapman, who would later play Sarah Johnson on *U.N.C.L.E.* and write for TV herself.

At the urging of two friends, Fields decided to try and write for *The Man from U.N.C.L.E.,* even though he had never seen the show. "I walked in, and met with a fellow named Doc Calvelli," he says. "And I showed him something and he handed me over to Sam Rolfe. And he gave me something, and he said can you rewrite this. I thought it was an audition, I didn't know they paid you for it. If I did I would have been nervous. And I just sort of never left the building."

He recalls, "They sent me into a back office, and there suddenly I was working at MGM, typing away at a typewriter, next to a guy who was composing music. He was playing the same thing over and over and over again, and it turned out to be the *Dr. Zhivago* theme. I was ready to break his neck, that's all I heard all day. I didn't know how long it was supposed to take to write four acts. I figured an act a day couldn't kill you. So four days later I appeared with the four acts at Sam's door. And he said, 'Oh, listen, Peter, have you finished the first act? I know you haven't written before but let me know.' I handed him all four acts and they shot it. That was 'The Fiddlesticks Affair.'"

Fields was immediately impressed with Sam Rolfe. "He was a very decisive man. He knew what he wanted, and very firmly would stick to his guns without being insulting in any way," he says. "With me, he was the instructor. He would tell me the why of things, and that way it would be more than just something for the script, but sort of a rule to remember. Sam was an excellent writer on his own."

Fields soon also met Dean Hargrove: "Dean came on while I was there. Although we never collaborated together, we always gave each other a hand, told each other what the problem was, and we'd kick it around. Dean and I had a lot of fun on that show. I'd pick him up for work at his house every morning, and somehow we got there on time. They were really wonderful days."

Fields became a good friend of Robert Vaughn's as well, becoming part of the Thursday Night Marching and Staggering Society, a group of dining companions that included *U.N.C.L.E.* publicist Chuck Painter and dialogue coach John Hackett along with Vaughn and Fields. In addition, Fields remembers that he and Vaughn "began having dinner together every night on the way home, at a place called the Aware Inn. We would discuss Vietnam, and I would take my little pad and write and he would take his little book and read." Fields wrote "The Dippy Blonde Affair" in the second season as a custom-made part for Vaughn's then-girlfriend, Joyce Jameson. The script made good use of Joyce Jameson's ample comedic talents.

Peter Fields feels that the writers could not have been successful had it not been for the highly professional nature of the *U.N.C.L.E.* production team. "Til Gabbani and Fred Koenekamp: I was exposed to the best in the business my first time out. Fred Koenekamp was always very serious, and he had these implosions. He was a very quiet guy. At first, I'd go down to the set, and I'd see these things I'd written being built. And Fred Koenekamp, every time something was rewritten it meant more sets and camerawork, and more hard work for him. And when he'd see me coming, he'd say 'Uh oh, another rewrite.' And after a while, he began calling me 'Rewrite.' I became very fond of him, he was such a warm human being. And Til Gabbani, I

didn't know it then, but everybody told me he was one of the best handheld operators in the business."

Fields and Dean Hargrove both came onto *The Man from U.N.C.L.E.* at about the same time in the first season. Each quickly showed they had a talent for the series, each displaying a feel for the relationship between Solo and Illya in their dialogue. They both clearly understood the two opposing spy organizations, Hargrove expanding on U.N.C.L.E. in such episodes as "The Never Never Affair," and Fields creating detail for THRUSH, as in "The Ultimate Computer Affair" and "The Arabian Affair."

Fields also had a firm grasp on the characters of the series. For example, in "The Minus X Affair," Fields masterfully defines the Solo-Illya relationship when Illya takes subtle pleasure in telling the penurious Mr. Waverly over the communicator that Solo has just ruined "another suit." Solo whispers to him to be sure and tell Waverly that it was a large truck that ran into him and ruined the suit. Illya intentionally ignores this and makes a point of telling Waverly it was a small truck to increase Solo's chances of being chastised by Waverly. Solo feigns a karate chop to Illya for this. Such friendly rivalry between the two leads made them seem more human, and endeared them to the audience.

Like McCallum and Victor, Fields felt that the details of the backgrounds of the characters, especially Illya, should remain unknown: "Illya was a character that had this mysterious past—nobody knew who he had been or what he had done. And in 'The Fiddlesticks Affair' I wrote a line that got a lot of mail. In a scene with Dan O'Herlihy, he said something about 'on my honor.' And Illya says, 'If you were a gentleman, sir, as I once was . . .' And that got a lot of mail, because people said 'Aha!' Illya became much more mysterious. I didn't know what the heck his background was either, so I figured I'd have him say that, and it would be ambiguous enough to titillate."

Fields recalls that there was no writer's guide for *The Man from U.N.C.L.E.* when he joined up in the first season. "For example," he says, "there was no THRUSH Central. I created that. I thought, 'Gee, who do these guys report to?' There was just Sam Rolfe telling me what kind of a thing he wanted,

and somehow, although it was a very difficult show for most people to write in, it was a piece of cake for Dean and for me. We worked very hard, but we had wonderful fun. There were no funny hats and the silliness that came later, it was simply tongue-in-cheek . . . we would take ordinary settings, and in those ordinary settings, we'd have extraordinary things going on."

Fields never got to write one *U.N.C.L.E.* story he had in mind: "I always wanted to do a story where you'd walk through a bank, and there would be all the equipment, the calculators, and it was really a THRUSH central

The U.N.C.L.E. trio plans its next confrontation with THRUSH. © *1964–1967 Metro-Goldwyn-Mayer, Inc.*

headquarters. I always wanted to do one like that, but I never got the chance. But that kind of thing, where all around you it could be going on, was what we used." Fields feels that that aspect of the show, the insertion of high adventure into everyday surroundings, was the main appeal of the show.

Although in later seasons there would be a formal writer's guide to help new writers get a handle on the format and the characters, it was Rolfe's prospectus that served this function for the first season. Rolfe gave the first-season writers one simple bit of advice: "We want plausibility, not realism." Rolfe's prospectus and Felton's memos on the format stressed several main themes that writers were to follow: sophisticated adventure, the involvement of an innocent person in every episode, situations that were outrageous but not unbelievable, a touch of what Felton liked to call "dash."

The later writer's guides spelled out what a writer needed to know to write for the series. The guide described U.N.C.L.E. as "a worldwide organization dedicated to the thwarting of grand-scale evildoers," and THRUSH as "a world power without real estate." But the guide cautioned that although most of the stories might involve U.N.C.L.E. and THRUSH, occasionally an independent villain should be brought in.

The guide described Waverly as being "faintly stuffy," Solo as "an urbane swinger" who always gets the girls, and Illya as "slightly jealous of this." The innocent was described for second-season writers as "frequently" an attractive girl, "who must stumble into the plot through no fault of [her] own, [who] must be in jeopardy, and [whose] presence must be necessary to the resolution of the story."

The guide offered an analysis of the show's appeal, which was thought to be on many levels. "To youngsters and some adults," it was simply an adventure series. But "as we move up the discernment level," it was seen as a spoof, and to the most discerning, "a sly commentary on our manners and morals." The show was self-described as "a mixture of physical excitement, with insouciant charm, parody." As for the plots, "credulity may be strained, but not shattered," there must be a "link with reality." As a final bit of advice, the guide urged, "Above all, have fun. If the writer doesn't, the audience isn't very likely to."

It was also well recognized that *The Man from U.N.C.L.E.* was not a *Twilight Zone,* trying to teach a moral lesson in each story. Rather, *U.N.C.L.E.* strove for entertainment through action and humor. Dialogue and action were more important than clever plot twists or surprise endings. The plot, usually, was only a skeleton for hanging several action sequences together.

In the first season, story lines were pretty much kept on track by Sam Rolfe. When the producer has also developed the series, it is easy for him to know which scripts keep the format in mind and which ones send the series off in the wrong direction. For the second season, the series stayed fairly true to its formula, thanks to David Victor, who also had a grasp of its essential elements and could affect scripts accordingly.

The innocent figured more prominently in first season scripts than in those of the other seasons. As the series went on, innocents were still in the stories, but they became more like bystanders than an essential part of the story. In the first season, we saw a secretary in "The Deadly Decoy Affair"; a college student in "The Love Affair"; a schoolteacher in "The Dove Affair"; a farmgirl in "The Iowa Scuba Affair"; etc. Yet, some episodes had a nonordinary person as the innocent, such as an U.N.C.L.E. clerk in "The Never Never Affair" or a retired U.N.C.L.E. agent in "The Odd Man Affair." The essence of the innocent's involvement was best summed up by Zohra Lampert's character in Dick Nelson's "The Mad, *Mad* Tea Party Affair," when she said: "In spite of being scared to death by everything that's happened here, I've really enjoyed it. . . . This is a day I'll always remember."

True to the guidelines, the writers did not always rely on THRUSH to provide the villainy. In the first season, only thirteen of the twenty-nine episodes used the evil organization. The other sixteen episodes featured a host of independent evildoers. The second season had more of THRUSH, with twenty-one episodes of the twenty-nine using the organization. The third season had twenty-one THRUSH episodes and the last season had THRUSH in thirteen of the sixteen episodes. *The Girl from U.N.C.L.E.* used THRUSH in eighteen of its twenty-nine episodes.

The villains, whether they were THRUSH or not, were an essential element in every script of *The Man from U.N.C.L.E.* They were many times idiosyncratic, always colorful, always egomaniacal, and usually fell victim to their own greed or other failings.

"The Ultimate Computer Affair" and "The Fiddlesticks Affair" by Fields and "The Discotheque Affair" by Hargrove were three of the few episodes in which U.N.C.L.E. took the offensive against THRUSH. "The Minus X Affair" by Fields contains one of the rare sad endings in the series, when the innocent girl's mother is killed. The only other examples of this type of ending in the series are "The Fiery Angel Affair" and "The Seven Wonders of the World Affair," both in the fourth season. Hargrove's "The Discotheque Affair" ends not in a victory for U.N.C.L.E. but a draw with THRUSH.

The use of humor in *The Man from U.N.C.L.E.* scripts was a precarious undertaking. *U.N.C.L.E.*'s unique claim to fame was as an adventure series that had just enough, but not too much, humor. Most of the humor was fairly obvious— Solo would fire off a wry remark, such as in "The Shark Affair," where, while being held painfully spreadeagled for a flogging, with a booted foot against each cheek, he remarks, "Is this grip really necessary?" Humor of this type acted as a counterbalance to the suspense, and made the heroes more human.

But some of the *U.N.C.L.E.* humor was more subtle. Many of the first-season villains were given the names of birds, in keeping with their connection to THRUSH, as in "The Mad, *Mad* Tea Party Affair" and "The Girls of Nazarone Affair," both of which feature Dr. Egret (originally called Dr. Byrd in the script). In "The Quadripartite Affair" and "The Giuoco Piano Affair," the innocent was Marion Raven. In both "The Gazebo in the Maze Affair" and "The Yukon Affair," we met a villain named Partridge. The same name was used again in "The Her Master's Voice Affair," and yet again in "The THRUSH Roulette Affair." In "The Take Me to Your Leader Affair," the antagonist was Simon Sparrow. In "The Birds and the

Bees Affair," we met Dr. Swan.

Other nonbird names were nevertheless subtle jokes as well. The molelike Mr. Elom in "The Project Deephole" used the word *mole* spelled backward. In "The Apple a Day Affair," the apple-orchard tycoon was named "Colonel Picks." In "The Concrete Overcoat Affair," a rather masculine acting female THRUSH agent was named Miss Diketon, and in the same episode a family of Mafioso-like criminals were named the Stiletto Brothers. In "The Deadly Decoy Affair," Solo runs into an Amish-like couple who use "thee" and "thy" in their conversations, and are named Thysen. In the same episode, the THRUSH agent he is escorting is named Egon, and his most noticeable feature is his colossal ego. In "The Deadly Smorgasbord Affair," a character was named Dr. A. C. Nillson, a reference to the TV ratings system. In "The Yellow Scarf Affair," Solo poses as an insurance investigator for the "Unified Northern Casualty and Liability Exchange" (U.N.C.L.E.), and in "The Hula Doll Affair," we see a haberdashery front for THRUSH named Thrale and Usher (THRUSH). Felton Avenue was referred to in both "The Monks of St. Thomas Affair," and in "The Hula Doll Affair." Similarly, in "The Thor Affair," a blackboard in the teacher's schoolroom has "RFK" written on it—free national advertising for Vaughn's friend Robert Kennedy for his presidential campaign the next year.

Episode titles always used the word "Affair," and no less than seven episodes used the word "Deadly." One episode title, "The Giuoco Piano Affair," referred to a classic chess opening used by J. R. Capablanca, world champion chess master, in the 1936 Moscow tournament.

Still other titles were puns, or references to mythology or classics of literature. "The Bridge of Lions Affair" title came from the book of the same name, written by Henry Slesar.

After each script was completed, a copy was sent to the MGM legal department to make sure it did not have any material that might libel, defame, slander, or embarrass any persons in real life and result in a lawsuit. Also, the network had broadcast standards that prescribed what types of material were appropriate for broadcast, and these had to be adhered to as well.

In addition, a third factor had to be considered. Each script had to be carefully perused to be sure it did not contain anything that might offend a sponsor of the series. For example, when Peter Allan Fields wrote the script for "The Fiddlesticks Affair," he had Korvel smoking a cigarette. One of the sponsors for the show was a cigar maker. So, Sam Rolfe had Fields change all cigarettes mentioned in the script to cigars.

Of course, sex was a taboo subject on television, since there was no way to control the age of the viewer. Although more adult, sexually suggestive scenes were made for the feature versions, the television episodes had to remain strictly G-rated. For example, the feature version of the pilot, *To Trap a Spy*, has a scene where it is clear that Solo and Luciana Paluzzi make love. But in the TV version, she is simply changing clothes in the next room. The closest the series came to nudity was in no less than three episodes with women in their slips— "The Mad, *Mad* Tea Party Affair," "The Gurnius Affair," and "The Thor Affair." In "The Ultimate Computer Affair," Peter Allan Fields wondered if the censors would allow a scene in which Charles Ruggles plays strip poker with his two nurses but it was kept intact. Use of dancing, hypnotism, and the treatment of animals all had to conform to network broadcast standards.

A special censorship problem *The Man from U.N.C.L.E.* had was a requirement that nothing even remotely resemble the James Bond novels or films, after the prior legal troubles with Albert Broccoli. Thus, it was suggested that the chess match that still appears at the beginning of "The Brain Killer Affair" be deleted, since it bore a resemblance to the chess match in the beginning of *From Russia with Love*. In "The Iowa Scuba Affair," the idea of a missile was switched to a manned aircraft to avoid similarity to either *Moonraker* or *Doctor No*.

At times the censorship bordered on the absurd. In "The Lethal Eagle Affair" on *Girl from U.N.C.L.E.*, the script described a scene as having Slate hiding in the crotch of a tree. Even this was warned against as being too suggestive—even though the "crotch" would only be seen and, after all, was only that of a tree. As producer Doug Benton recalls, "For 'The Carpathian Caper Affair,' the story concerned a Mother Magda who sold chicken soup. And when we sent it through, the NBC people who read it thought it was a lovely idea but it was too Jewish. They wouldn't let us do it until we moved it to the Carpathian mountains. All we did was went through the script and anytime it talked about the Catskills, we'd make it Carpathians, and it went through." Writer Les Roberts originally set "The Apple A Day Affair" in an Amish community, but Boris Ingster insisted it be changed to a hillbilly setting

when NBC expressed fear it would offend the Amish—even though the Amish have neither TV nor electricity.

Although their requirements at times seemed ludicrous, the censors did fulfill a purpose. Lawsuits did occur over program content, and one episode of *The Man from U.N.C.L.E.* led to legal action that eventually resulted in the episode being withdrawn from the series and not shown again for nearly twenty years.

"The Pieces of Fate Affair" grew out of a story idea by writer Yale Udoff. Originally titled "The Novel Affair," the story involved a set of missing THRUSH diaries with top secret information both U.N.C.L.E. and THRUSH were after. Udoff recalls: "I met with Boris Ingster, who was producer at the time, and an old Hollywood hand. And we tried to make the story fun. But I was a young writer at the time, and writing for a show that is successful, the usual course is for someone else to rewrite it, because they have more contact with the characters. It really got changed in the rewrite."

The rewrite was assigned to Harlan Ellison, who rewrote many scripts for U.N.C.L.E. even though his name only appears on two episodes. Ellison retained only the basic premise, rewrote the script, and called it "The Pieces of Fate Affair."

Ellison's script poked fun at both authors and literary reviewers. For the book reviewer, Ellison chose the name Judith Merle, and thereupon the trouble began. As Ellison explains, "In the world of science fiction, there is a literary device called Tuckerisms, named after Bob Tucker, who wrote science fiction. And Bob would use the name of friends of his as characters throughout the books. The

Vaughn and McCallum with guest star Sharon Farrell in the "lost" episode, "The Pieces of Fate Affair," which suffered for years from legal problems. © *1964–1967 Metro-Goldwyn-Mayer, Inc.*

characters did not resemble the people at all. It was a way of saying hello to your friends, and it was a kind of a group joke. When I did 'The Pieces of Fate Affair,' since it was a literary background, I thought I'll have a little fun with it and drop a bunch of my friends in here. So there was an assassin named Simian Spinrad, because one of my best friends was Norman Spinrad. And there was a bookstore called Jack Vance's Bookstore,

and Jack Vance was one of my favorite players. And there was a THRUSH agent who was a book reviewer and critic, and it was played by Grayson Hall, who was an Academy Award nominee, a very elegant woman who played it with great high style, and the character was called Judith Merle. She was named after a book reviewer and critic of my acquaintance named Judith Merril."

The real Merril was, at the time, a

well-known and much respected writer, editor, and critic in the world of science fiction. Ellison remembers, "Soon after the episode aired, everybody enjoyed it and it got great reviews. Judith Merril had apparently been to England, and when she came back from England one of her daughters had seen the segment and was offended." Merril's attorney threatened legal action against the show. "I believe Judith Merril thought that it was possible to sue MGM and NBC without suing me. And I got a call from the airport, from Judith Merril, saying don't worry about this. But her attorney still pressed the matter, and MGM was furious at me and everyone else. Granted, it was silly of me to use the names of real people, but it was such an accepted kind of thing in the field. Everybody did it, but this was the first time I had done it of any consequence."

Ellison was, at this point, still not involved in the suit, but decided he would try and get the matter resolved. "The case went on, and MGM was going to sue me for recovery. I said I'll take care of this. So I had a meeting with Judith Merril in New York in the office of my then-agent, who is also an old friend of Judith's. I said 'Look, Judy, this is gonna hurt me, it's gonna hurt me a lot. People in Hollywood don't work with people who get sued. It's foolish, you know I meant no harm.' And she said, 'Yes, I know you meant no harm.' We had this long conversation, and I said 'Look, Judy, I'll give you all the money I have, two thousand dollars, which is every cent I have, and I'm happy to give it to you. Just please knock off this damn thing.'"

But "It went on for years and years and years and no one ever did anything

about it, because it wasn't a real lawsuit, it was one of those nuisance suits," Ellison says. "It never came to trial, never went to depositions, or anything like that. Eventually, years later, I think five or six years later, Judith Merril settled for . . . substantially the same amount of money I had offered her."

But the suit had the long-term effect of pulling "The Pieces of Fate Affair" out of the U.N.C.L.E. series. According to Ellison, "What happened was simply that because the thing was ongoing for five or six years, NBC put a flag on it in the files that there was a problem, and they never bothered to reshow it." MGM dubbed in the new name of Jody Moore in the dialogue and in the opening and closing credits so the episode could be shown in England in November of 1967, but it was not rerun in the U.S. and in fact was not seen on U.S. TV again until 1985.

But even that was not the end of the controversy. Ellison adds, "Years later, MGM called me and said 'We have settled for two thousand dollars,'" whatever it was, "and we would like you to chip in on this, or to recompense us.' And I said 'No way.' I said, 'I will only share the expenses on a judgment that is finally found in a court of law.' It never was. Well, they never asked me again, and that was the end of it. I never paid a penny." Norman Felton also recalls the aftereffects of Ellison's script for "The Pieces of Fate Affair": "I remember it cost us quite a bit of money, because the episode was not shown for some time. And that cost the writer a lot of money, as well as the actors, who did not receive any payments for reruns."

The plots of the scripts for *The Man from U.N.C.L.E.* can be broken down into three broad categories: plans by THRUSH to gain world power (often with new technology); efforts by U.N.C.L.E. and THRUSH to destroy each other; and U.N.C.L.E.'s battles with independent villains. Also, three episodes, "The Bow Wow Affair," "The Terbuf Affair," and "The Secret Sceptre Affair," were not actual U.N.C.L.E. assignments at all but cases taken on as personal favors.

The stories themselves also evolved into a predictable scenario. Act I nearly always began at Waverly's office, where he would explain the problem to the two agents and then send them out to resolve it, often in opposite directions. They would work independently, then meet up later and defeat the villain in the climax as a team. Following this, there would usually be a scene back in Waverly's office wherein Solo would escort the girl out to dinner to celebrate the victory. A running joke developed in these denouement scenes, wherein Waverly would try and get everyone to go out to celebrate, suggesting dinner or tea at his club, but would often find that Solo had already made plans with the pretty girl.

Throughout the story, a main staple of *U.N.C.L.E.* writing was continual setbacks. Typically, Solo and Illya would lose every battle but win the war. They were constantly being captured, knocked unconscious, or losing what they were supposed to protect or regain. THRUSH would prevail at every turn, only to be defeated in the end by a clever ploy of the two U.N.C.L.E. agents, a failing of the villain's, or a combination of these. THRUSH and other villains never simply shot and killed Solo and Illya, even though they had hundreds of chances to do so. Instead, they went to

great pains to set up exotic methods of death and then left the scene, smugly assuming there was no way for them to escape this certain death.

Many of the *U.N.C.L.E.* stories revolved around THRUSH trying to get or use new technological developments, often requiring the kidnapping of the scientist who had created the device. A deadly gas was the object in "The Quadripartite Affair"; a thought translator in "The Foxes and Hounds Affair"; a suspended animation device in "The Deadly Smorgasbord Affair"; a rare heavy metal in "The Yukon Affair"; a formula for antimatter in "The Suburbia Affair"; a sense-heightening drug in "The Minus X Affair"; a miniaturized nuclear device in "The Indian Affairs Affair"; and a virus that destroys the ability to reproduce in "The Adriatic Express Affair." Others included an aging chemical ("The Finny Foot Affair"); a sophisticated polygraph machine ("The Yellow Scarf Affair"); a space ship ("The Love Affair"); a healing serum ("The Girls of Nazarone Affair"); a computer ("The Ultimate Computer Affair"); a will gas ("The Alexander the Greater Affair"); a vaporizing machine ("The Arabian Affair"); a rejuvenation process ("The Bridge of Lions Affair"); a strain of deadly bees ("The Birds and the Bees Affair"); and a ray projector ("The Moonglow Affair"). Devices to control nature were also sought, such as a volcanic activator ("The Cherry Blossom Affair), an earthquake activator ("The Project Deephole Affair" and "The Man from THRUSH Affair"), and a tidalwave machine ("The Yo-Ho-Ho and a Bottle of Rum Affair").

Another favorite plot was THRUSH attacking or infiltrating U.N.C.L.E.

headquarters; this was seen in "The Vulcan Affair," "The Birds and the Bees Affair," "The Discotheque Affair," "The Mad, *Mad* Tea Party Affair," "The Waverly Ring Affair," and "The Summit Five Affair." Some episodes, such as "The Shark Affair," involved various independent villains. The group that produced the most non-THRUSH villains on the show was the Third Reich, with Nazis or their descendants appearing in "The Deadly Games Affair," "The Gurnius Affair," and "The Recollectors Affair."

With 134 episodes of *The Man from U.N.C.L.E.* and *The Girl from U.N.C.L.E.,* eventually the basic plots and some scenes began to repeat themselves. The location of an U.N.C.L.E. conference was the basis for the plots in "The Children's Day Affair," "The Summit Five Affair," and "The Montori Device Affair." An old girlfriend was used to get at a THRUSH agent in both "The Vulcan Affair" and "The See Paris and Die Affair" (this seems surprising since they were both first-season episodes). An opening scene showing a man driving down a country road at night and then being killed before he can complete a message to U.N.C.L.E. to warn of an assassination plot, used in "The Vulcan Affair," was repeated almost exactly in "The J for Judas Affair" opening. Concern over assassination plans against a boy lama from the Himalayas formed the basis of the plot in both "The Four Steps Affair" and "The Abominable Snowman Affair." Gypsies using murder to buy up controlling interests of stock in companies was a plot element in both "The Bow Wow Affair" and the *Girl from U.N.C.L.E.* episode "The Romany Lie Affair." Illya finds himself placed in a

guillotine in both "The Virtue Affair" and "The When in Roma Affair," and Solo finds himself in a far worse predicament—a shotgun wedding—in three episodes, "The Deadly Goddess Affair," "The Concrete Overcoat Affair," and "The Apple a Day Affair." A shy, naïve American tourist girl was used as the innocent in both "The Foxes and Hounds Affair" and "The When in Roma Affair," and was even played by the same actress in both episodes.

The same murder methods came up often as well. In "The Iowa Scuba Affair," "The Summit Five Affair," and "The Napoleon's Tomb Affair," a shower stall emitted deadly gas. A jaguar was used to hunt Solo down in both "The Green Opal Affair" and "The Deadly Quest Affair," and an elevator shaft proved to be lethal in "The Brain Killer Affair," "The THRUSH Roulette Affair" (with Michael Rennie, who died the same way in the movie *Hotel),* and "The Project Deephole Affair." An exploding handkerchief was used in both "The Foxes and Hounds Affair" and "The Thor Affair," although here the borrowing from an earlier episode was acknowledged.

Not all the similarities were mere repetition. Some involved the writer's particular style. For example, Dean Hargrove apparently liked action scenes involving a person going from one vehicle to another while in motion, as they appear in three of his scripts: "The Project Deephole Affair" (car to car); "The Alexander the Greater Affair" (car to plane); and "The Indian Affairs Affair" (motorcycle to truck). In both of Harlan Ellison's episodes, "The Pieces of Fate Affair" and "The Sort-of-Do-It-Yourself-Dreadful Affair," there is a scene where a THRUSH agent pleads for his life by pointing out his years of loyal THRUSH service.

As the series went on, the role of the gadgets in the scripts changed as well. Originally, the gadgets were simply a novel adjunct to the skills of Solo and Illya. Like James Bond, they were still required to use their wits to escape danger—as in "The Iowa Scuba Affair," where Solo constructs a makeshift bomb from his aerosol shaving can and his cigarette lighter, or in "The Never Never Affair," where Illya escapes a THRUSH fire assault by ducking into the city sewer system through a manhole. In "The Adriatic Express Affair," where Solo and Illya are locked in a jail cell without any devices along, they burn the wooden floorboards by lighting some cognac.

In Fields' "The Foxes and Hounds Affair," they escape a jail cell by tying the guest star's stockings across the door, then getting the guard to rush in and trip. But in Hargrove's "The Children's Day Affair," they again try to escape a jail cell by having Solo crouched on a ledge above the door, ready to spring onto the guard when he enters the cell. Instead, the guard opens the door and beckons them to come out, and Illya steps out and calmly asks the chagrined Solo, "Are you coming?" This is a superb example of both *U.N.C.L.E.* humor and the agents using their wits instead of a gadget. By the end of the second season, however, gadgets were relied on exclusively for escapes, and sequences like this were no longer seen.

Each season, more scripts would be written than produced. In the first season, "The Diamond Affair," "The Mortar Affair," "The Middle East Affair," and twenty other scripts were never filmed. The second season of the series saw scripts prepared for "The Button Affair," "The Jigsaw Affair," "The Cotton Candy Affair," "The Gypsy Traveler Affair," and nineteen others that were not used. In the third season, stories titled "The Volcano Affair," "The Black Widow Affair, "The Fu Manchu Affair," and ten others were passed over for production, while on *The Girl from U.N.C.L.E.*, Peter Allan Fields's "The Applebaum Affair" and others were written but never made.

Overall, the *U.N.C.L.E.* stories were superb. The writers faced a monumental task: providing thrilling, "save-the-world" adventures every week—twice a week when *The Girl from U.N.C.L.E.* was also running. The James Bond movies have sometimes been criticized as being too repetitious in their stories, yet the Bond movies only involve sixteen scripts spread out over twenty-five years, with two years between films. The *U.N.C.L.E.* series produced 134 spy adventures on a weekly basis in only three and a half years—a phenomenal writing feat.

Chapter 12

The *U.N.C.L.E.* Sets

The Man from U.N.C.L.E. was a show that involved international espionage. Consequently, many of the story locales were set in foreign countries. The limited budget of a television series did not permit the *U.N.C.L.E.* production crew to shoot on location, so they had to simulate the foreign locales.

Producer David Victor states that the nonuse of location shooting was not completely dictated by economics, but was in part intentional. "My philosophy was that you didn't need locations. The danger with locations is if you have too much travel you pay too much credence, put too much emphasis on the background. If you're not careful, the background takes away from the sheer audaciousness of the chief aspects *The Man from U.N.C.L.E.* always had. We gained something by not going to France, for instance, and instead putting a legend on the screen saying 'Somewhere in France' with the Eiffel tower in the background. In other words, we winked at the audience, saying, 'Come on, you know it's all nonsense, we're having fun, join in.'"

Thus, although the *U.N.C.L.E.* stories spanned the globe, not a single scene in an *U.N.C.L.E.* episode was shot outside of Southern California. David McCallum says, "To this day, people come up to me and say it must have been wonderful to have been in all of those foreign countries, but in fact, we never left the MGM Lots 1, 2, and 3 and up into the hills within a fifty-mile radius of the city." For *The Girl from U.N.C.L.E.*, absolutely no location work was done. "Every frame was shot on the MGM lot," Douglas Benton confirms.

Occasionally a nearby location would be used on *The Man from U.N.C.L.E.* For filming of "The Neptune Affair," the camera crew and cast went to the beach by the Santa Monica Pier. There, director of photography Fred Koenekamp and his camera crew stood waist deep in the ocean in swimsuits to film the final scene. The policeman who appears in the scene played his part in bare feet with his pant legs rolled up, and real policemen, in the form of studio security personnel, kept onlookers away from the cast and crew. Because using the regular camera would have been impossible due to the need for electrical power, the battery-operated Arriflex camera was used. Fred Koenekamp and cameraman Til Gabbani often had to wait until the rough waves subsided before they could get a steady shot.

Besides the location work at Lever Brothers for the pilot, another first-season foray beyond MGM's walls was done for the twin episodes, "The Giuoco Piano Affair" and "The Quadripartite Affair." Since part of these stories involved mountainous terrain, filming was done in the nearby Santa Monica hills. For "The Double Affair," the nearby Griffith Observatory was used for THRUSH headquarters.

But for the most part, shooting was done on the MGM grounds. The interiors were filmed on soundstages on the main lot, mostly on Stages 10 and 28.

McCallum poses on the stage rafters and next to some lights used to illuminate the Del Floria's tailor shop set below. © *1964–1967 Metro-Goldwyn-Mayer, Inc.*

The exterior, or outdoor, scenes, were shot on MGM Backlots 2 and 3.

A set is the whole of the background of a camera shot, exclusive of actors and props. A set can be a room, the interior of a vehicle, such as a car or plane, or it can be an open outdoor area such as a desert, jungle, or street. Interior sets are constructed as needed, and often with just the minimum amount of effort and expense needed to present a given visual image. The standing sets, such as Del Floria's tailor shop, Waverly's office, the reception room, and the various U.N.C.L.E. hallways and offices, were "standing," or permanent sets housed on the soundstage. These sets did double duty during the third season when *The Girl from U.N.C.L.E.* was on the air. Other interior shooting for *Girl* shifted between Stages 4, 21, and 22.

The number of sets needed for a given episode, whether interior or exterior, varied considerably. For "The Double Affair," for example, nine exterior and twenty-five interior sets were used. Fred Koenekamp counted the number of sets used on one particular single episode and found that forty-four sets were used in the six-day shooting period. By contrast, for the two-part episode "The Prince of Darkness Affair," more than eighty sets were used.

Exterior scenes were shot mostly on Lots 2 and 3, sometimes referred to as "the backlot." The backlot was an area adjacent to the studio itself that contained several outdoor standing sets. MGM, in the mid-1960s, boasted one of the best Hollywood backlots. For the most part, Lot 2 housed the forests, lagoons, and other uncivilized areas, while Lot 3 had the street sets and buildings. As producer Sam Rolfe recalled,

"You could shoot almost anything there—from a New York street to a jungle lagoon. I could go to France, I could go to London, I could go to the bottom of the sea and never leave the lot. I could go into castles, or little French cafés, or to New York City. On Lot 2, they had a little French country road, a little railroad station, a little Andy Hardy family town, and lots of units with woods. Lot 3 had a tank of water where we could use squids and whales, and throw people in and drown them, as well as a jungle area." Writer Peter Allan Fields remembers, "It was the Disneyland of the time, it was marvelous. It was right for any situation, you didn't have to worry about logistics much." Til Gabbani says, "We didn't have to go anywhere, because it was all there."

George Lehr also felt the availability of the MGM backlot was an important factor in the look of the show: "We never left Southern California the entire show. MGM had the best backlot in town then. They had three enormous exterior complexes that were twenty or thirty acres each. There wasn't a place in the world that you couldn't duplicate," he says. *Girl from U.N.C.L.E.* producer Doug Benton concurs: "We could go anywhere just by going down the road."

MGM charged a fee to Arena Productions every time the backlot was used, and this also threatened the budget. As Norman Felton describes it, "The costs on the backlot were like two thousand dollars a day. This was acceptable for a movie, but not for a TV budget. I finally got MGM to cut up the backlot into areas, and we would be charged for certain areas only. If you shot by the lake, it would cost a thousand dollars if you showed the water, but if you shot away

from the water, it would be less."

One problem encountered by Sam Rolfe in filming *U.N.C.L.E.* on the backlot in the first season was competition with other MGM TV productions: "The big problem I had with *U.N.C.L.E.* was there was a series called *Combat* which was shot out at Metro at the time, and somehow they got on the set we wanted the week before we hit it. And they'd blow it up. We'd be forced to go into the village with the little bridge across it, and we'd get down there the day before to look it over, and *Combat* would have been there the day before. We'd have to say, 'Get the booby traps out and patch it up, because we're coming in.'"

But the *U.N.C.L.E.* crew was not above pulling the same trick on other productions vying for the sets. Lehr says, "If a feature had been shot on the lot, and there was a set there, you were allowed to use it as long as you changed it so it wasn't recognizable. We'd change a window, or a curtain, or a sign. Set decorator Merrill Pye was very good at that." Rolfe recalls that when the MGM feature *Ice Station Zebra* was filming on the backlot, "We snuck in behind the producer's back and shot it and got out of there, but he found out and he came after us because he didn't want us to use it." On another occasion, an NBC producer was making a circus film on the backlot, and the *U.N.C.L.E.* crew, according to Felton, redressed part of that feature set and used it. As he explains, "They had a rule at MGM that you could not use a set from a movie until six months after it was released in the theaters. But by then, of course, the sets would be torn up. I got them to say we could use them if we redressed them so they were not like the movie. But in this

THRUSH robots attack Illya outside Del Floria's. © *1964–1967 Metro-Goldwyn-Mayer, Inc.*

case, the producer built a set, and before he could use it we went in, repainted it, used it, and then repainted it back for him so it looked like it did for him before he knew it. After that, the head of the studio told me to try and not use sets at least until they were done with them."

Associate producer George Lehr recalled that Norman Felton advised him to be constantly on the lookout for standing sets on the MGM lot that could be used for *U.N.C.L.E.* This would pro-vide visual variety for the series and save the cost of constructing new sets. Thus, the MGM backlot still contained Scarlet O'Hara's Tara plantation from *Gone with the Wind*, the original boat from *Showboat*, and other sets from MGM feature productions. The jungle portion of the backlot seen in such episodes as "The My Friend the Gorilla Affair" and "The Prince of Darkness Affair" had earlier been used for many of the old MGM Tarzan movies. The old courthouse building used in the Andy Hardy movies was redressed as a university building for the *Girl from U.N.C.L.E.* episode "The Faustus Affair" by repainting it and putting a SCIENCE BUILDING sign in front of it.

The New York set was of course the location for Del Floria's tailor shop, the secret entrance to U.N.C.L.E. headquarters. Interestingly, the exterior of the tailor shop was on the backlot and the interior on a sound stage. "That was a mockup," George Lehr explains, "as out on the street, all you had was a door. You saw him walk down the street to the door, and as soon as he started opening the door, because it was deadheaded on the back, we ended there. So what we had on the stage, was a double-faced door. On this side was the interior of the tailor shop, and on the other side, we had it faced exactly like the one on the lot, with rails and all. We could then do a reverse and have them coming through the door."

The tailor shop also appears, unmarked as such, in the background of several other scenes. In "The Sort-of-Do-It-Yourself-Dreadful Affair," it appears in the background of the scene where the model is wearing a bikini in a cologne commercial. The twin pillars she is standing in front of were located directly across the street from the tailor shop on the New York street, and they appear in several episodes as well. In "The Shark Affair," the Del Floria's exterior appears as itself and as the exterior of the apartment building the kidnapped librarian's wife lives in. Amazingly, they appear in adjacent scenes, simply by removing the Del Floria's sign. The crew was thus able to use a relatively small set, one or two blocks of the New York street, over and over again without noticeable repetition, simply by using different camera angles and slight alterations.

The New York street set used so extensively on *U.N.C.L.E,* including Del Floria's tailor shop, was destroyed by a fire in 1967. For the fourth season, only stock footage of Del Floria's exterior could be used. However, for the fourth-season episode "The Deadly Quest Affair," the burnt rubble of the set itself was used for scenes supposedly taking place in a run-down condemned section of Manhattan. The MGM backlot was eventually sold for a housing development in the early 1970s when MGM experienced the financial difficulties that led to the auction of most of its props and costumes. Today, condominiums stand where Del Floria's once was, and only the small lake remains.

Since keeping the costs down is a prime concern of any business, sometimes even the studio itself was used as a set. When a used car lot was needed for "The Matterhorn Affair," the visitors' parking lot outside the MGM main gate was used. When Solo and Illya blow up a water tower filled with deadly gas in the teaser for "The Deadly Toys Affair," it is the MGM water tower they climb. The MGM lot is also seen in the special U.N.C.L.E. car scenes in "The Take Me to Your Leader Affair," and the lot is featured in the *Girl from U.N.C.L.E.* episodes "The Prisoner of Zalamar Affair" and "The Garden of Evil Affair."

In the fourth and final season of *The Man from U.N.C.L.E.,* part of the revitalization effort involved new sets for the headquarters scenes for the series. Massive computer banks, with flashing lights, were borrowed from the National

Aeronautics and Space Administration. These computers were set up in a special computer "alley" corridor just off Waverly's office. In the fourth-season episode "The Summit Five Affair," the computer corridor does double duty as part of London U.N.C.L.E. headquarters, but the computers are cleverly matted out of the shot by an automatic door closing partially.

The sets used on *The Man from U.N.C.L.E.* contributed significantly to the illusion of international locations without the expense of location shooting—another example of the outstanding teamwork of the *U.N.C.L.E.* crew.

Chapter 13

The *U.N.C.L.E.* Guest Stars

With the requirement of an "innocent" person's involvement each week, at least one guest star per episode was called for. With the exception of Jill Ireland as Marion Raven in "The Giuoco Piano Affair" and "The Quadripartite Affair," there were no recurring "innocents." A guest star appeared once and did not make another appearance on the series (in the same role). Also frequently featured on the show were guest villains. As with the innocents, most were seen and not heard from again—usually because their evil deeds resulted in a well-deserved death at the end of the story.

At an average of two per episode, the two *U.N.C.L.E.* series eventually would cast approximately 278 guest star slots, and had the reputation of paying the lowest guest-star fee of any prime-time show of its time. One report put the figure at $2,500 per episode, while another stated that when Don Francks appeared as a guest star in "The Roundtable Affair," the going rate was $3,500 for a guaranteed seven-day shooting schedule.

To David McCallum, the *U.N.C.L.E.* series was an opportunity to meet the talent Hollywood had to offer. He particularly recalls "The Concrete Overcoat

David McCallum is besieged by blondes, including Sharon Tate (center), in "The Girls of Nazarone Affair." © *1964–1967 Metro-Goldwyn-Mayer, Inc.*

Affair" and the veteran gangster movie actors that appeared, as well as Joan Crawford, Herbert Lom, and Curt Jurgens ("The Five Daughters Affair," parts 1 and 2) and Elsa Lanchester ("The Brain Killer Affair").

Joan Crawford's guest appearance on the show marked the first time she had been on the MGM lot in twenty-five years. David McCallum says: "I remember Joan Crawford vividly. With the red carpet, and the flowers, and the wallpaper on the dressing room, everything beautifully done but nothing matching. It was a wonderful Hollywood moment when she arrived on the set." As a memento of her appearance, she was presented with a toy THRUSH rifle, and in a note to Norman Felton later said she was having great fun showing it to her friends. "My one great regret of the whole series," McCallum says, "is that I never kept an autograph book."

Robert Vaughn lists as one of his favorite actors on the show Maurice Evans, who appeared in the two-part episode, "The Bridge of Lions Affair." He says, "Maurice Evans was an actor I had idolized. When I was appearing as a young actor, I met him backstage at a stage production he was in. He gave me a lot of good advice on acting. And when he appeared on *U.N.C.L.E.*, he remembered that."

As for female guest stars, Vaughn recalls Patricia Crowley, the first of the "innocents," fondly: "She had played my wife in an episode of *The Lieutenant*. That's where I first met her. And Sharon Tate comes to mind, she was quite beautiful. And Leigh Chapman, one of the U.N.C.L.E. girls. There were many pretty girls." And indeed there were. Other recognized beauties included two former Miss Americas, Lee Meriwether in the role of Dr. Egret in "The Mad,

Sam Rolfe, Norman Felton, and Joseph Calvelli, along with guest star Jill Ireland, play a rare stint in *front* of the camera. *Courtesy of the Norman Felton collection.*

Mad Tea Party Affair" and Mary Ann Mobley in "The Moonglow Affair," as well as two Playboy Playmates of the Year, Donna Michelle in "The Double Affair" and Angela Dorian in "The Indian Affairs Affair."

The *U.N.C.L.E.* producers cast many veteran horror film actors in the series, always, naturally enough, as villains. Boris Karloff, the king of horror who played the original *Frankenstein* and *The Mummy* and hundreds of other classic horror roles, made an unusual appearance in the *Girl from U.N.C.L.E.* episode, 'The Mother Muffin Affair," as a woman. Like his role as Frankenstein's monster, Karloff injected a note of pathos for his character who, though evil, also craved human affection.

Many people were surprised that Karloff would do a guest-starring role on a television series. But *Girl from U.N.C.L.E.* producer Doug Benton had an inside track: "I had worked with him on his earlier series," he recalled. "I was the story editor and associate producer on *Thriller,* and that was one of the reasons he appeared on *The Girl from U.N.C.L.E.* for us."

The *Bride of Frankenstein* also made an appearance. Elsa Lanchester played Dr. Dabree in "The Brain Killer Affair," and appeared with the same static-charged, silver-streaked hairdo she had in her famous *Bride of Frankenstein* role more than thirty years earlier.

Other classic horror guest stars on *U.N.C.L.E.* included Vincent Price, who played a THRUSH villain in "The Foxes and Hounds Affair," and John Carradine, who appeared in both "The Prince of Darkness Affair" and in the *Girl from U.N.C.L.E.* episode "The Montori Device Affair."

Although there are exceptions—Bill

Dana in "The Matterhorn Affair," Glenn Corbett in "The Hong Kong Shilling Affair," and William Shatner in "The Project Strigas Affair," for example—most of the "innocents" were female. Robert Vaughn once said in jest that they didn't allow too many handsome men on the show. This statement probably contained more than a grain of truth, since the use of female innocents provided script opportunities for a romantic relationship with either of the two stars. Children were also only sparingly used; they included Kurt Russell in "The Finny Foot Affair" and Jay North, who played "Dennis the Menace," in "The Deadly Toys Affair."

Perhaps the most famous pairing of guest stars occurred in the first-season episode "The Project Strigas Affair." In that episode, William Shatner played a young chemist "innocent," and Leonard Nimoy played an East European intelligence agent. This episode was the first time the two appeared together, a full two years before they were to become immortalized in their roles as Captain James T. Kirk and Mr. Spock in *Star Trek.*

In addition to using both known and unknown acting talents, *The Man from U.N.C.L.E.* was unique in that it used several nonacting performers in guest-starring roles. Football player Roosevelt Grier made an appearance in "The Brain Killer Affair." Narrator Alexander Scourby played a villain in "The Deadly Games Affair," and puppeteer Shari Lewis played an acting role in "The Off Broadway Affair." Even the spouses of Hollywood actors got into the act, with Kamali Davi, the wife of Chuck Connors, and Neeli Adams, Mrs. Steve McQueen, both appearing in "The Yellow Scarf Affair."

Pop-music star Sonny Bono is menaced by McCallum in "The Hot Number Affair." *Courtesy of the Norman Felton collection.*

Several comedians played more or less dramatic roles on the series. Victor Borge, the comic pianist, appeared in "The Suburbia Affair." Wally Cox played a role in the *Girl from U.N.C.L.E.* episode "The Little John Doe Affair," as did Dom DeLuise in "The Double-O-Nothing Affair." Comedian Shelley Berman appeared on both *Man* and *Girl*, in "The Super-Colossal Affair" and "The Moulin Ruse Affair."

Musicians and singers also made guest appearances. Sonny and Cher made a request to Boris Ingster to appear on the show, so a script was written ("The Hot Number Affair") that featured both of them. Nancy Sinatra, Frank's daughter and a pop-music star in her own right,

appeared in "The Take Me to Your Leader Affair." Two musical groups made appearances—Every Mother's Son in "The Five Daughters Affair," (parts 1 and 2), and the Daily Flash in "The Drublegratz Affair."

Nepotism occasionally occurred on the *U.N.C.L.E.* set when it came to picking guest stars. Vaughn's longest-running girlfriend, comedienne Joyce Jameson, gave entertaining performances in both "The Dippy Blonde Affair" and on *Girl from U.N.C.L.E.* in "The Carpathian Caper Affair." David McCallum's wife, Jill Ireland, appeared in no less than five episodes: "The Giuoco Piano Affair," "The Quadripartite Affair," "The Tigers Are Coming Affair," and "The Five

Daughters Affair" (parts 1 and 2).

Robert Vaughn recalls that in spite of the awkward position the scripts put him and his costar's wife in on these episodes, no problems developed: "We were all very friendly with each other and saw each other a lot because Jill and the children were on the set even when she was not appearing." The only problem that did develop was that when the script called for Jill to kiss Robert Vaughn, she could not keep from laughing.

But it was uncomfortable for David McCallum the first time he was to have his wife as a guest star, as they had not worked together for over six years. But after some initial tension, they talked it over in the dressing room and cleared the air, and there were no problems after that. Their scenes together for "The Quadripartite Affair" were shot in the Santa Monica mountains in 110-degree heat.

Even the stars were occasionally required to serve as guest stars. Nearly everyone played a dual role in at least one episode: Robert Vaughn in "The Double Affair"; David McCallum in "The Gurnius Affair"; Leo G. Carroll in "The Bow Wow Affair"; Stefanie Powers in "The Prisoner of Zalamar Affair"; and Noel Harrison in "The Kooky Spook Affair."

This was offset by some episodes where the stars did not have to appear at all. David McCallum was only signed for seven of the first thirteen episodes, so he does not appear at all in "The Yellow Scarf Affair," "The Iowa Scuba Affair," "The Dove Affair," and appears only briefly in "The Neptune Affair" and "The Green Opal Affair." But McCallum carried the ball alone in "The Bow Wow Affair," with Vaughn appearing only briefly at the beginning and end. McCallum explains: "Those were occasions when Robert took a well-deserved holiday. And secondly, he was completing his PhD and he needed time off to work on that, such as the week he actually wrote the thesis. So it wasn't because my character was in the ascendancy, it was because Robert needed the time off."

Later episodes relied on one of the leads alone also. "The Yo-Ho-Ho and a Bottle of Rum Affair" was essentially an Illya story, while "The Deadly Smorgasbord Affair" relied on Solo's character. In "The Man from THRUSH Affair," there is no Illya, while in "The Survival School Affair," there is no Solo.

One member of the cast, Leo G. Carroll, actually requested more time in front of the camera. Carroll went to Rolfe and asked for more action scenes, as his grandchildren were wondering why he sat behind a desk all the time. So a script was changed to allow him to administer a karate chop. Because of his age, several takes were necessary, but when he did get it right the entire crew erupted in spontaneous applause.

The production staff itself also appeared as guest stars. For "The Giuoco Piano Affair," a party scene was staffed by Norman Felton as a chess player, Sam Rolfe as a Texan, Doc Calvelli as a sleeping writer, and director Richard Donner as a drunk. The appearances were just for fun, and are indicative of the atmosphere on the set. Calvelli later stated, tongue-in-cheek, that his sleeping performance was the best of the four. When asked how it felt to direct himself, Richard Donner says, also tongue-in-cheek, "I was the most versatile actor I've ever worked with."

One aspect of this scene came back to

haunt Felton, however. He says, "I made a few chess moves in the episode. And everybody got a big kick out of it. And about six months later, I happened to be on the backlot at MGM when they were filming an episode outdoors. And a man was there, an extra, sitting at a table under an umbrella. And a prop man came up to me and said, 'Mr. Felton, I have a chess set, why don't you do your chess thing.' So he put it on the table where the extra was sitting, and we did a little scene with the chess set."

But that was not the end of the incident. Normally, there was a second assistant on the set who would take care of things like union waivers that were required any time a nonactor, like Felton, played a scene. But in this instance, it was not done. "Several months later," Felton recalls, "I was called to a meeting with a representative of the Screen Actors Guild, and the industrial relations man at MGM, because I did not have a waiver. We paid a two-thousand-dollar penalty for my sitting there. But the man who complained was the man who was sitting there, and he got paid an extra fee for sitting there. I really got a ribbing out of that. It was an expensive scene to do."

Felton and his producers did at various times give consideration to a continuing role for some of the more popular villains. George Sanders's portrayal of Squire G. Emory Partridge in the first-season episode "The Gazebo in the Maze Affair" was considered good enough to bring Sanders back as the same character in "The Yukon Affair" in the second season. Anne Francis reappears as Gervaise Ravel in "The Giuoco Piano Affair" and "The Quadripartite Affair." The character of Dr. Egret appears in both "The Mad, *Mad* Tea Party

Affair" and "The Girls of Nazarone Affair," but she is played by different actresses. Many other actors made dual appearances on the show as villains, but played a different character each time (with the additional exception of Arthur Malet, who played the same role in two *Girl from U.N.C.L.E.* episodes, "The Mother Muffin Affair" and "The Garden of Evil Affair").

The idea of recurring villains was clearly part of the first-season episodes. Dr. Egret, in both of her appearances, is shown as wearing a rubber mask which she discards at the end of the episode to make her escape. This clever idea would have allowed a different actress to play the role each time she appeared. But the idea was dropped and Dr. Egret was not seen again after the first season. Elsa Lanchester's performance as Dr. Dabree in "The Brain Killer Affair" was so diabolical that the script was rewritten so that her character would survive instead of being killed; she vows to return and wreak revenge upon Solo, but she never did. And, in "The Deadly Games Affair," we are introduced to the beautiful Angelique, a THRUSH agent who we learn has opposed Solo more than once before. They share an attraction for each other that makes for an interesting relationship. She, too, survives the affair; but she did not appear again in the series.

Producer David Victor acknowledged the plan to reuse those villains who had proven to be popular. In addition to Elsa Lanchester, there were plans to reuse other villains from the first season such as Ken Murray from "The Fiddlesticks Affair," Cesar Romero from "The Never Never Affair," and Alexander Scourby from "The Deadly Games Affair." But those plans were not carried out.

Although no villainous character was repeated, several actors did such a good job of being evil on the screen that they were brought back again as different villains. Theodore Marcuse played a bald, malicious THRUSH agent in no less than three episodes of *The Man from U.N.C.L.E.*: "The Recollectors Affair," "The Pieces of Fate Affair," and "The Minus X Affair." Tragically, he was killed in a car accident on November 29, 1967, just nine months after he was seen in "The Pieces of Fate Affair."

Another often-seen actor in a villain's role was Bernard Fox, who appeared in "The Bridge of Lions Affair" (parts 1 and 2), in "The Thor Affair," and on *The Girl from U.N.C.L.E.* in "The Mother Muffin Affair."

Two actors often played secondary roles as huge henchmen who carried out the villain's bidding. In "The Vulcan Affair" pilot, we received a brief glimpse of seven-foot tall Richard Kiel, who played a more expanded role in the first-season episode "The Hong Kong Shilling Affair." Kiel was later chosen by the producers of the James Bond movies to play a similar role, that of Jaws, for the Bond films *The Spy Who Loved Me* and *Moonraker*. The second actor chosen mainly for his size was Cal Bolder. Bolder played a heavy in "The Alexander the Greater Affair" (parts 1 and 2), where he roughs up Solo in his role as a fitness instructor. He appeared again as a chauffeur in "The Bridge of Lions Affair," at one point lifting Solo's car up with Solo in it. He also appeared in the *Girl from U.N.C.L.E.* episode "The Romany Lie Affair."

Although Jill Ireland was the only "innocent" character to make two appearances, several guest stars were used more than once. Pat Harrington, Jr., for example, appeared in "The Bow Wow Affair," "The Hula Doll Affair," and "The Come with Me to the Casbah Affair." He utilized an Italian accent and recreated a character he had done on the old *Tonight Show* with Steve Allen for his role of a dog expert in "The Bow Wow Affair." Harrington later played a regular role on the series *One Day at a Time*.

Woodrow Parfrey appeared frequently as well, in "The Project Strigas Affair," "The Sort-of-Do-It-Yourself-Dreadful Affair," "The Take Me to Your Leader Affair," "The Cherry Blossom Affair," and "The Moonglow Affair."

The most often seen female guest star was Sharon Farrell. She was seen in "The Minus X Affair," "The Pieces of Fate Affair," and "The Double Affair." She also appeared on *The Wild Wild West,* and in several movies, including *Marlowe* and *Night of the Comet*.

In addition to the role of Alexander Waverly, a continuing female role as a secretary to Waverly was contemplated. However, over the series several actresses were used, and no memorable character emerged. The pilot episode used Leigh Chapman as Sarah Johnson in the TV version; but the movie version had a character named Margaret Oberon, who liked to work on her tan under a sunlamp at her radio console. Leigh Chapman appears as Sarah Johnson in about half of the first-season episodes, and as a receptionist in "The Mad, *Mad* Tea Party Affair." She returned in the second season as Wanda in three episodes. Chapman was born in North Carolina, and worked for the William Morris agency in LA as a legal secretary to attorney Peter Allan Fields, who would later write for the *U.N.C.L.E.*

series. She herself turned to TV writing for *Burke's Law, Dr. Kildare, The Wild, Wild West, Mission: Impossible,* and *My Favorite Martian.* She guest-starred on *Iron Horse* and *The Monkees,* and eventually wrote screenplays for *Dirty Mary and Crazy Larry* and *The Octagon.* The other secretary of the first season was Heather McNab, played by May Heatherly, who had appeared on *Hawaiian Eye, The Real McCoys,* and *Gunsmoke.* This character also liked to sunbathe in the office.

The receptionist in the first season was Wanda Mae Kim, who was played by Grace Lee, Miss Free China of 1962 and runner-up in the Miss World contest. Although her character was dropped, she appeared later as a geisha in "The Cherry Blossom Affair." Yvonne Craig, who guest starred in "The Brain Killer Affair" in the first season, appeared as a secretary and Waverly's niece Maude Waverly in the added scenes for *One Spy Too Many,* and in *One of Our Spies Is Missing* as Wanda.

Sharon Hillyer played many secretarial roles on the series, such as Wanda in five episodes, "Miss Gorgeous" in another; in other episodes she played an U.N.C.L.E. girl, an U.N.C.L.E. agent, an U.N.C.L.E. technician, and a stewardess. Sarah was played by Maurine Dawson in "The Ultimate Computer Affair," and

by Kay Michaels in "The Take Me to Your Leader Affair."

For the fourth season, part of the "new look" of the series was to be a more regular secretary, Barbara Moore as Lisa Rogers, who was seen in ten of the seventeen episodes. She was chosen after winning eighteen beauty contests, and beat out fifty other applicants for the role. Moore landed a recording contract while doing promotional work for the show in Nashville.

The remaining continuing character was Del Floria, the tailor that would be seen when Solo and Illya entered headquarters. Del Floria, a single surname like Del Monte, first name unknown, was played in the pilot by Mario Siletti. Irving Steinberg played Del Floria in "The Mad, *Mad* Tea Party Affair," "The Double Affair," "The Ultimate Computer Affair," and "The Foxes and Hounds Affair." Rick Bernard played the role in "The Hula Doll Affair" and "The Concrete Overcoat Affair," and Charles Mayer in "The Maze Affair."

The guest stars added variety to the series, and gave each episode a new character the audience could identify with. The large number of guest stars, and the great talent that was obtained for these roles, was yet another element in the success of *The Man from U.N.C.L.E.*

Chapter 14

The *U.N.C.L.E.* Format

To introduce the audience to the world of *U.N.C.L.E.* and the main characters, a special opening sequence was used for the first thirteen episodes ordered by the network after the pilot. The sequence begins with a long-range shot of Manhattan, near the United Nations. The camera pans over to the right, and begins to zoom in and down on a particular area. There is then a cut to the Del Floria's street front, showing a daytime scene with casual passersby. The narrator tells the audience that the location is "somewhere" in the East Forties, and then Solo and Illya appear as they enter Del Floria's, an "ordinary tailor shop—or is it ordinary?" As the two agents enter headquarters, the narrator explains what the initials "U.N.C.L.E." stand for, and the purpose of the organization. As the agents walk down the shiny corridor, steel doors automatically open and close. They enter a room full of computers and radios; Waverly is seated at a console. As Illya proceeds to assemble the U.N.C.L.E. Special gun, Solo turns to the camera and introduces himself. Illya then does the same, as does Waverly, absentmindedly caught off guard at first. He turns away, as the camera pulls back to take in all three men. Superimposed now is the title of this week's episode. The logo then appears,

accompanied by the theme song and the opening credits, which list Vaughn, McCallum, Carroll, and the guest stars. In a few seconds, the first-time viewer is told the characters' names and their relationships—"my friend, Napoleon"—and is introduced to U.N.C.L.E., its headquarters, its purpose, and even some of its gadgetry.

Early on, it was decided that both the fictional organization U.N.C.L.E. and the show itself would have a distinctive logo. With Felton and Rolfe's help, the MGM art department came up with a unique symbol, consisting of a silhouetted globe surrounded by concentric circles, flanked by a man in suit and tie holding a gun in his right hand. Both were mounted on a horizontal bar, underneath which the letters "U.N.C.L.E." were printed in profil-style print, a kind of three-dimensional raised lettering. This logo was used at the start of every episode. For the first season, a two-dimensional map of the world appeared on the screen. The words *The . . . Man . . . from . . .* came out of infinity to the center of the screen and then popped off. The word *U.N.C.L.E.* would then come on, letter by letter, and slip to the bottom of the frame as the logo then appeared above it.

This long opening was replaced halfway through the season, with "The Deadly Decoy Affair." There, instead of a walk through headquarters, we saw a replay of the break-in through Del Floria's from the pilot episode, using a silhouette for the intruder. The shots crack and splinter a sheet of bulletproof glass in front of the figure, and as the lights come up we see it is Napoleon Solo as he raises his gun and looks directly into the camera. The picture freezes and the episode title is superimposed over the image.

This new opening was to be used for the remainder of the first season. But for "The Deadly Decoy Affair," a bit more was added. In addition to the above, Solo steps out from behind the splintered glass and addresses the audience about that night's episode. Although this was the only episode to use this approach, similar introductions were written for other first-season episodes.

Following the opening sequence would be the episode title, which, at Felton's suggestion, always had the word "Affair" in it. Each episode was divided into four acts. This was Sam Rolfe's idea, as he felt it made a logical way to organize the action. In addition, treating each segment as an act of a play made it easier to cut in with commercial breaks at logical points in the action without interrupting the flow of the story.

Each act was given its own subtitle, often incorporating a line of dialogue from that act. The act titles were originally decided upon by Norman Felton and Sam Rolfe, but eventually they became the responsibility of George Lehr. Lehr would cast about for ideas among the crew and cast. The predominant thought was for the act titles to help tell the story, or provide humor, or both. For

the fourth season, however, it was decided that the episode title set up the first act sufficiently, and in those episodes there is no Act I title.

In the first season, only the pilot episode had a teaser. A teaser is a short sequence at the very beginning of an episode, appearing before the title or credits appear, designed to whet the appetite of the audience. The teaser for "The Vulcan Affair" pilot was the break-in sequence to *U.N.C.L.E.* headquarters, which ended with the splintered glass scene. The remainder of the first-season episodes did not have a teaser, and began with Act I immediately after the opening sequence and opening credits and commercial break.

But starting with the second season, a teaser was added to every episode to set up the story before the title and credits appeared. The teaser would fade into a blur, and the logo would appear, the theme music would come up, and shots of Vaughn, McCallum, and Carroll would come on: "Starring ROBERT VAUGHN as Napoleon Solo, DAVID McCALLUM as Illya Kuryakin, and LEO G. CARROLL as Alexander Waverly." These would be followed by shots of the guest stars while the *U.N.C.L.E.* theme continued to play. This same format was followed for the rest of the series.

Following the commercial, after the Act I title was established, often the setting would be established with a still shot of some famous landmark—the Eiffel Tower, Big Ben, the Acropolis, etc.— with a superimposed designation, such as "Somewhere in Greece," or "Somewhere in Iowa." The acts were designated by Roman numerals, and acts II-IV would have the episode title in small print in the upper right-hand corner of the screen.

After the episode was completed, often the *U.N.C.L.E.* logo would appear and a female voice-over would softly say "Our man from U.N.C.L.E. will be right back with a look at next week's show." The preview would be narrated by McCallum or Vaughn in a voice-over, promising lots of action and adventure and announcing the name of the episode— "Join us next week for 'The Test Tube Killer Affair.'" Sometimes the last-minute nature of television production would result in one title being used in the preview, and another on the following week's broadcast. Thus, on New Year's Eve 1965, McCallum narrated a preview tag that urged us to tune in to "The Very Grave Affair," which turned out to be "The Dippy Blonde Affair."

For the first season, while the end credits were given, five or six still scenes from that episode served as background. Curiously, for one episode, "The Four Steps Affair," the background scenes were not stills but moving scenes from the episode. For the second and subsequent seasons, stock color stills of Vaughn, McCallum, and Carroll were used as a backdrop for the closing credits of every episode, although a different set was used for each of the last three seasons.

A technical problem in the show itself concerned how to show the transition from one scene to another. For the first season, two main types of transitional device were used. On some shows, a "freeze frame" technique was used. The image would simply freeze in place, then blur or fade out. On others, the switch was made with a straight dissolve, or a blurring of the image to obscurity, followed by a blurred image of the next scene that gradually came into focus (or with a commercial). On some occasions, the blur fade-out would be used within a scene as well, to show the passage of time.

But later, blur fades were considered too expensive. A "whip" pan, involving rapidly moving the camera horizontally to give a fast blurring effect, was developed. George Lehr recalls, "It was created by Sam Rolfe. He's the one who wanted the idea, and he expressed what he wanted as a transitional device. Sam said, 'I want some kind of visual element to use, and I think what we could do is at the end of a scene, spin the camera so

A closing credit background for the third and fourth seasons. © *1964–1967 Metro-Goldwyn-Mayer, Inc.*

that the last shot of the scene would spin away from the shot, and the next scene, would spin into the shot.'"

But it turned out that Rolfe's idea was not workable, Lehr said: "When you're directing a show, you don't know which scene you shoot is going to be your last one. So, it had to be created from separate images, so it could be cut in editorially."

Lehr recalls "We tried to do it optically, by using a piece of negative. That didn't work. So then we took some enlarged pictures down to the insert stage, and whip-panned on and off those. And that didn't work. So then we took great big pieces of posterboard and splashed colors on them and panned on and off those, because it had to be nebulous. They didn't want to see anything in the blur, just colors. But they wanted you to feel as if you were moving across actual pictures." The pans finally decided on were soon being emulated by other studios and shows, Lehr says: "Suddenly they were being used all over town, and other studios were renting them from our library." Eventually the transitional blurs were accompanied by music—bongoes, or a xylophone.

The episodes were often filmed in one order and broadcast in another. For example, the third episode to be filmed was "The Brain Killer Affair," which was not broadcast until the twenty-third air date. The number of episodes also varied from one season to the next. For the first season, twenty-nine episodes were broadcast. For the second season, thirty episodes were shown. For the third season, again thirty were broadcast. For *The Girl from U.N.C.L.E.*, twenty-nine episodes were produced. *The Man from U.N.C.L.E.*'s fourth season only lasted for sixteen episodes before its cancellation. George Lehr states that a new show would receive authorization from the network for only a few shows at first, such as thirteen or seventeen. Once the show had established its ratings and was into a second or third season, the network would authorize twenty-four episodes with an option for five or six additional episodes.

Chapter 15

U.N.C.L.E.—Day By Day

The costs of producing *The Man from U.N.C.L.E.* were paid by sponsors purchasing commercial time from the network. With six sixty-second commercial positions—one after the opening sequence, one after each act, and one between the preview of the next week's episode and the closing credits—as well as the credits, titles, and station identification, the actual running time of an episode was forty-eight minutes of the one-hour time slot. The cost of a one-minute commercial on *The Man from U.N.C.L.E.* was approximately $51,000, and $39,000 on *The Girl from U.N.C.L.E.*

Although several companies served as sponsors, sometimes a sponsor would purchase an entire episode's commercial spots for their products, as Chevrolet did for the first two episodes. At one time it was contemplated that as a by-product of this, Norman Felton, Sam Rolfe, and Robert Vaughn would all be given Chevrolet automobiles to drive for their personal use, but this was found to violate the anti-payola rules of the industry. Other first-season sponsors for *The Man from U.N.C.L.E.* included Polaroid, Union Carbide, Chanel, Beechnut, Proctor and Gamble, Carnation, Bristol Meyers, Vicks, Maybelline, and Hawaiian Punch.

The commercial revenues were of course designed to offset the costs of producing the series. The average cost of an episode from the second season was $155,785. The average cost of the *Girl from U.N.C.L.E.* episodes was $160,486, even though that show was budgeted at $154,000 per episode. For the fourth season of *The Man from U.N.C.L.E.* the average cost was approximately $167,000 per episode.

When an episode did go overbudget, it was pointed out and the reason why was made known so steps could be taken to prevent it from happening too often. Sometimes the overruns were minor, such as in "The Off-Broadway Affair," where the budget ran $205 over because of the cost of purchasing tights and leotards for the performers. But on "The Bridge of Lions Affair" two-parter, the production came in $20,000 overbudget.

The costs attributable to the producer, director, writer, and the cast are commonly referred to as "above-the-line" costs, because in most accountings of episode budgets these costs are treated separately from the other costs and subtotaled. For a typical third-season episode, the producer fee was $6,000, the director's $3,500, the writer's $6,500, and the cast's, including guest stars', $22,000. The total above-the-line costs were $38,000.

The "below-the-line" costs included such things as technical crew salaries, props, sets, etc. Set construction costs averaged $7,000, lighting $8,000, props $7,000, and extras would cost $5,000. It was necessary to pay MGM for stage rentals, and this was budgeted at $3,800. The cost of film and its laboratory processing was put in at $18,000, and editing and projection costs were set at $7,000. Sound work would cost $4,500. With other miscellaneous items, the below-the-line costs would total $95,000. With fringe benefits and studio overhead added in, the total budget for a single color episode came to $155,000.

But even with the success of *The Man from U.N.C.L.E.*, the network was still not paying Arena and MGM the full cost of producing the series. As Felton pointed out to Stan Robertson of NBC in August of 1967, "We deliver, at a price nowhere near the cost of episodes, a remarkable amount of performance and production in the *U.N.C.L.E.* shows, because of terrific stress and strain on the part of the production company." Innovativeness on the part of the crew, such as Til Gabbani's use of the Arriflex camera, allowing the episodes to be filmed in the budgeted six days, made this possible, as did the creative thinking of men like Bob Murdock and Arnold Goode, property masters, who would save the production company thousands by constructing props from everyday items at minimal cost. But with the high costs of making an action series like *U.N.C.L.E.*, eventually offshoots like merchandising items and revenue from the theatrical versions of the episodes were needed to generate a profit.

At any given time, the *U.N.C.L.E.* production team would have several shows in progress. It was not a matter of starting up an episode, following it through to completion, and then starting another. After a script was accepted, the actual production of the episode took place in three distinct stages: preproduction (choosing the director, the guest stars, locations, etc.), production (shooting the actual film footage), and postproduction (editing, dubbing, mixing, scoring, etc.). As George Lehr explains, "When you are under the gun on shooting that many shows a season, we'd have three, four, or five in story stages. And Sam and the story editors would be working on development. And we'd have one preparing, one shooting, and two or three in postproduction. So at any one time, we had five or six shows going simultaneously."

But the assembly line of shows was geared to the all-important shooting schedule, the episode actually being filmed. Robert Vaughn remembers that the hours on the show were long and demanding: "We had a very tough schedule. We shot the show in six days, as opposed to today, where you shoot a show in seven or eight days." George Lehr agrees: "The show was actually shot in six or seven days, constantly. We never went over seven days the whole four years I was with it. A lot of the shows that were two-parters and would be turned into foreign theatrical releases, we would shoot eight, nine, ten, or twelve or even fourteen days on, but what we would do is we would do the key parts first and then shoot the additional material, which was maybe a little racier, for the foreign feature."

Another reason the shooting schedule was so tight was that both *U.N.C.L.E.* shows involved an extraordinary number of sets and set changes, since the stories involved many different locales. "It was amazing how much we did in so little time," recalls Doug Benton. "We had six days, and we used to average forty-five to fifty setups a day. And if you want to judge that by today's standards, the average TV movie does about twenty setups a day, and the average TV episode does about thirty-five setups a day."

Assistant director Bill Finnegan recalled that "On a feature, it was a big thing to move one or two times from one set to another. On *U.N.C.L.E.*, we would move five times a day. On a feature, you might do ten or fifteen camera setups a day. On *U.N.C.L.E.*, Fred Koenekamp was able to do forty. On a feature, you might do two or three script pages a day. On the show, we would do up to ten pages a day. One day, when John Brahm was directing, we had to do nineteen pages. When I came in in the morning, I ordered dinner for the crew, knowing we would still be there then. Brahm questioned that, and I told him if we didn't need them I'd eat them myself. I regretted saying that, because we finished at seven P.M. But the dinners went to a good cause—we sent them to a home for unwed mothers."

Finnegan had reason to expect long hours. He says, "The first year, we worked after dinner every single night of the week. The second assistants would start at six A.M., and usually finish up at ten P.M., and on Fridays at midnight. I lived an hour's drive from the studio, so many times I'd sleep in a dressing room for two or three nights because it was easier. I remember waking up one morning and wondering what was the matter, and found that I had slept over on a Friday night and we weren't shooting the next day. But it was the best training, be-

cause every week you were doing something different."

The shooting schedule normally called for ten- to twelve-hour days for the cast and crew, five days per week. David McCallum recalls those early mornings on the *U.N.C.L.E.* set: "They gave us a dressing room. I had mine right next to Elvis Presley's suite, and he had the Colonel, his agent, with him, and he was over the dance studio where Fred Astaire used to rehearse for those MGM musicals. I had two rooms, a little bedroom and a little dressing area, and I had put in my stereo and all that. And I would stay there most of the time when I wasn't working on the set. I had a small trailer, which they'd haul around, and which I kept everything in. And I would go in probably around six-thirty, and give myself breakfast in that trailer, and I'd go to makeup usually around seven-fifteen or seven-thirty, and be ready to shoot at eight."

Leigh Chapman, who played U.N.C.L.E. secretary Sarah Johnson in some of the first-season episodes, also recalls early-morning calls. "We had to report in at seven A.M. for makeup," she remembers. "You're sequestered away in your little chair, with the lights hitting you, and the makeup people going about their business. And the wardrobe people had an easy job with me, because I was wearing the same thing every time."

Following makeup application and wardrobe sessions, the next step was rehearsals of the day's dialogue. Leigh Chapman recalls, "There was a brief period for rehearsals. And then they started with the takes. We were pretty much limited to one rehearsal. It was a very fast shooting schedule, and the day was over really very quickly." According to Noel Harrison, Mark Slate of *Girl*

With specials in hand, the men from U.N.C.L.E. undertake ''The Prince of Darkness Affair.'' © *1964–1967 Metro-Goldwyn-Mayer, Inc.*

from U.N.C.L.E., the time between receipt of the script and the time to perform in front of the camera was occasionally nonexistent: "Sometimes you would get new pages during rehearsal. You learned to memorize instantly."

George Lehr recalls that the start time varied with the season. "In the summertime, in order to get the benefit of all the daylight, you would start at maybe six-thirty, with a six-thirty crew call for a seven-o'clock shooting," he explains. "In the fall when the days were shorter, you would have a seven-thirty or eight-o'clock call. And you'd go until maybe nine, ten o'clock at night." This was a longer schedule than normal for a television series at the time. "U.N.C.L.E. was unique because it was a combination of a lot of action and a lot of exteriors," Lehr

asserts. "Whereas on *Dr. Kildare,* their normal workday would be seven-thirty or eight in the morning, and they'd knock off at eight o'clock at night." George Lehr also recognizes that today's union regulations would have made the *U.N.C.L.E.* show difficult to do. "Today," he says, "after twelve hours, a lot of your people go into double or triple overtime. In those days, you could work twelve or fourteen hours a day without getting into the heavy penalties that you do today."

For each episode, a shooting schedule was devised. This consisted of several sheets, each setting forth exactly which scenes would be shot when, on what stage, what actors were needed, etc. In movies and television, scenes from a script are never shot in the order they appear in the story. Rather, they are shot according to availability of actors, sets, props, lighting, etc. If several scenes are to be shot on one set, they will all be filmed at the same time, even though they may come in very different places in the story. This saves moving the cast, crew, and camera back and forth to the set over and over again.

Similarly, if a particular member of the cast is only available at certain times, the shooting schedule is adjusted accordingly. For example, Leo G. Carroll, because of his age, could only work one or two days per week toward the end of the series. For that reason, all of his scenes were scheduled to be shot on the same day. When Robert Vaughn was attending college classes at USC in preparation for his PhD, his shooting schedule was adjusted to allow him to leave at three P.M. each Wednesday so he could attend a night class.

Unforeseen factors sometimes changed the contemplated shooting schedule.

Filming of "The Minus X Affair," which began on February 25, 1966, was interrupted by an illness in the cast. To keep the cameras rolling, production on the next episode, "The Indian Affairs Affair," began on March 4, and "Minus X" was finished later.

Some dubbing of dialogue is always necessary on a show. But on *U.N.C.L.E.* the dubbing was not always planned. For one first-season episode, "The Neptune Affair," it was an emergency. The script concerned an underwater base that housed, among other things, a deadly gas. The scriptwriter, Henry Sharp, had chosen the name *freon* for the gas. The episode was completely filmed and all postproduction work was done. The week before the show was to be broadcast, a preview of it was tagged on to the end of the *U.N.C.L.E.* episode. One brief scene in the preview had the word *freon* in it. The episode happened to be seen by an executive of the E. I. DuPont de Nemours Company. DuPont had patented a refrigerant gas called Freon, commonly used today in air conditioners and refrigerators. The executive called NBC, who in turn contacted Felton. With only two days before broadcast, a mad scramble was on to dub in another word to stave off legal action by DuPont. As Sam Rolfe says, "I guess they were worried some people might not buy their refrigerators if we told them it had a deadly gas in it."

Unfortunately, the word *freon* appeared in the episode thirteen times. It was spoken by no less than three actors, at different emotional levels and with different inflections each time. With only forty-eight hours before air time, since the original guest stars were long finished with the show, it was too late

and too expensive to bring them back to do their own dubbing. Further complicating the problem was the fact that two prints of the episode had to be redone, since one print was broadcast from New York and one from California. So a new word, *hydro,* was formulated, and one actor spent a full day sitting in front of a microphone speaking the word over and over, each time trying to match both the voice and tone of the actor he was dubbing for. George Lehr recalls, "It was as if we kidnapped this guy off the street, and nailed his shoes to the floor, and made him say *hydro* over and over again until he went mad."

Another reason for dubbing was to clean up any speech or sound problems overlooked during filming. Many times this could be done electronically without having to reshoot the scene. George Lehr, who supervised much of the postproduction work, including dubbing, recalled that Robert Vaughn had a tendency to have trouble with any words with the letter *S:* "Bob we used to kid a lot about his S's. When I dubbed him, I always had to put him through a high-pass filter to chop all the high ends. All his *S*'s sing at you. So on one of the blooper reels we put together for a party, I just put all of his *S*'s I could find together, all the clips of film. Then we just played it normally, and it just made him hiss like crazy, and everyone got a big kick out of that."

Sound effects were also dubbed in. One of the most famous sound effects of the series was the two-tone alarm made by the U.N.C.L.E. pen communicator. A similar alarm was used for security crises at U.N.C.L.E. headquarters. For the pen alarms, George Lehr recalls, "That was manufactured. What we did was, we took tones to make the communicator sound. We took a frequency oscillator and recorded various treatments on intermittent. Then we cut a high one and a low one, and paired them together and cut a film loop and ran that through the dummy." The U.N.C.L.E. communicator alarm was also used in the MGM movie *Around the World Under the Sea,* in which David McCallum appeared.

For the sound of the U.N.C.L.E. Special gun firing, a similar approach was used, according to Lehr: "I would dub the show with sound effects for the gun, and Sam would say I don't like this shot, do something else. He wanted it to sound different, to sound silenced. But when we gave him an authentic silenced shot, he didn't like that. It didn't sound deadly enough. So what we did, we took a silenced, straight half-load 9-mm shot and clipped the high end and clipped the low end, and that's what we got."

John Hackett worked on *The Man from U.N.C.L.E.* during the third season of the show as dialogue coach. Hackett was a friend of Robert Vaughn's, and had written some speeches against the Vietnam War for Vaughn. Hackett found that neither McCallum nor Vaughn needed any dialogue coaching: "Bob was phenomenal with lines. He almost could read a script once and know it, he had a photographic kind of memory. He never needed any help," he recalls.

But Leo G. Carroll was another story. The veteran actor was in his seventies at the time, and in poor health. As the series went on, he had more and more difficulty with his lines. George Lehr states, "He was a super guy, just a sweetheart, and he tried very hard, but he started having trouble. He was a total pro, and funnier than a crutch. But he did have

trouble memorizing his lines. And he realized it, and he was very embarrassed and refused to use a TelePrompTer. We said, 'Leo, there's no sense in you having to work this hard.' Because he was so professional, he said 'I can't use the teleprompter.'"

Carroll's lines were especially difficult. As Lehr puts it, "He had a lot of technical stuff, and a lot of stuff he just didn't feel comfortable with in a lot of cases. In some scenes he used the script in front of him disguised as some U.N.C.L.E. document. That was one reason he said he didn't use the TelePrompTer, he never knew where to look for it. When you use a TelePrompTer, you have to stage it in a fashion so that when you cut from angle to angle, you don't have the guy searching for his prompter. So it takes a different kind of shooting. So as a result, with the director's understanding of the problem, lots of times we'd shoot it with the script there, and he'd look down as if looking at his notes."

Norman Felton and Sam Rolfe would both often find a reason to visit the set. Rolfe liked to visit the set "because it was so much fun." On one occasion, Felton went to the set of *The Man from U.N.C.L.E.* and was not recognized by a stage hand, who asked him to leave. But his presence virtually always commanded attention, according to David McCallum: "Norman Felton's style as a producer was to engage the most professional director and writer, and leave them to it. That really was the best way to do it. Should an episode ever look as if it were going to go over schedule, Norman would appear on the set. Absolute quiet—you could have heard a pin drop—and Norman would say that there were *x* number of pages to do, and two hours to do them, and they would be shot in that time, well shot. And then he'd walk off the set. In other words, whenever things appeared to be falling apart, he'd come down and pull things together. What he said was law, and he made things happen."

Another consideration in shooting the series was continuity. Continuity, broadly defined, is the process of making sure that the fictional myth the audience is immersed in does not get shattered by mistakes in the production that remind the audience that this is just people acting, and not real characters in a real setting. For example, in "The Green Opal Affair," a girl supposedly unconscious on the floor blinks when a gun is fired. In "The Never Never Affair," in Waverly's office, Illya is standing in the recessed cubicle behind Waverly's desk. As he steps out of the cubicle, he bumps into the wall and stumbles momentarily. In "The Quadripartite Affair," a gun hits Solo in the chin when guest star Roger Carmel turns around. In "The Brain Killer Affair," football star Roosevelt Grier is holding the U.N.C.L.E. Special when he is supposedly put into a trance. He collapses into a chair, still holding the gun. But a moment after he is "frozen," he adjusts his grip on the gun.

Other lapses in continuity are harder to spot. For "The Quadripartite Affair," we see already in U.N.C.L.E.'s files a picture of Anne Francis in a masquerade ball gown and headpiece, a costume she does not wear until the masquerade party occurring much later in the story. Similarly, a large polar projection map is seen on the wall of Waverly's office in several episodes, showing the country of Siam. Since Siam was changed to Thailand in 1939, the map is either very old

or the name of Thailand was changed back to Siam to avoid any reference to the war in Southeast Asia.

The Girl from U.N.C.L.E. had its share of continuity lapses as well. In "The Lethal Eagle Affair," April is tied to the top of a moving car while an eagle soars overhead, ready to attack her. Stock footage of a golden eagle in flight was used for this scene. However, the script called for the eagle to be transported via a molecular device into a cage in a THRUSH laboratory. When the "eagle"

© 1964–1967 Metro-Goldwyn-Mayer, Inc.

appears in the cage, we see a California vulture instead.

The badges sometimes caused continuity lapses; on occasion people inside U.N.C.L.E. headquarters would appear without badges but not set off any alarms, as in "The Vulcan Affair" and "The Love Affair." Originally, too, only the receptionist at U.N.C.L.E. headquarters could affix the badges, as a special chemical on their fingertips was what kept the alarms from activating. George Lehr recalls: "If you remember, in one of the shows Bob Vaughn schmoos the gal so that he could put the badge on himself. He gave her a big line about something, and was on the make for her, and took the badge from her. And Sam raised holy hell, and said you can't do that."

But after Sam Rolfe left the series, that attention to detail disappeared. Lehr states, "Eventually, after Sam left, the guys would walk in and take their numbers off the card themselves. And we said you can't do that, her hands have to touch it or it will set the alarm off." Those who took over began to think of the badges as similar to a policeman's badge, rather than a headquarters security device. In "The Waverly Ring Affair," Solo leaves Del Floria's still wearing his badge. In the fourth-season episode "The Summit Five Affair," Illya is seen wearing his badge outside of U.N.C.L.E. headquarters as well. In the *Girl from U.N.C.L.E.* episode "The Lethal Eagle Affair," Waverly and a squad of U.N.C.L.E. agents come to April Dancer's rescue wearing their badges like so many deputy sheriffs. The U.N.C.L.E. identification cards also caused their share of continuity problems, as in "The Candidate's Wife Af-

fair," where the card is displayed upside down.

This is not to say that the *U.N.C.L.E.* series were rife with mistakes in continuity; considering that the two series consisted of over 134 one-hour episodes, they did quite well. There were also examples of good continuity, mostly in the first season. In "The Love Affair," Solo uses a small explosive charge to blow off some wires binding his wrists. In a later scene, we see a darkened, burned spot on his shirt from the escape. In "The Yellow Scarf Affair," he uses his jacket to decoy a sniper. We later see the bullet hole in the jacket, just as it should be.

Of course, most of the continuity errors were removed in postproduction; the above examples are those that got through. Chuck Painter recalls, "One of my extracurricular activities was sitting and looking over the shoulder of the cutter to pick out outtakes for the soiree at the end of the year. All the goofs and blats and all of that stuff, we'd put them on a goof reel. And toward the end of the party, when everybody was feeling good, we'd show it and they'd be falling all over the floor in hysterics." But, George Lehr recalls that these outtake reels were not kept for long. "We made goody reels. But in those days, as it is today, the studio was very nervous about them, so the bloopers and all of the outtakes that existed were systematically destroyed so that they didn't get into the wrong hands."

In each scene shot, the visual image, of course, had to be accompanied by sound. A boom microphone usually was used, consisting of a cylindrical mike on a long, overhanging rod. The trick was to position the mike so that it would pick up the conversations of the actors without being in the shot. A noticeable lapse in this area is visible in "The Hula Doll Affair," in the scene where Illya is entering the front of THRUSH headquarters disguised as a taxi driver. The microphone boom dips noticeably into the shot for an instant.

Close attention to detail added to the cinematic experience. In "The Mad, *Mad* Tea Party Affair," in the chase through headquarters at the episode's climax, the double agent fires his gun at his pursuers. We see this from floor level, and realism is heightened as the spent shells clatter to the floor in the foreground.

Camera angles were sometimes utilized to mask or hide a part of the scene. When it was felt it would be too gruesome to show the double agent in "The Mad, *Mad* Tea Party Affair" homogenize the brain of the U.N.C.L.E. technician, we instead see his pipe fall to the floor as he dies.

At other times, camera angles and matchcuts were used for transitional effect. In "The Minus X Affair," a glass breaking in one scene is instantly replaced by an insert of Eve Arden cleaning up different broken glass from an earlier scene in her laboratory. A similar transition was used in "The Green Opal Affair," where in one scene we see Solo rehearsing his adopted role as a bookkeeper, and after a fast cut we see him actually playing the role for his new employer, played by Carroll O'Connor.

Occasionally, the speed of the camera was varied for effect. Slow motion was used in the opening credit sequences of the *U.N.C.L.E.* movies. Isolated uses of slow motion appeared in the episodes themselves, such as the assassination scene in "The Fiery Angel Affair." Fast motion was also used in some episodes, such as "The Sort-of-Do-It-Yourself-Dreadful Affair" and "The Moulin Ruse Affair" in *The Girl from U.N.C.L.E.*

Although some scenes in *U.N.C.L.E.* were shot at night, such as the water-tower sequence in the "Deadly Toys Affair" teaser, others were shot in daytime but made to look like night by the use of filters, such as the scene with Illya climbing over a fence in the same episode.

When it was necessary to imply a given location in the world, stock footage of some recognizable landmark from that locale would be used in a brief establishing shot. For instance, a stock shot of the Golden Gate Bridge and San Francisco cable cars were used in "The Candidate's Wife Affair." For "The Five Daughters Affair," Norman Felton asked George Lehr to find stock footage of a jet shooting rockets from *The Lieutenant*. Thus, the same stock footage of a plane exploding in midair was used repeatedly as a substitute for all sizes and shapes of planes throughout the series, even a helicopter. Another example of the misuse of stock footage took place in "The Gazebo in the Maze Affair," when Illya is supposedly traveling on a double-decker bus in New York City. Instead of seeing stock footage of New York City outside the windows, we see California parking lots and development tracts.

Occasionally, the same footage shot for one episode would be reused in another. In "The Green Opal Affair," we see Illya improving his coordination with a spiked training block and a ball bat. He is interrupted by an alarm, and rushes to Waverly's cubicle to shut off the switch. The alarm part of this sequence was used in "The Mad, *Mad* Tea Party" as well, but it creates a continuity lapse because Illya is in shirtsleeves in the former episode; in the latter episode, he runs out into the hall and suddenly has his suitcoat on. In "The Maze Affair," the same bomb-disposal sequence is used twice in the same episode.

Chapter 16

The *U.N.C.L.E.* Stunts

On *The Man from U.N.C.L.E.*, action scenes were as common as commercials. Every episode included a number of fight scenes, as well as other types of physical action. The production company had too much money invested in the actors to risk any injury, and the actors were not trained to perform stunts without injury. Thus, professional stunt people would stand in for the actors for these sequences.

On occasion, the main actors did do their own stuntwork. In "The Alexander the Greater Affair," Illya is pursued by a farm tractor, but climbs up the scoop of the tractor and jumps down onto the driver. McCallum performed much of this sequence himself, with bed mattresses piled on top of the tractor to cushion his landing.

John Hackett states that "Bob Vaughn always had a lot of courage to try new things. He's not a good swimmer, and I remember one time the script called for him to be in the water, in the ocean off Santa Monica pier. So he got in the water and did the best he could. He tried to give the impression he wasn't drowning, acting his way through it. He was a good athlete in other sports, but coming from Minnesota he didn't have the ocean swimming background we do here in California. You have to put your-

self in his position: as an adventurous character, it's an awkward situation to say he doesn't want to go in the water. And for the show, he'd get in there and do his best. If you're an actor, when they ask you if you can ride a horse, you say yes and you jump on and disguise it. But swimming in the ocean was a life-threatening activity, so it displayed even more courage on his part to get in there and try it." Hackett recalls that another time, "Vaughn had to ride a motorcycle, and he had never done so before. But he got on the thing, and because he was athletic he got control of the mechanics of it and pulled it off."

But on another occasion, the star was not so lucky. As Vaughn recalls it, "I was on a boat, and I was to jump off it. And I grabbed what I thought was a cold smokestack pipe on the boat, but it turned out to be a red hot smokestack, and I burned my hand."

For most such scenes, however, stunt doubles were used. Robert Vaughn's stunt double was commonly Richard Geary. Finding a stunt double that resembled David McCallum was not so easy. His blond hair and distinctive hairstyle made it hard to find a stuntman that would look like him, even from behind. McCallum states "I did a lot of the physical work, but I don't think I ever did anything that would be considered life-threatening, for the simple reason that (a) I wouldn't be that stupid, and (b) they wouldn't let us do it, because if anything happened to Robert or me it would be foolish. When we got hold of my stuntman, who had been a circus performer, he and I designed the stunts so that I would do a certain amount of the physical things within the shot, and he would complete them. I'd go behind a wall and he'd go flying out the other side."

The circus performer who doubled for McCallum was Fred Waugh. Waugh was an avid gymnast in high school, and after graduation he joined a circus and worked as a trapeze artist for over fourteen years. He worked in circus movies doing aerial stunts until he was hired for *The Man from U.N.C.L.E.* He remained with the show for over three years, doing fights, car chases, fires, and aerial work. He later did extensive work on the *Spiderman* series.

Besides doubling for McCallum, Waugh played bit roles on the series as well, appearing in "The J for Judas Affair," and for *The Girl from U.N.C.L.E.*, "The Drublegratz Affair," "The Paradise Lost Affair," "The Double-O-Nothing Affair," and "The Kooky Spook Affair." Waugh was even asked to double for Stefanie Powers on occasion. Waugh continues in stuntwork to this day, having worked as stunt coordinator on both *Splash* and *Porky's Revenge*.

Another steady *U.N.C.L.E.* stuntman was Jay Jones. In addition to stuntwork for television, Jones was an avid racquetball player who later turned professional. Jones also played a small role in "The Yo-Ho-Ho and a Bottle of Rum Affair." For *The Girl from U.N.C.L.E.*, Dick Crockett filled in on many occasions, and Tyler Hillman stood in for Mark Slate. Crockett also played secondary roles in *The Man from U.N.C.L.E.* in "The Off-Broadway Affair," "The Gurnius Affair," "The Her Master's Voice Affair," and "The Five Daughters Affair."

Occasionally a stuntperson would double for a guest star as well, such as when Nancy Sinatra's character climbed down a drainpipe in "The Take Me to Your Leader Affair." On other occasions the guest stars endured the discomfort, such as Patricia Crowley's scene hanging from steam pipes in "The Vulcan Affair": "We did that all ourselves," she remembers. "And it wasn't all that difficult. In the scenes that were above our

Robert Vaughn undergoes a dousing in the name of realism. © *1964–1967 Metro-Goldwyn-Mayer, Inc.*

133

David McCallum finds that stunt work is sometimes a dirty job in "The Alexander the Greater Affair." © *1964–1967 Metro-Goldwyn-Mayer, Inc.*

feet, they had a little box for us to stand on, although we were hanging down there for quite some time."

Some serious injuries did occur on the *U.N.C.L.E.* set. Director Darrell Hallenbeck remembers, "We had a full lake on the backlot, and we had two stuntmen on a speedboat. And one of them lost control and he told the other guy to jump, and he did. But the boat turned around and ran over Freddie Waugh. You could hear the bump, and see the motor kick up. And we thought, 'Oh my God, he's chopped up to pieces.'" George Lehr witnessed the same incident, recalling, "The boat wobbled and went right up over Fred Waugh, right up his back from the tailbone to his head. And when we pulled Freddie out and got

him on shore, his back was open from his tailbone to his shoulders, just laid open, exposing his spine. It was the worst thing I ever saw in my life. And I thought then, he was dead. He was unconscious, and we had medics there inside of four minutes. But he recovered, it was miraculous."

Another stuntman was not so lucky, however. In the second episode, "The Iowa Scuba Affair," George Lehr recalls that a stuntman "was to jump through a fire, and he broke his back. He had to dive through a wall of fire, and we rehearsed and rehearsed and rehearsed it. Everything went okay, then when we went to get it on film, instead of jumping over the fire and tucking and rolling into the pit, he took kind of a horizontal leap, with not enough height on it so he could tuck and roll. And he landed in the pit on the back of his neck and on his shoulders and he broke his neck. He's totally paralyzed to this day." The fire scene was omitted from the episode.

Most of the other mishaps on the set were minor. On one occasion, while Richard Donner was directing an episode, a prop man missed his cue to close the "automatic" doors of U.N.C.L.E. headquarters, which were merely wooden panels on tracks manually operated by offscreen prop men. The door closed too soon, catching Vaughn on the temple. A system of hand signals was developed after that.

Once, a set collapsed around the two stars when a set hand forgot to nail the walls in place. On another occasion, David McCallum was practicing the quick draw with the prop guns on the set with some members of the crew when a blank cartridge went off, momentarily making McCallum fear he had shot one of the crewmen.

McCallum remembers another incident on the set: "I had to drive a forklift for ["The Arabian Affair"]. I knew how to drive it and how to turn it, but they didn't tell me how to stop it. I took the whole set down. I let Freddie Waugh do the driving after that." Another time, the half-globe of the world mounted on Waverly's desk was destroyed when a wooden panel fell on it and shattered it—while the actors were seated around the table.

Other incidents on the set did not turn out to be so harmless. On the set of *The Girl from U.N.C.L.E.* episode "The Faustus Affair," veteran actor Raymond Massey, who had worked with producer Douglas Benton before on Felton's *Dr. Kildare* series, made a guest appearance. Benton recalls, "At the end of the show, we had him turn white. And the special-effects people did it with silicate powder, which nobody thought anything about at the time. But it irritated and aggravated a lung condition that Raymond had, and it put him in the hospital. He was doing this as more or less a favor to me, and I just felt awful about it."

For "The Hot Number Affair," rock music star Sonny Bono suffered a bloody nose when he caught a roundhouse punch from McCallum in a fight scene. In "The Hong Kong Shilling Affair," guest star Glenn Corbett was required to fall through a window to the floor below. When the scene was shot, Corbett requested to do it himself, and he was placed on a platform seven feet off the floor, above a pile of mattresses. Corbett fell through to the mattresses below, but landed in such a way that he fell between the mattresses to the floor. He was hospitalized at Culver Memorial Hospital with a back injury.

Normally, such an injury would bring the production to a halt, which could cost thousands of dollars. But this particular scene was one of Corbett's last ones. His only remaining scene called for him and his romantic interest in the episode to stand behind a bar and wave good-bye to Solo and Illya. Since he was hospitalized and unavailable, an even better ending was written for the episode: we see only their hands waving, then slowly sinking out of sight behind the bar, allowing the use of a stand-in's hand.

Chapter 17

The *U.N.C.L.E.* Crew

The production staff and crew for *The Man from U.N.C.L.E.* was drawn, to a large degree, from other Norman Felton productions. From *The Lieutenant,* besides Robert Vaughn, *The Man from U.N.C.L.E.* gained the services of director of photography Fred Koenekamp and cameraman Til Gabbani, special-effects man Marcel Vercoutere, several assistant directors, and many others. From *The Eleventh Hour* came Sam Rolfe and associate producer George Lehr, and from *Dr. Kildare* came *Girl from U.N.C.L.E.* producer Douglas Benton and others. From *The Twilight Zone,* another MGM series, came assistant director E. Darrell Hallenbeck, and set decorators Keough Gleason, Frank R. McElvy, Robert R. Benton, Jerry Wunderlich, and Budd Friend.

Certain positions in the credits were supervisory only. Recording supervisor for the entire series was Franklin Milton, music supervisor was Frank E. Anderson, and John Dunning was supervising film editor. These men were heads of their MGM departments and their names automatically appeared on the credits.

The job of putting together the various portions of finished films into a cohesive order was done by the film editor. Film editor for the pilot was Henry Ber-man, who also edited ten other episodes for the first season, and ten for the second season. Other film editors included Joseph Dervin (thirty-one episodes), Bill Gulick (thirty episodes), and Ray Williford (ten episodes). Most of the editing for the series was done by these men, along with Elmo Veron, Fred Maguire, Harry Knapp, Albert Dervin, and Jack Rogers. Assistant film editor was Harry Komer.

The role of film editor is a crucial one. According to George Lehr, "The three creative people on a show are the writer, the director and the editor. The producer hires all three. The writer is assigned to develop a story, working hand in hand with the producer. The director, with the script, sits down with the producer and decides pretty much what the look of the show will be. In the process of making a film you first have got to have the written word, then you've got to have somebody to transcribe that to film, which is the director. He gets the actors to perform what has been written. And then you have the next step, which is the film editor. He sits up in a little room and gets all the film from the stage that the director sends him. Now he's got to put it all together. And the only thing he has to go on is the notes the script supervisor sends him with the script, to guide him as to how the director feels the scene should be handled. So he has the job of putting it all together. He has the key creative element in the process at that stage."

The film editor's role is so creative because he is given wide discretion on how to assemble the raw film sent to him. "Every second of the day he's making those kinds of decisions," says Lehr. "The director will send a note saying 'I want to use this particular scene because Illya Kuryakin seems to be a little bit better.' Maybe there's a technical flaw where Illya is looking in the wrong direction or the timing is wrong, and the editor won't use that. So he has to decide, 'Well, here's another take, I think I

know what the director is trying to do here, so I'm going to use a portion of another take, and see how it works.' The director will work with the editor, and tell him this is what I wanted, or it isn't what I wanted, or it's better than what I wanted."

Third-season film editor Ray Williford explains, "On *The Man from U.N.C.L.E.*, they always had three editors. And each show was picked up by a new editor, as it took about three weeks to completely edit a show. An editor's responsibility is to take the film after it has been exposed and developed, and the dailies are presented to him with the sound, if there is any, and his assistant takes the picture and the soundtrack, and they syn-

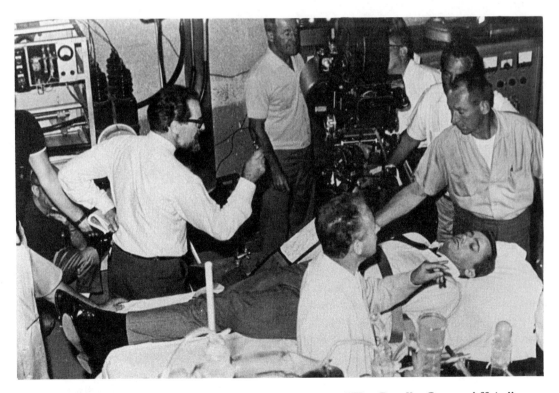

Sound and camera crews prepare for a scene in "The Deadly Games Affair."
© *1964–1967 Metro-Goldwyn-Mayer, Inc.*

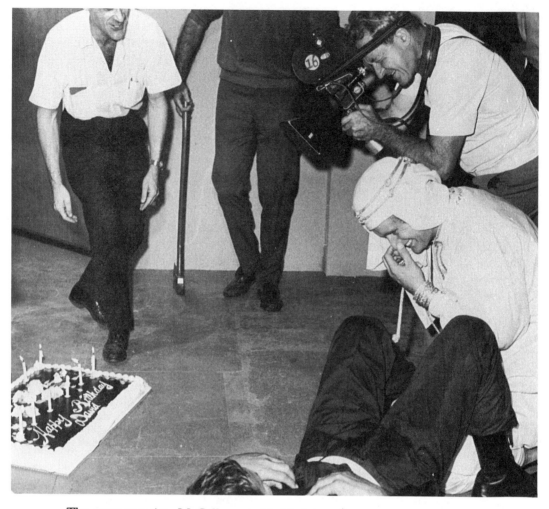

The crew surprises McCallum on his birthday. *Courtesy of Chuck Painter.*

chronize that film. Then each individual setup that is shot for the film daily that you receive is synchronized. Then the assistant codes it, with a number code to identify the individual setups, the scene and the take. They are then broken down and boxed, and when the editor is ready to edit the film, the assistant presents it to him in chronological order for the sequence, and the editor edits the sequence. The scenes are not shot in con-

tinuity, as they might shoot the last of the picture first, then the middle, and all over the place. You do them sequentially, then you put them all together."

Williford agrees that the editor has considerable control over the final product: "The editor has complete discretion. The first edit is the editor's responsibility, he can put it together any way he sees fit. And you don't do it by script, you do it by the way you see it dramatically. You're actually directing the picture the first time you put it together, because you have the responsibility of selecting whether you want a close-up shot, or an over-the-shoulder, or a master, or if something doesn't work throwing it away or redirecting it if it's possible on film. Then, secondly, you show it to the director. If he disapproves of anything, he tells you what he wants and you have to redo it. The next thing is the producer, for the same thing. But usually they are not too dissatisfied, because of the time element with the air date."

Once their approval is obtained, according to Williford, the editor "makes dupes, black-and-white reversals. And one of those goes to the sound-effects people, and the other print goes to the music people. Then it goes into dubbing, and from there it goes back into the lab for negative cutting. Then they get what they call a first trial print, which is to check sound and also to check the color. And if it is approved, you go to the final stage, an answer print."

Henry Grace's name appears as set decorator in every episode of *The Man from U.N.C.L.E.* and *The Girl from U.N.C.L.E.*, again, because of his position as the head of the MGM department. The second set decorator on the pilot was Frank McElvy. The rest of the first season, set decorators traded off each episode, with these duties being performed by Jerry Wunderlich, Robert Benton, and Budd S. Friend. For the second season, Charles S. Thompson, Francisco Lombardo, and Jack Mills decorated sets. For the third season, Lombardo returned, and was accompanied by Richard Pefferle, Keough Gleason, and Don Greenwood, Jr. For the last season of the series, Richard

Spero, James Berkey, Hugh Hunt, and Joseph Stone worked on set decoration. Spero would later do set decoration for *Riptide.*

Sam Rolfe credits the set decoration department on *The Man from U.N.C.L.E.* with the versatility that made it possible for rapid shifts of locale in the story. "On each stage there was a loft," he says, "places where they stored the sets. They just folded them up and stored them on the back of the lot. And the set designers, the guys who had charge of those things, knew where they were. And if you had a need for a set from Mars, we'd say 'Get Mars,' and they'd go out to the lot and get it." If for some reason they did not have the required set handy, Rolfe says, they were still able to solve the problem: "If we needed to go to the North Pole, they would simply paint everything white. If we then needed to go into a coal mine, then the guys with the paint brushes would color it black, and just move it around. They were constantly in the same set, just changing the color on it or moving the furniture around. Those guys were very, very imaginative in those days, and they didn't have all the high tech to work with. It was done with their hands and shovels and brushes."

The duties of the set decorator were varied. George Lehr describes them thus: "The set decorator is the person responsible for all the furnishings on the set. The hand prop man, on the other hand, handles all the props that are handled by the actors. The set decorator is responsible for the pictures, the chairs, the tables, the lamp fixtures, anything that is not handled by the actors are set decorations. He works very closely with the art director."

George Davis was the head of the art department, and was credited in every episode for that reason. For all of the first season, art direction on the show itself was done by Merrill Pye. In the second season, Pye again performed this duty for the first seven episodes, then was replaced by James Sullivan for the rest of the series.

According to Lehr, "The art director is responsible for the overall look. He would build the sets, constructionwise, supervise that, and design it. Then he and the set decorator would get together and the two of them would work very closely hand in hand."

The above positions were cited in the closing credits. But many more people were involved in the making of *The Man from U.N.C.L.E.* than appeared in the credits. For example, the gaffer, responsible for the movement and placement of lights, was Joe Frazer, and later Gene Stout. The best boy, or chief helper to the gaffer, was originally Lloyd Peters, followed by Seymour Rubin and George Holt. They were in turn assisted by three to four electricians.

The lighting was an important part of the production. Lighting was obviously crucial for indoor stage filming, but was also used in outdoor shoots in bright sunshine, to eliminate shadows. Test strips of ten to twelve frames of film would be examined each day to make sure the image was adequately lit.

The key grip, or head of the construction crew, was originally Al Hunter, and later Don Lambert, assisted by second grips George Serjeant and Dick Boreland. The crab dolly operators for the camera were Art Austrian and Roy Seelye.

The sound mixer was originally

Charles E. Wallace, and later Fred Fauss. Recordist was John Chandler. Jimmy Utterback was the main microphone boom operator, and these duties were at one time also performed by Michael Joe Clark. Originally, the sound for *The Man from U.N.C.L.E.* was recorded on 17½-mm magnetic film equipment. But in the third season, Franklin Milton, head of the MGM sound department, purchased a new, lightweight sound unit that used ¼-inch tape, and held 200 feet more than the old unit. Another technological development on the show was a portable looping room in a soundproof trailer. This allowed the actors to "loop," or re-

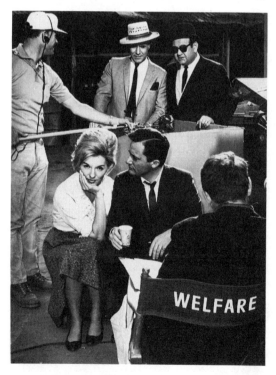

Sound man Jimmy Utterback tests a microphone between takes in "The King of Diamonds Affair." © *1964–1967 Metro-Goldwyn-Mayer, Inc.*

cord additional dialogue, right on the set instead of at the sync room.

Among the unsung technicians of *The Man from U.N.C.L.E.* were the people responsible for the appearance of the actors. Men's wardrobe person Gene Ostler and women's wardrobe person Rose Rockney and others were required to keep all the clothing, jewelry, and personal effects in top shape, and to have them on the set when needed. Hairstylists from MGM made sure everyone who appeared in front of the camera was well-groomed.

But perhaps the biggest job in this area fell on the makeup people. Every actor appearing in front of the camera needed makeup—to hide blemishes, to accent certain features, to remove shad-

Illya in yet another disguise in "The Project Strigas Affair," with Werner Klemperer at left. *Courtesy of the Norman Felton collection.*

The many faces of Illya Kuryakin. © *1964–1967 Metro-Goldwyn-Mayer, Inc.*

ows. But special makeup jobs were common on *The Man from U.N.C.L.E.*, and these fell to Stan Smith and Bob Littlefield. In the first season, many scripts treated the character of Illya Kuryakin as a master of disguises. He appeared as a Balkan intelligence agent with mustache and graying temples in "The Project Strigas Affair." He also appeared in a heavy fur piece with slanted eyes, bald head, and Fu Manchu mustache as a Mongolian warlord in "The Hong Kong Shilling Affair." For the latter episode, makeup expert William Tuttle received special mention in the closing credits. Although the makeup and appliances applied to McCallum for this episode were quite bulky, David McCallum said he didn't mind the discomfort: "I think the disguise people remember the most is the one where I played a Mongolian warlord. And it wasn't uncomfortable at all. It was great fun. The idea is, if you are going to disguise your physique, you have to do it in a grand fashion."

John Shaner served as Robert Vaughn's stand-in for 2 years of the show, and John Hackett served as dialogue director for two years. Both men were friends of Robert Vaughn's. Bill Tynan previously served as dialogue director. Shaner was also a writer, and cowrote the script for "The Pop Art Affair." He also played a role as an U.N.C.L.E. technician in "The Waverly Ring Affair," and as the air force sergeant in "The Iowa Scuba Affair."

Sam Rolfe's secretary in the first season was Marilyn Cantrell. Later producer's secretaries included Katharine Bliler and Jean Miller. Budgeting was done by Seymour Winston, and Bill Snyder served as cost advisor. Fred Houghton was legal advisor to the show. Casting was done by Don McElwaine and Jane Murray, and stills were handled by Eric Carpenter.

Together, the above individuals made up the "U.N.C.L.E. Team," a smooth-functioning group of men and women who every week produced a slick, well-orchestrated, and successful product.

Chapter 18

The *U.N.C.L.E.* Props

Another essential element of the success of *The Man from U.N.C.L.E.* was the seemingly endless array of technology that U.N.C.L.E. and THRUSH used against each other. Although only one "gadget"—the cigarette-case communicator—appears in the pilot, it was planned early on that futuristic devices would play a strong role in the series. Any series needs props, usually everyday items. But *The Man from U.N.C.L.E.* had special property requirements, and an important part of the show would be the futuristic technology the agents used.

Sam Rolfe was an advocate of stressing gadgetry from the beginning, and his theory was proven wise. On August 10, 1964, Felton acknowledged to Rolfe that preliminary testing of two episodes filmed showed that audiences liked those "gadgets and gimmicks."

To produce these "gimmicks," a team of practiced professionals was assembled at MGM. A prop team usually consisted of a prop master and two assistants, but could encompass more people. Bob Murdock was brought to the *U.N.C.L.E.* special-effects team by virtue of his work for Norman Felton on *The Eleventh Hour.* Murdock was joined by Arnold Goode, a veteran prop man who originally worked on the old Our Gang and Laurel and Hardy pictures for Pathé Studios

and the Hal Roach studios. It was at the Hal Roach studios that Goode met Rudy Butler, who would head the MGM prop department in 1964; this connection resulted in Goode being assigned to *U.N.C.L.E.*

Bob Murdock's title on the show was "property master." "There were two of us," Murdock explains. "Arnold Goode and I both. I was the senior member of the group as far as the show was concerned because I worked on the pilot. Arnold would do every other show. That way, it gave us a few days to get the stuff together for the next show."

The chief problem with providing props for *The Man from U.N.C.L.E.*, according to Bob Murdock, was the lack of time for preparation. Many times, he says, they would have only three days between receiving the script to see what was needed and the time when props would be needed on the set. This often required improvising props on the spot from whatever was available, and on occasion props were made on the run on the way to the backlot at MGM for filming. One of the problems was that the prop department was never given a blueprint as to what was needed, only a vague reference in the script.

Murdock recalls, "Sometimes we'd get the script a week ahead of time, which was unusual. Most of the time we'd get only a script outline. We'd go through it, and lots of the stuff was routine. But any new stuff that came in, we'd underline it and write it down on a special sheet of paper, called a breakdown sheet, and then go talk to the director and get his ideas on it. Then we'd go to a budget meeting two days before the show started shooting, with the director, and the producers, and the special-effects man, and the cameraman, or his representative if he was working. That's when everything must solidify. And we would hammer out this thing, and figure out the cheapest way to do it. And if we came up with an answer, that's the answer we'd use on the show. Once we set it up, we'd usually go with it."

Next to the lack of time, the next biggest challenge facing Murdock and Goode was the budget. "It varied with the show," Murdock says. "We had to buy all the ammunition, all the props, and everything else out of our budget, and our salaries came out of there too." But on occasion, the script would call for something that could not be economically produced. Murdock remembers that in a case like that, "We'd go down and find prices and find something that costs two thousand dollars to make up a certain item, and we'd put our heads together and we'd go to the producers and say 'Well, we can do *this* for fifteen dollars, and it would be just as effective.' And they'd say 'Lets's go.' That's the way we kept the show going."

As an example of this, Murdock recalls: "One morning I read a script that had come out with changed pages, and about seven-thirty in the morning I thought we'd better take a look at these. They were going to shoot about eleven

o'clock, and the script called for a three-meter-range cyanide bomb. And it was short, he just had it in his hand and handed it to this guy. So I took a cigar case, and I filled it half full of milk, and put a little red syrup in it, and then closed the top with a cork and put a little silver paper over the top and painted it. And it was a three-meter-range cyanide bomb. But that's the way we did things. We'd get away with murder in those days."

Arnold Goode remembers that the prop department would take each script as it was received and break it down into three categories of prop needs: those that would need to be bought, those that would need to be manufactured, and those that could be rented. Expensive items were either written out of the script or deleted altogether. If an item could be purchased at a reasonable price, it was; then it was modified to fit the story.

If the item could be rented from another source, this was usually preferable to spending the time and money to manufacture it. When a bank of computer panels was needed for a background in U.N.C.L.E. headquarters, the Maxwell Smith company was consulted and several obsolete computer banks, complete with flashing lights, were provided.

Since the *U.N.C.L.E.* show involved a lot of firearms, the property masters had the additional responsibility of maintaining safety on the set. Arnold Goode recalls shooting on the set of "The Her Master's Voice Affair": "We had something with some girls at an academy, with some shotguns. Barry Shear, the director, was a wild man, and the way he wanted to shoot all these things, it was impossible. So Bob refused to let him have the guns. He said, 'Well, I'll get your job.' Bob said, 'Yeah, but you're not going to shoot the guns,' because the way he wanted to shoot it would have deafened half the girls, ear by ear. So Fred Koenekamp, the cameraman, backed Bob up and they shot it another way, after holding up the show for a half hour."

Goode found himself in a similar position: "We were shooting on the backlot, and the director wanted to shoot the gun so close to someone, it was dangerous—even with blanks it could have killed them. So I refused to give him the gun. So an MGM executive finally showed up and said I was holding things up and costing them a lot of money. So I gave him the key and said, 'Here, you can unlock the gun and give it to him.' He said no, and they changed the shot. At that time we were having quite a few accidents, and a few more might have closed us down."

When Director Richard Donner worked on *U.N.C.L.E.*, he ordered that his special director's chair be brought on the set. Arnold Goode recalls that "Bob Murdock went to get it, and he came back laughing. I went to see it, and it was the biggest director's chair I've ever seen. Bob told Donner he wasn't going to move it onto the set because it was too big and heavy, but Donner said we had to have it there. So the next day, I had Ken Swartz make up a six-inch miniature replica of the chair. The next day, Donner starts screaming on the set for his chair, and I said, it's right behind you, Mr. Donner. Needless to say, it didn't go over very well. He never did get his chair."

Murdock and Goode were assisted by several assistant prop men. The first as-sistant was Billy Graham. Arnold Goode states, "To put it bluntly, Billy Graham should have received more credit than we did for the props. Bill was a very ingenious and quite a capable man. But he didn't want the responsibility of being the first man on the show." Other assistants included Ken Swartz, as well as his brother, George Swartz, and Glen Cook. Goode states, "Normally, the assistants would carry out the ideas we would come up with, and quite often they would have the idea. It was a whole lot of teamwork on *U.N.C.L.E.*"

Sometimes a prop idea would come from a member of the cast as well. Goode recalls the "Waverly rings" from "The Waverly Ring Affair": "The script

A sampling of the myriad gadgets and devices used on "The Man from U.N.C.L.E." *Courtesy of the Norman Felton collection.*

called for an U.N.C.L.E. ring, which glowed. People have often wondered how we made them glow. I was having quite a bit of trouble with the rings, and I didn't know how to get enough light into this ring so it would photograph. That's usually a big problem, because lights from the set would overpower those small ones, because they have so much more candlepower. So I was talking to Leo G. Carroll, and he mentioned using a small wheat bulb to me, which is a very small, fifteen-watt bulb. So I went to a hobby shop, and put two of them in the ring, and waxed it over on the bottom, put thin red glass over the top, and ran wires down through and onto a battery. So if you touched the battery, the lights would flash on and off when you rubbed them. That was quite an ingenious prop, and Leo G. Carroll was the one who suggested how to make it glow."

At other times, cast members were not encouraged to become involved in the props. Goode states, "David McCallum would take all of our props, and if you didn't watch him he would disassemble the thing to see what made it click."

A third important member of the prop team was Marcel Vercoutere. Vercoutere was the special-effects side of the team, as opposed to Goode and Murdock, the prop men. Often their areas would overlap, such as when a bomb was to be thrown. Murdock and Goode would construct the bomb seen in the thrower's hands, and Vercoutere would create the explosion when the bomb went off. For example, an exploding ashtray in "The Mad, *Mad* Tea Party Affair" was accomplished by attaching a piece of tinfoil coated with gunpowder onto the bottom of the ashtray and toss-ing it onto an electrically charged nail.

Vercoutere was responsible for all gunfire as well. To simulate gunfire, Vercoutere would plant small gunpowder charges in the walls or ground near the actors and set them off electrically. His cautious and careful approach to this potentially dangerous work earned him the respect of the cast and crew, some of whom had to literally trust him with their lives. Sometimes the effect called for Vercoutere, an expert marksman, to shoot pellets near the heads of the actors. David McCallum says, "Marcel was the only man I would trust to put bullet shots around my head."

George Lehr recalls that the particularly difficult episodes were those involving the U.N.C.L.E. rocket-firing helicopter, seen in "The See Paris and Die Affair," "The Quadripartite Affair," and "The Finny Foot Affair." Civil Aeronautics Board regulations prohibited the use of a real rocket on a civilian helicopter. So Vercoutere rigged up a pipe to the bottom of the helicopter from which he could pump steam from behind the pilot's seat to simulate a rocket firing. A sound effect would then be added during editing. It was scenes like this that earned Vercoutere the nickname "more smoke Marcel," according to David McCallum.

The helicopter scene in "The See Paris and Die Affair" caused problems on the ground as well. The script called for a rocket to strike a car but it proved difficult to coordinate the preplanted explosive charges in the ground with the movement of the car to give the desired effect of the rocket striking. The best take showed the explosions occurring near the front of the car. So the script was rewritten and the final version only shows a near miss that nevertheless stops the car.

Another source of props was other MGM shows. *The Twilight Zone,* in particular, provided many props for use on *The Man from U.N.C.L.E.* The triple-lensed camera mounted behind Waverly's desk and the intercom panel on his desk were both from that show, as was the laser gun mounted on the roof of U.N.C.L.E. headquarters in "The Mad, *Mad* Tea Party Affair." A series of lights resembling an octagon with a wedge cut out of it is seen in "The Neptune Affair," and these were not only used previously in a *Twilight Zone* episode, but had originally been used in the classic science fiction movie, *Forbidden Planet.* The head of Robby the Robot from that same movie was used as a rejuvenating helmet in "The Bridge of Lions Affair."

The favor was repaid when several *U.N.C.L.E.* props were later used on other series. The laser gun seen in "The Cherry Blossom Affair" and "The Monks of St. Thomas Affair" was later seen in an episode of *Wonder Woman;* the observation platform in "The Minus X Affair" and several other episodes was later used in *Medical Center;* and the Ultimate Computer in "The Ultimate Computer Affair" had its bubble cover removed and was seen in an episode of *The Monkees.*

The special triangular badges worn in U.N.C.L.E. headquarters scenes had the numbers silkscreened on in the MGM shop, and had safety pins attached to the back, but were difficult and hazardous to use. Eventually a clip was attached to the back of the badges, as evidenced by a rivet mark on the front.

Communications devices were also an important part of the *U.N.C.L.E.* stories.

Solo and Illya needed to be in communication with Mr. Waverly and with each other in nearly every episode of the series. In the pilot, a gold, square cigarette case was modified into a radio for Solo to use. When the flip top was opened, it appeared to be holding cigarettes, but inside was a concealed radio. This communicator was used throughout the first season and part of the second. George Lehr remembers, "What we did was we made the speaker section underneath, so it was concealed when you closed it. And it had an artificial cigarette glued to the panel, and you could put real cigarettes down the side."

The communicator underwent an evolution on the series, however. Lehr recalled that Sam Rolfe thought the original cigarette-case communicator looked too bulky. Another cigarette-case communicator was developed in the second season, consisting of a larger, flatter leather-covered case that opened like a book to reveal several cigarettes. However, the cigarettes were phony and when they were flipped over, a radio and small reel-to-reel tape recorder was revealed. A chrome silver cigarette lighter mounted on top twisted around to serve as an antenna. A second, matching version had a .32-caliber pistol inside.

Eventually a fountain-pen communicator was developed to replace the cigarette case, and became one of the most frequently seen props on the show. The U.N.C.L.E. pen communicators were made from an aluminum tube with a microphone grill at one end and a 2½-inch antenna at the other. Arnold Goode states that "For the pen communicator, we just picked up a pen, sawed it off and put a grid on the top of it. A lot of these things we would just pick out of the air,

Robert Vaughn displays the U.N.C.L.E. pen communicator. © *1964–1967 Metro-Gold-wyn-Mayer, Inc.*

spontaneously—there was very little planning. But we all had good imaginations."

On the show, Solo or Illya needed only to pull out their pens, pull off the cap and place it on the other end, then twist, and, when the antenna appeared, speak that immortal line, "Open Channel D," to contact Waverly. But the pen communicators served other functions on the series besides communications. They also contained an amnesia pill in "The Nowhere Affair," were magnetic in "The Concrete Overcoat Affair," served as a bomb detector in "The Test Tube Killer Affair," and emitted a knockout gas in "The Bat Cave Affair." The agent's name was printed on the barrel in both "The Lethal Eagle Affair" and "The Jewels of Topango Affair" of *The Girl from U.N.C.L.E.*

The U.N.C.L.E. car featured a futuristic body style and gull-wing doors. © *1964–1967 Metro-Goldwyn-Mayer, Inc.*

There were also definite plans to provide Solo and Illya with a special U.N.C.L.E. car, similar to James Bond's gadget-equipped Aston Martin made so famous in "Goldfinger." The Dodge Charger was chosen to be the U.N.C.L.E. car and was seen in a few episodes, but the Chrysler Corporation canceled the plan, fearing that sales, especially to families, would be hurt by the image the car would get if used in the series as a secret agent's car.

For the third season, Gene Winfield, who had started to modify the Charger for the show, went to Felton with three different cars to consider as a totally unique car for U.N.C.L.E. Along with Dan Dever, Winfield, who worked for AMT model car company's speed and custom division in Phoenix, Arizona, started with a stock Piranha, a two-seated sleek sports car he had designed, featuring gull-wing doors and made of thermoplastic. He outfitted the car with a rear-mounted six-cylinder Corvair engine and a manual four-speed transmission, and added concealed twin flame throwers in the front grill, a mock laser beam on the top, mock rocket launchers built into the doors, machine guns, and a parachute in the rear behind the license plate. The car had propellers to be amphibious, and a revolving wood-grain dash board that housed radar and sonar screens, infrared TV, and a revolving console that hid the controls. The car was metallic blue in color, had a wheel base of 88 inches and a length of 156 inches, but was only 45 inches tall.

But the U.N.C.L.E. car was plagued with problems. George Lehr recalls, "It was a disaster. The car wouldn't start, the battery was always dead, the devices hung up." *Girl from U.N.C.L.E.* producer

Douglas Benton had similar recollections about the car: "It was one of the bad jokes of the whole thing. I don't think it ever ran over ten feet without completely falling apart. We could almost follow it around the studio by the oil it left. We would see it and it would be sitting in a pool of motor oil."

Both Vaughn and McCallum had trouble getting in and out of the low-slung car in a hurry, and when they complained there was not enough headroom, bubble-type windows were added in the fourth season. George Lehr said Stefanie Powers had a particularly difficult time using the car on *The Girl from U.N.C.L.E.*: "You should have seen Stefanie try to get in and out in a skirt in those days. Trying to get up over that step and into that gull wing in a hurry was a feat. She told us, 'You guys are crazy.'"

Because of the difficulties with the car, it was seen only briefly in a handful of

Stefanie Powers and the car's rocket boosters. *Courtesy of the Norman Felton collection.*

149

episodes: "The Five Daughters Affair," "The Take Me to Your Leader Affair," "The Man from THRUSH Affair," "The Napoleon's Tomb Affair," "The Test Tube Killer Affair," and the *Girl from U.N.C.L.E.* episode "The UFO Affair," the only time the devices were used to any extent. Norman Felton recalls that "The car did cost a lot to make, but the company that made it expected to get considerable publicity from it in return." Those costs, between thirty and forty thousand dollars, were paid by AMT, which marketed a plastic model kit version of the car.

After the show was canceled, the car made the rounds of custom car shows for a few years, and later ended up on blocks, rusted and minus an engine, in Colorado. It was found there by Bob Short, an *U.N.C.L.E.* fan from the Los Angeles area, who completely restored it to its original condition. He was recently stopped in the car by a policeman, not because he was speeding, but because the officer was an old fan of the show and wanted a closer look at the car.

The most famous prop of the show was, of course, the "U.N.C.L.E. Special" gun. It was decided early on by both Norman Felton and Sam Rolfe that Napoleon Solo would need more than just an ordinary gun to carry out his missions. Since Solo was the top agent of a supersecret multinational agency that would be fighting crime on a grand scale, it was logical that his weapon would be not only state-of-the-art, but slightly beyond anything available in the real world of 1964.

Bob Murdock says, "The U.N.C.L.E. gun is a whole story in itself." In designing the needs of the U.N.C.L.E. gun, Felton and Rolfe decided that the gun must

Robert Vaughn with the original Mauser version of the "U.N.C.L.E. special." © *1964– 1967 Metro-Goldwyn-Mayer, Inc.*

contain, as a minimum, four characteristics: adequate stopping and firing power, meaning a large caliber; the ability to operate fully automatic (as a machine gun); the ability to be concealed on the person or in an attaché case, since secret agents would be using it; and the capacity to be silenced, for discreet operations. In addition, it was decided that the U.N.C.L.E. gun should be based on an actual gun, so as to give the illusion of reality.

In April 1964, Norman Felton consulted with Lou Gray and the MGM armory about the guns, which would have to be completed by June 1, when filming of the series began. Reuben Klemmer, assisted by Richard Conroy, Hank Gilbert, and Bo Clerke, designed and developed a specially modified 1934 7.65-mm German Mauser pistol for the show. The original U.N.C.L.E. Special was designed by Richard Conroy to be convertible into a machine gun/rifle by the addition of various attachments, such as a shoulder stock, extended barrel with silencer, scope, and extended magazine. The original model had a wooden grip on the extended barrel, but the grip was only used in publicity photos. This conversion design was similar to a Stoner 63 system then being tested in the Far East by the U.S. Marines.

Actually, many features of the U.N.C.L.E. gun were derived not from story needs, but from merchandising considerations suggested by Stanley Weston, the agent in charge of merchandising offshoots from the show. Ideal toys, the company that actually marketed the toy version of the U.N.C.L.E.

Robert Vaughn converts the U.N.C.L.E. pistol into the "special." *Courtesy of the Norman Felton collection.*

gun, thought the Mauser version looked too "Mickey Mouse," and came up with their own design, with the help of Reuben Klemmer. Ideal liked the idea of a "long" Special, feeling that it would make an attractive toy item for the Christmas season. Klemmer had helped design the Mauser for the show, and had also constructed a bipod stand for the front end of the gun. Since Klemmer designed both the Mauser and the Ideal version, the bipod appears in the Ideal version of the "Napoleon Solo Gun" even though it never appeared on the series.

The original Mauser gun was soon thought to be aesthetically unattractive. It did not photograph well, and it seemed overwhelmed by all the gadgets attached to it. It also jammed frequently, and was hard to find blank ammunition for. Arnold Goode recalls that "We were on location on our first day of shooting, and they brought the Mauser out. We'd waited two weeks for it, and it wouldn't work, and I mean literally that. It not only wouldn't fire blanks, it wouldn't fire anything."

So Goode went to Bobby Henderson, a friend of his working as property master on *Combat*, and borrowed three or four Walther P-38 pistols. George Lehr recalls that "The parts for the Mauser were harder and more expensive to work on. Since we could get P-38s dirt cheap, we thought, why not? Besides, the Mauser would heat up from firing, but the Walther could be fired all day without heating up, and you could drop it in mud, water, or sand and it would still fire." The gun would now be the P-38, but would still utilize an add-on barrel, stock, scope, and longer clip.

Since the episodes were broadcast in a

different order than they were filmed, there is no clear transition point between the use of the Mauser and the Walther on the series. Generally, episodes using the Mauser were "The Iowa Scuba Affair," "The Brain Killer Affair," "The Neptune Affair," "The Deadly Games Affair," "The Quadripartite Affair," "The Dove Affair," and "The Yellow Scarf Affair." The Walther is used exclusively in "The King of Knaves Affair," "The Green Opal Affair," and subsequent episodes.

The P-38 was a large gun, weighing two pounds as a pistol and three pounds, eight ounces as a carbine. It fired 9-mm ammunition, which was similar to the American .38-caliber, which made finding blank cartridges much easier. The very same stock and Phantom Bushnell 1.3 to 5.0 scope was used on the Walther as on the Mauser, but the scope had to be reversed to permit the shells to eject.

Fully assembled, the Special was similar in length to an M-1 carbine. Disassembled, it could be carried in a suit pocket or a special pack worn on the trousers belt, in back, as seen in only one episode—"The Yellow Scarf Affair." The attachments were developed for only two of the six Walthers. An extended magazine clip holding sixteen rounds was developed by simply attaching two normal eight-round clips together. The Special was only capable of firing blanks, as the screwthreads to attach the barrel would have caused a real round to lodge in the barrel.

Bob Murdock recalls, "We only had two Mausers with attachments made. When we switched to the Walther, we started out with two, then four, and eventually we had six. Whenever they broke, Manuel Zamora would fix them, so we always had one for shooting. We bought the guns for around two hundred to three hundred dollars, but they ended up costing around fifteen hundred per gun." Additional guns made of resin or plastic mold were constructed for scenes where the guns were required to be dropped, or carried in water, and several foam rubber versions of the Walther pistol were made for scenes where someone needed to be hit over the head.

An additional attachment was developed for the Walther in its pistol form. Variously called a "flash arrester," "muzzle compensator," or, because of its appearance, a "bird cage," a small metal device was attached to the muzzle of the pistol when the extended barrel was not used in order to give it a balanced look, since the barrel had been sawed off for the attachments. But they also served a practical purpose. The Walther P-38 relied on the "blowback" of gas from the exploded round to kick back the slide to inject another round. With the barrel cut short, there was not enough gas pushing backward to do this. The bird cages helped trap some of the exploding gas from the blank cartridges and propel it backward.

The grips, the pieces that fit over the "handle" of the gun, were made from one solid piece of aluminum. Early in the show, Solo's gun displayed a large white letter *S* on the grip, and Illya's gun a *K*, but this was discontinued when the aluminum mailbox letters, purchased at a hardware store, kept falling off.

In the series, the Special supposedly fired sleep-inducing darts as well as bullets; this was fictional. But one aspect of the gun—its machine-gun capacity—was real, and caused more than a few problems. Arnold Goode states, "One day I got a call to come over to our prop office, and here's two very well dressed gentlemen, and they begin asking me a lot of questions. Nobody introduced me or anything. They want to know about the guns. And I just clammed up. Finally, I said 'Well just who in the hell are you guys.' That's when they pulled their little badges out. That was the Treasury Department. They found out that we were manufacturing automatic guns without any license whatsoever. That was the whole thing, the guns actually worked. The question became then, were they going to take all of our guns. But before they did that, it was lunchtime. And I asked the two if they'd like to go to the commissary and have lunch with me, and I introduced them to quite a few stars that were around, and they thought it was nice. Then we came back after lunch, and I took them on all of the sets of the shows that were shooting on the lot. We finally got back to the office, and they decided they wouldn't take them all, they would just take one to inspect it and see how many things we had really violated, and we could keep the rest to use and to operate. I think MGM was fined two thousand dollars for manufacturing guns without a license. But we almost lost the guns at that point."

To everyone's utter astonishment, MGM started to receive fan mail addressed to "The Gun." *U.N.C.L.E.* publicist Chuck Painter stated that gun fan mail began pouring in two days after it was first seen, and at one point reached the rate of five hundred letters per week. The Ideal toy version of the gun proved to be a best-seller at $4.99 each. A U.S. Army Ordinance general inquired about availability of the weapon for the armed forces, and asked to borrow some mod-

THRUSH, too, had its distinctive weaponry. © *1964–1967 Metro-Goldwyn-Mayer, Inc.*

els for testing. The U.N.C.L.E. gun had become a fourth star of the show.

The final item to be completed for the U.N.C.L.E. armory were shoulder holsters. Special black leather harnesses, with extra wide tops, were constructed. A problem arose when the U.N.C.L.E. agents were required to be tied up or held upside down. To keep the holster and gun from flopping down, David Mc-Callum suggested that a leather belt be run through the bottom of the holster and around the agent's waist, with the belt concealed by cutting a slit in the actor's shirt to pass it through. When ex-football star Roosevelt Grier guest-starred in "The Brain Killer Affair," a special holster was constructed for him

in light of his huge size. When the script called for Solo's holster to be ripped off his shoulder in "The Cherry Blossom Affair," a special breakaway holster was made up. Female employees of U.N.C.L.E. seen in headquarters scenes carried their guns—actually plastic Eldon water pistols—in special holsters worn at the small of the back.

The THRUSH gun was based on an M-1 carbine. The THRUSH gun seen in such first-season episodes as "The Iowa Scuba Affair" and "The Yellow Scarf Affair" was later modified for the rest of the series. According to Arnold Goode, "There's been lots of stories on how the THRUSH gun came about. But the truth is, there were never any blueprints on it.

I went to a surplus store in Pasadena and got an old obsolete night scope the Army had developed. Bob Murdock and I put that together, with Manuel Zamora's help. The original scope was real, but later they were molded." At least six THRUSH guns, both real and resin replicas, were made, as that many are seen in "The Children's Day Affair."

Props on *The Man from U.N.C.L.E.* often were used on more than one episode. Thus, the Ultimate Computer from "The Ultimate Computer Affair" was seen again in "The Off-Broadway Affair" and in "The Survival School Affair." The brain killer machine from "The Brain Killer Affair" was reused in "The Never Never Affair," "The Virtue Affair," "The Odd Man Affair," and in the *Girl from U.N.C.L.E.* episode "The Danish Blue Affair."

The "U.N.C.L.E. special" versus the THRUSH rifle. © *1964–1967 Metro-Goldwyn-Mayer, Inc.*

The hard work and imagination of Bob Murdock, Arnold Goode, Ken Swartz, Marcel Vercoutere, Billy Graham, and the others did not go unnoticed by their peers in the industry, as the prop team of *The Man from U.N.C.L.E.* was nominated for a special Emmy award. Arnold Goode says, "That was the only nomination for unusual props that has ever been given out. It was a special thing."

Murdock regards his *U.N.C.L.E.* experience as one of the highlights of his forty-two-year career, but feels that after the second year, "They were taking the money away from us, and the gimmicks and gags, which it was originated on. And they were hiring more money into guest stars. And consequently, the story would slip us back into actors instead of gizmos and gadgets as it was originally. And bringing in new gimmicks and gags went down the drain, because of the money we had to spend on them. They couldn't go both ways, they couldn't have both gimmicks and name actors. That's why, in my opinion, you saw the series go down the drain. Because they quit dreaming."

Chapter 19

U.N.C.L.E. Around the World

The Man from U.N.C.L.E. premiered in the United States, and it was only later that it was sold to foreign television markets. The show was broadcast on the Canadian Broadcasting Corporation on Thursdays at eight P.M. in 1966. The show became phenomenally popular in Great Britain, where it was seen weekly

David McCallum and present-wife Kathy field questions at an U.N.C.L.E. news conference in Japan in 1967. © *1964–1967 Metro-Goldwyn-Mayer, Inc.*

by over nine million Britons on the BBC on Thursday evenings at eight P.M., after *Top of the Pops* at seven-thirty and before the news at eight-fifty. The *Radio Times* carried a full-page article on the "U.N.C.L.E. Cult" in England, and requests for U.N.C.L.E. ID cards topped 200,000. The show was sold to the British market in lots of thirteen episodes each.

Beginning with "The Ultimate Computer Affair" on December 23, 1965, the second-season color episodes were broadcast in England also, again in a different order, through May 19, 1966. However, the BBC was not yet broadcasting them in color. Starting on May 26, the BBC broadcast *The Best of U.N.C.L.E,* repeating four first-season episodes. From October 20, 1966, on, the BBC broadcast *The Man from U.N.C.L.E.* and *The Girl from U.N.C.L.E.* alternately, every other week, interspersing an odd mixture of second- and third-season episodes of *Man from U.N.C.L.E.* with *Girl from U.N.C.L.E.* episodes. Two episodes, "The THRUSH Roulette Affair" of *The Man from U.N.C.L.E.* and "The Carpathian Caper Affair" of *The Girl from U.N.C.L.E.* were never broadcast in England, and those episodes that formed the basis for the movies were also withheld.

The Man from U.N.C.L.E. was released virtually all over the world, eventually being telecast in over sixty countries, including Argentina, Australia, Bermuda, Brazil, Costa Rica, El Salvador, Ger-

Full-time secretaries were hired to handle the demand for U.N.C.L.E. ID cards in England. *Courtesy of the Norman Felton collection.*

many, Austria, Japan, Mexico, Panama, Peru, the Philippines, Uruguay, Venezuela, Egypt, Thailand, Belgium, Chile, the Dominican Republic, Ecuador, Finland, Gibraltar, Honduras, Hong Kong, Kenya, Portugal, Puerto Rico, Singapore, Kuala Lumpur, and South Korea. In Japan, the show gathered a huge following, as evidenced by the receptions afforded Vaughn and McCallum on a promotional tour there in 1967. The show was translated into several languages, including French, German, and Japanese, with the episode and act titles, opening (but not closing) cred-

its, etc., all spoken by a narrator since they appeared in English. In France, the show was *Des Agents Très Speciaux;* in Germany, it was *Solo für O.N.C.E.L.*; in Brazil, the Portugese translation was *O Agente da U.N.C.L.E.,* and in Danish it was *Manden fra U.N.C.L.E.*

One place where *The Man from U.N.C.L.E.* was not appreciated was in the Soviet Union. Not only was *U.N.C.L.E.* seen as capitalistic and imperialistic, but *Pravda* denounced the use of Illya, Russian agent, calling him "bloodthirsty."

Chapter 20

Merchandising
U.N.C.L.E.

The Man from U.N.C.L.E. was intended from the very beginning to generate profits from more sources than just advertising revenues. It was recognized early on that the show would have an appeal to teens and preteens, the primary market for games, toys, books, and comics.

Arena utilized the services of the Stanley Weston company to set up marketing offshoots of *The Man from U.N.C.L.E.* As early as February 1964, months before the show even started shooting, Weston suggested to Felton that certain aspects of the show be developed with an eye to merchandising, such as a logo and a gun that would make an attractive toy.

Another major area of merchandising was in paperbacks and magazines. Terry Carr, an editor at Ace Books of New York, decided that the time was ripe to cash in on the James Bond craze and signed a licensing agreement with MGM for one *Man from U.N.C.L.E.* book on November 3, 1964, and asked

Norman Felton (second from left), Vaughn, McCallum, and Ideal toy executives announce the toy version of the U.N.C.L.E. gun. *Courtesy of the Norman Felton collection.*

U.N.C.L.E. car toys. *Courtesy of George Zivic.*

Michael Avallone to write *The Thousand Coffins Affair* for a fee of one thousand dollars. Avallone based part of the story on his war experiences in Oberteisendorf, Germany. The book was simply titled *The Man from U.N.C.L.E.*, as further works were not contemplated.

But the book was a big success, selling over a million copies, and was translated into over sixty languages. Ace decided to continue the series. Even though Avallone had already written about fifty pages of a second novel, *The THRUSH and the Eagles Affair,* Ace decided to turn to other writers.

Souvenir Press published the first U.N.C.L.E. novels in England. But from that point on, the publishing order of the American and English U.N.C.L.E. paperback series diverged. The U.S. series ran for twenty-three novels, the British series for sixteen.

David McDaniel was the most prolific writer of the U.N.C.L.E. paperback novels. McDaniel, who was an U.N.C.L.E. fan as well as writer, coined the acronym "The Technological Hierarchy for the Removal of Undesirables and the Subjugation of Humanity" for THRUSH in *The Dagger Affair,* the fourth U.S. entry. In *The Utopia Affair,* paperback number fifteen, he put in two characters named

Some of the U.N.C.L.E. books and magazines. *Courtesy of George Zivic.*

Gene Coulson and Buck DeWeese—references to his friends and fellow writers Buck Coulson and Gene DeWeese, who cowrote the eleventh and twelfth entries in the series as "Thomas Stratton." McDaniel was fond of inside jokes in his books; he used MGM's street address as the location of U.N.C.L.E. headquarters in LA in *The Dagger Affair.* In *The Monster Wheel Affair* (number eight), he gave his chapters titles from the verses of a song, whose first initials spelled out "A A WYN IS A TIGHTWAD"—referring to the president of Ace Books. Even his name was an example of his sense of humor: he used his real name, David

McDaniel, in all of his writing: but he used a pseudonym, "Ted Johnstone," in real life, and even dedicated *The Monster Wheel Affair,* to Ted Johnstone. McDaniel also wrote *The Final Affair,* a story in which both U.N.C.L.E. and THRUSH are destroyed, which was to be the twenty-fourth and final book in the series. In 1977, McDaniel died following a household mishap.

Ron Ellik and Fredric Langley were friends of David McDaniel and wrote *The Cross of Gold Affair* (number fourteen), under the name "Fredric Davies," which was taken from a combination of their first and middle names. Like

McDaniel, these two writers liked inside jokes, and they wrote their real names in as U.N.C.L.E. agents encountered in the story. Tragically, Ellik died in a car accident just two days after Carr showed him the galley proofs of his novel. David McDaniel dedicated *The Utopia Affair* (number fifteen) to Ellik's memory.

The Girl from U.N.C.L.E. inspired its own short-lived paperback series from Signet books, with two books by Michael Avallone, *The Birds of a Feather Affair* and *The Blazing Affair*. A third entry by him, *The Devil Down Under Affair,* was not published. In England, a series of *Girl from U.N.C.L.E.* books ran for four novels.

A series of *Man from U.N.C.L.E. Magazine* novelettes appeared at the same time, published by Leo Margulies and his wife Cylvia. Although each issue claimed to be authored by "Robert Hart Davis," actually several writers were used. Dennis Lynds was hired to do six stories the first year, each about thirty thousand words, for which he was to be paid $450 per story. Misreading a studio press sheet, he erroneously referred to the research girl at U.N.C.L.E. as May Heatherly instead of Heather McNab (May Heatherly was the name of the actress who played McNab). Harry Whittington wrote both *U.N.C.L.E.* novels and magazine novelettes. Another of the magazine *U.N.C.L.E.* authors was John Jakes, now famous for his historical novels, such as *North and South*.

The magazine ran for two years, or twenty-four issues. A twenty-fifth issue, "The Vanishing City Affair," was written by frequent contributor I. G. Edmonds, but was never published. Margulies also published a *Girl from U.N.C.L.E. Magazine* that ran for seven

The U.N.C.L.E. comic books. *Courtesy of George Zivic.*

issues and also used the "Robert Hart Davis" pen name for its authors.

Gold Key Comics produced twenty-two comic books based on *The Man from U.N.C.L.E.* and five based on *The Girl from U.N.C.L.E.*, with artwork by Mike Sekowsky, Mike Peppe, Werner Roth, Don Heck, and Mike Roy for *The Man from U.N.C.L.E.* comics, and Bill Lignante and Alden McWilliams for *The Girl from U.N.C.L.E.* The writing was done by Dick Wood and Paul Newman.

Whitman Publishing Company produced three hardcover *U.N.C.L.E.* books, aimed at juvenile readers. *The Affair of the Gentle Saboteur* was the first hardcover, by Brandon Keith, followed by *The Affair of the Gunrunner's Gold,* also by Keith. Whitman also produced a hardcover "Big-Little" book, *The Calcutta Affair.*

Wonder Books of New York in 1965 brought out an oversized *U.N.C.L.E.* book by Walter Gibson, creator of *The*

Some of the U.N.C.L.E. gun and radio sets. *Courtesy of George Zivic.*

Shadow, and illustrated by I. H. Guyer, called *The Coin of El Diablo Affair.* Coloring books based on *The Man from U.N.C.L.E.* were produced by Watkins-Strathmore Company.

One of the most popular paper items among *U.N.C.L.E.* fans was a paperbound photo book called *Illya: That Man from U.N.C.L.E.* This was essentially an extension of an article the author, Chandler Brossard, had written for *Look* magazine. Brossard was a senior editor at *Look,* and used the name "Iris-Marie Brossard" on the book, which was taken from the first names of his two daughters, who were Illya fans.

Marx, Ideal, Milton Bradley, A.C. Gilbert, and a host of others would eventually make very profitable licensing agreements with Arena and MGM to produce *U.N.C.L.E.* toy items, and the diversity of these items illustrated the popularity of the show among children and teens.

A number of board games based on the show appeared. The original *U.N.C.L.E.* game sold for three dollars when it came out in 1965 from Ideal. A second game, the THRUSH Ray-Gun Affair Game, was also made by Ideal. A smaller card game by Milton Bradley was simply called the *Man from U.N.C.L.E.* Card Game, but was followed by an Illya Kuryakin Card Game.

Undoubtedly the biggest sellers were the toy guns by Ideal. According to Chuck Painter, "The toy gun was the big thing, probably the most popular thing made from the show." The gun sets came with a plastic U.N.C.L.E. triangular badge and a silver ID card. The premier set, the Napoleon Solo Gun, included the U.N.C.L.E. plastic cap-firing pistol and all the accessories, including the scope, extended stock, and extended barrel. This gun was used in all the Ideal U.N.C.L.E. gun sets except the Illya Kuryakin Gun Set, which had a larger gun. In 1965, Ideal also produced a smaller set, featuring the Solo gun without any attachments, called the *Man from U.N.C.L.E.* Secret Service Gun Set, and used the gun and an assortment of devices in the *Man from U.N.C.L.E.* Secret Weapon Set. The gun and several other items were put together by Ideal in the *Man from U.N.C.L.E.* Attaché Case. Ideal made an Illya K. Special, a cigarette lighter communicator with concealed gun, and made a toy THRUSH rifle with target silhouettes in the scope as well.

Even *U.N.C.L.E.* dolls were produced. A. C. Gilbert Company in 1965 produced twelve-inch Napoleon Solo and Illya Kuryakin dolls, with removable clothes and a spring-action arm that fired a small cap pistol. Gilbert also made seven different accessory sets to go with the dolls, which included small guns, binoculars, grenades, etc. Similar to the dolls were 5½-inch solid plastic figures of Solo and Illya by Marx, along with figures of Waverly, three different THRUSH agents, and two generic agents.

Cragston Industries produced a *Man from U.N.C.L.E.* Secret Transmitter Set, essentially walkie-talkies resembling the cigarette case communicator. The *Man from U.N.C.L.E.* Spy Magic Tricks Set by Ideal was an ordinary magic kit trying to cash in on the *U.N.C.L.E.* craze. Marx produced a replica of the THRUSH cane-pistol often seen on the show, as well as a Counter-Spy Outfit with a multitude of disguises and concealed devices and a *Girl from U.N.C.L.E.* doll with snap-on plastic clothes. Sears distributed

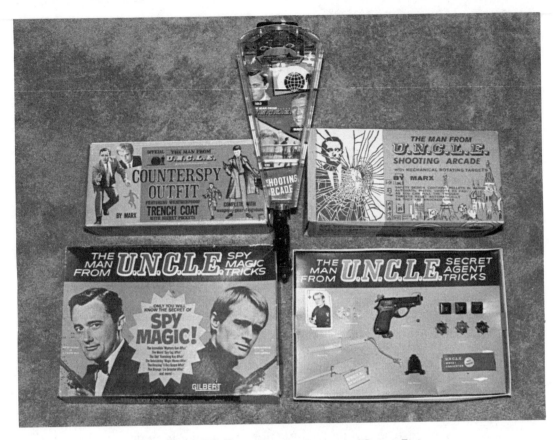

Various U.N.C.L.E. toy items. *Courtesy of George Zivic.*

an *U.N.C.L.E.* Secret Code Wheel pinball game, and Marx made an *U.N.C.L.E.* Shooting Arcade.

The U.N.C.L.E. car was produced in miniature die-cast metal by Corgi and called a Gun Firing THRUSH Buster. The first version was simply a 1961 Oldsmobile Super 88 sedan, with a miniature Solo and Illya inside that would take turns firing out the window as a button on top was depressed. Corgi later produced a version of the Piranha U.N.C.L.E car in both Husky Extra and Corgi Junior labels, complete with a hood that opened and fired a rocket.

For modelers, Aurora Plastics produced one-twelfth scale plastic model kits of both Solo and Illya in 1966. The two models were designed to be bought separately and then displayed together to make one diorama. AMT produced a one-twenty-fifth scale plastic model version of the U.N.C.L.E. car in 1967.

Milton Bradley produced *U.N.C.L.E.* jigsaw puzzles in both junior (hundred-piece) and adult (six-hundred-piece) versions, and tray puzzles were made by Jaymar Specialties.

Baseball cards received competition from a set of black-and-white *U.N.C.L.E.*

photo gum cards by Topps Chewing Gum, with a slightly smaller version of the same set sold in Great Britain. Great Britain also produced a color set of gum cards combining both *The Man from U.N.C.L.E.* and *The Girl from U.N.C.L.E.*, as well as a set of small Cadet Sweet Cards. The Ed-U-Cards Company produced a pack of *U.N.C.L.E.* playing cards. Halco, a division of the J. Halpern Company of Pittsburgh, Pennsylvania, made two Halloween costumes based on *The Man from U.N.C.L.E.*, while Eberhard Faber came out with *U.N.C.L.E.* Photo-Fantastiks, a set of drawings with colored pencils.

There were three main music albums issued for the music on *The Man from U.N.C.L.E. Original Music From the Man from U.N.C.L.E.* was arranged by Hugo Montenegro. It was also released on reel-to-reel tape, and a 45-rpm single of the theme was separately released. The album was popular, and a second album *More Music from the Man From U.N.C.L.E.*, was made, also conducted by Montenegro. An album of TV themes from several shows was released by MGM, but relied on the popularity of *The Man from U.N.C.L.E.* for the title and jacket cover. The album *The Girl from U.N.C.L.E.: Music from the Television Series* was released in 1967.

Miscellaneous *U.N.C.L.E.* toy offshoots included an Illya rubber hand puppet by Gilbert, Viewmaster reels by Sawyer, an *U.N.C.L.E.* lunch box and thermos, numerous posters, *U.N.C.L.E.* Secret Print Putty, and bicycle license plates by Marx. There seemed no end to the uses the *U.N.C.L.E.* name could be put to: *The Man from U.N.C.L.E.* was put on socks, hosiery, slippers, sweatshirts, pajamas, toy rings, raincoats, water pistols, notebooks, swim trunks, bop bags, roadrace sets, etc. In England, Lone Star toy company produced many *U.N.C.L.E.* toy guns and other items.

Clearly, the extent of the sales bonanza based on the *U.N.C.L.E.* series was indicative of the extent the public, particularly children, were affected by the show. *The Man from U.N.C.L.E.* was not only a phenomenon in the world of television, but a major merchandising product as well.

Chapter 21

The *U.N.C.L.E.* Movies

Norman Felton had considered the generation of additional revenue from movie versions of the *U.N.C.L.E.* series quite early on. Because its startup costs were so high, the pilot, "The Vulcan Affair," was a natural choice of an episode to expand into a feature in order to recoup some of those costs.

To gain the extra footage, Felton had additional scenes with Luciana Paluzzi shot at a later date and edited into the pilot to make a ninety-two-minute feature movie, to be called *To Trap a Spy*. For one scene, Rolfe used Old Post Road in Virginia, his own former address. A second first-season episode, "The Double Affair," was also turned into a film with the addition of more adult scenes with Sharon Farrell; it became *The Spy with My Face*. Although none of these scenes involved nudity, they did suggest sexual activity. As Darrell Hallenbeck explains, "In some of the feature scenes, you'd be a little more liberal with the censorship."

Since time and money had gone into shooting the extra footage for the first two movies, Felton put that footage to good use by cleverly combining it with some more original footage and a different soundtrack to make a first-season TV episode, "The Four Steps Affair." In January 1964, Felton gave consideration to

combining "The Quadripartite Affair" and "The Giuoco Piano Affair" into a feature with an additional day of shooting "bridging" scenes at a cost of $75,000, but this was not carried out.

After the first two movies were made and released, they were successful enough that Felton knew it would be profitable to continue to turn *U.N.C.L.E.* episodes into films. Second-season producer David Victor recalls, "At first, we simply extended one of the shows, shooting another hour to it. Then we finally came to the conclusion that, why not simply start with two-hour shows, to run over two weeks, and then simply put them together for motion pictures. And that's what we did from that point on."

"One of the reasons for that, from a producer's point of view," he says, "is that we were able to go to the studio and say, 'Look, this is going to be released internationally. Why don't you put big stars, the bigger names, in right from the beginning so that they will have some validity and credence when they are released?' So we were able to use people like Joan Crawford." He found that this enhanced the entire process: "Instead of taking two episodes and splicing them together, or expanding them somehow, we went in knowing that those two hours would be released theatrically. This gave a little more production value with the bigger names."

Another advantage was more money to make the episodes with: "We had a bigger budget, because it would be absorbed over two hours. Some of the stories were my stories, and some came from conversations with writers. But they were designed, essentially, as movies that would be shown first on the network."

Victor was able to put his theory to work on the two-part opener for the second season, "The Alexander the Greater Affair," which became the movie *One Spy Too Many*. The average cost of $300,000 for the two-part TV production costs were increased to $550,000 for the finished feature version.

One Spy Too Many came out at the height of *The Man from U.N.C.L.E.*'s popularity, and hit England and Europe as the show was debuting there. MGM's British distribution manager Michael Havas set into motion an ambitious publicity campaign, which included such devices as giving Personna razorblades to theater managers to commemorate the "Pit and Pendulum" scene in the film. In March of 1966, *One Spy Too Many* set an all-time record in the history of MGM in England on its London premiere, grossing $282,000 in the first week of it's engagement there in fifty-five North and South London theaters. Norman Felton was in London at the time and saw long lines around the corner from the large Empire Theater waiting to see the first morning show. *One Spy Too Many* even outsold the James Bond film *Thunderball* in it's fifth week of play.

The first three movies were released

Turning the TV episodes into movies allowed the use of major Hollywood stars such as Joan Crawford, here seen accepting a toy THRUSH rifle as a souvenir. © *1964–1967 Metro-Goldwyn-Mayer, Inc.*

David McCallum and Dorothy Provine in a rare scene from "The Alexander the Greater Affair." This scene was cut from the feature version. © *1964–1967 Metro-Goldwyn-Mayer, Inc.*

in both the United States and overseas, and earned more than seven million dollars, better than any other MGM movies at the time. The second two-parter of the second season, "The Bridge of Lions Affair," was also made into a feature, *One of Our Spies is Missing.* No additional scenes were shot except for a few using Yvonne Craig as the U.N.C.L.E. secretary; but the order of the scenes was changed. This film was not released extensively in the United States, because of complaints and reviewer criticism about enticing an audience to buy a ticket to see something they then found they had already watched on TV for free. Eventually the advertising for the movies was changed from "the new

U.N.C.L.E. adventure" to "a feature-length hit from the TV show." The rest of the feature versions were released only overseas; this was not a problem since most of the TV versions had not yet been seen there. For the first three, which *had* been seen on TV in Europe, the movie version offered a chance to see the story in color, since most Europeans did not have color TV then.

For the third season, "The Concrete Overcoat Affair," became *The Spy in the Green Hat.* Felton contacted NBC and proposed showing *The Spy in the Green Hat* in U.S. theaters first, *then* airing it on the series, but NBC declined. "The Five Daughters Affair," was made into *The Karate Killers.* These movie versions are essentially identical to the TV versions, although in *Karate Killers,* for some unknown reason, when Kim Darby asks a group of geishas for help, in the TV version the head geisha says "Okay, kid, stick with us," but in the feature version, she says "Okay, teenybopper, stick with us."

Two-parters were made into features again in the fourth season of *U.N.C.L.E.* "The Prince of Darkness Affair" became *The Helicopter Spies.* Additional bedroom scenes were again shot, with Vaughn confronting Julie London in bed with Roy Jensen. The final two-parter, "The Seven Wonders of the World Affair," was made into *How to Steal the World.*

All together, eight feature films were made from the *U.N.C.L.E.* series. *Variety* reported that in just three years, the *U.N.C.L.E.* movies had grossed over $12 million. Episodes that had cost $150,000 to make were grossing over $2.5 million dollars each in theaters—another indication of the remarkable success the series was having.

Chapter 22

The *U.N.C.L.E.* Awards

The cast and crew of *The Man from U.N.C.L.E.* received the plaudits of their peers in the form of numerous awards for achievement. One of the most prestigious of these was the Golden Globe Award, presented by the Hollywood Foreign Press Association to *The Man from U.N.C.L.E.* for Best TV Series in 1966. Both Robert Vaughn and David McCallum were also nominated as Best Actor.

U.N.C.L.E. also was nominated as best series by the Screen Producers Guild, by the Motion Picture Sound Editors, and by the American Cinema Editors. The music for the show won a Grammy award for Best Original Score Written for a Motion Picture or Television Show, and was the only show even nominated that season.

The American Legion named *The Man from U.N.C.L.E.* the Best Family Entertainment Series for 1966, the result of polling over a million members. Robert Vaughn won the *Photoplay* Award as Most Popular Actor of 1965, and David McCallum won the Motion Picture Costumers' Adam and Eve Award for Most Popular TV Actor of the Year.

But the most prestigious award was the Emmy, presented each year since 1949 by the Academy of Television Arts and Sciences. For the 1964–65 season, the first season of *The Man from U.N.C.L.E.*, Felton submitted "The Double Affair," "The Project Strigas Affair," "The Never Never Affair," and "The Vulcan Affair" for consideration. The show itself was up for Outstanding Dramatic Series. Also nominated that year were David McCallum for Individual Achievement as an Actor or Performer, as well as Fred Koenekamp for Individual Achievement in Cinematography,

McCallum and Vaughn wage a mock battle over a Golden Globe award. *Courtesy of the Norman Felton collection.*

and Henry Berman, Joseph Dervin, and William Gulick for Individual Achievement in Film Editing. In addition, for Individual Achievement, Special Photographic Effects, a nomination was given to *The Man from U.N.C.L.E.* "production team" instead of to an individual.

In 1966, the second season of the show, *U.N.C.L.E.* was nominated for no less than ten Emmys. The series itself was nominated again for Outstanding Dramatic Series. David McCallum was nominated for Outstanding Continued Performance by an Actor in a Leading Role in a Dramatic Series, and Leo G. Carroll was nominated for an Emmy for Outstanding Performance by an Actor in a Supporting Role in a Drama. Composer Jerry Goldsmith was nominated for Achievement in Music, Composition.

Also nominated in the second season was Fred Koenekamp, again for Individual Achievement in Cinematography. George Davis, Merrill Pye, and James Sullivan were nominated for Individual Achievement in Art Direction, while Henry Grace, Francisco Lombardo, Jack

Mills, and Charles Thompson were nominated for Individual Achievements in Set Decoration for their work on *U.N.C.L.E.* A nomination for Individual Achievement in Film Editing went to Henry Berman, Joseph Dervin, and William Gulick. An Individual Achievement in Sound Editing nomination went to John J. Lipow and William Rival. A special Emmy nomination under this category was made for Arnold Goode, Bill Graham, and Bob Murdock for "creation of unusual props"—a special nomination never given before or since.

For the third season, for the first time, *The Man from U.N.C.L.E.* was not nominated for Outstanding Dramatic Program, not surprisingly in light of the shift in direction and the flavor of the scripts that season. The sole nomination was for Leo G. Carroll, for Outstanding Performance by an Actor in a Supporting Role in a Drama. In spite of the numerous nominations for Emmys the show received—more than any other dramatic series in the second season—no Emmy award was ever won by the show.

Snatching Defeat from the Jaws of Victory: How a Good Show Went Bad

Chapter 23

The Third Season

The third season of *The Man from U.N.C.L.E.* opened at a strange time. The American television public had already experienced the *U.N.C.L.E.* phenomenon, and the show had an established audience. But in *U.N.C.L.E.*'s second season, the copycat shows had appeared, and there were not one, but several spy shows to choose from on all three networks. The spy craze was starting to run its course.

It was in this atmosphere that the direction of the third season of *The Man from U.N.C.L.E.* was planned. Believing that what was then being called "camp" was in vogue at the time, it was decided to emphasize the humor in the series. What actually happened was a turn from humor to comedy, a very different thing. Humor in an adventure series can, as was the case in *U.N.C.L.E.*'s first two seasons, enhance the sense of danger by showing that the heroes can laugh in the face of that danger. But comedy in an adventure series detracts from any suspense built up by distracting the audience from the danger. Comedy, as opposed to humor, puts the situation and even the hero in a ridiculous light, and it is impossible to sustain suspense at the same time.

This almost fatal oversight was helped along by another television series that was beginning to cause a stir almost like *The Man from U.N.C.L.E.* had two years earlier. *Batman* on ABC was a blatant and intentional attempt to poke fun at its subject matter. One of the appeals of *Batman* was that it was supposed to look ridiculous. The producers of that show had an understanding with the audience that the show was intended to be so bad that it would be good, that we would be entertained by how hokey it could be.

But *The Man from U.N.C.L.E.* was not based on any such premise. Indeed, when first brought to the screen by Felton and Rolfe it promised to be an adventure series, with elements of danger and suspense. Humor eventually not only became a part of the series, but an asset to it. But it was never at any time meant to be a comedy.

The trend toward comedy made the show more of a slapstick Mack Sennett short than an adventure series. There were scenes like the one in "The Five Daughters Affair" where the Rome fire department arrives on the scene amid mass confusion and runs around a castle like Keystone Kops, at one point even showing a fireman splitting the rungs of a ladder with his head as his fellow firemen rush by. Or the one in "The My Friend the Gorilla Affair" where a man in a gorilla suit (played by George Barrows, who used the same costume in the 1953 "Z" movie classic, *Robot Monster*) dances the watusi with Solo.

The sophisticated gadgets of the first and second season, a popular element of the show in themselves, now also gave way to the absurd. The use of Popsicle hand grenades in "The Suburbia Affair" is one example, and a golf cart cannon in "The Pop Art Affair" is another. An entire plot was based on exploding apples in "The Apple a Day Affair." Such perversions of the original nature of the show prompted the general public to switch channels, and even offended diehard *U.N.C.L.E.* fans. Indeed, the scene in the third-season episode "The Super-Colossal Affair," with Illya riding a bomb filled with essence of skunk in free fall over Las Vegas, prompted Sam Rolfe, watching the show some two years after his own involvement had ended, to turn to his wife and say, "Don't expect any more royalty checks from this show if that is what it has become."

For the third season, 1966–67, *The Man from U.N.C.L.E.* was kept on Friday nights, but was moved from ten P.M. EST to eight-thirty P.M., opposite *Time Tunnel* and *The Milton Berle Show* on ABC, and *Hogan's Heroes* and the beginning of *The Friday Night Movie* on CBS. (Halfway through the season, *Time Tunnel* would be replaced by *Rango*.)

The third season was a mixed bag in terms of stories. "The Super-Colossal Affair" contained some ridiculously awful scenes, exemplifying how silly the show had become. "The Abominable Snowman Affair" was not much better; it featured Illya sneaking into a country in disguise—as a yeti, which of course would not attract any attention. These episodes, along with "The Five Daugh-

Vaughn and McCallum in a scene from "The Sort-of-Do-It-Yourself-Dreadful Affair." © *1964–1967 Metro-Goldwyn-Mayer, Inc.*

ters Affair," show how the series had deteriorated from the heights of such first-season episodes as "The Mad, *Mad* Tea Party Affair."

George Lehr states that this shift from adventure to comedy was not the fault of the producer: "Boris Ingster, the producer the third season, was being pushed in the same direction that *Girl from U.N.C.L.E.* was being pushed by the network," he says. "They wanted stories that were more humorous, to go into that slapstick area. Scenes like the one with Illya riding the bomb sent us all up the wall. I remember saying, 'I can't believe this. We've gone from walking the line between reality and legitimate spy stories to this.' The network is the one you have to blame, because they're the ones who first pushed both *Man* and *Girl* in that direction."

David Victor, supervising producer for both shows, became concerned about the direction the scripts were going and issued a five-page memo saying the stories had become "quite predictable, highly formularized, and too similar in form to be exciting to the viewer. . . . The basic adventure Solo and Illya are involved in is too familiar—usually some formula that THRUSH is determined to get . . . via the threadbare cliché situation of the scientist and his daughter." He also felt that the formula had become so rigid that "we have more of a ritual than a drama," with Waverly always appearing at the beginning, the heroes always getting captured just before the commercial, etc. Victor also felt that Solo and Illya bickered too much, that Solo was no longer seen as a suave ladies' man but a "leering lecher," and that the gadgets were becoming fewer and lacking originality.

Victor reminded the writers that "*The Man from U.N.C.L.E.* should be a high-intrigue adventure with the light touch, which has been its hallmark in the past. It must stop being comedic with villains you cannot believe. The situations must be witty, and sometimes outrageous, but the behavior of Solo, Illya and Waverly must be legitimate. . . . You can then believe the danger, the suspense, the story itself."

This memo shows that Victor saw the writing on the wall. For the third season, *The Man from U.N.C.L.E.* was no longer ranked in the top twenty shows on TV, placing thirtieth among sixty shows with an overall rating of 19.8. Looking to the fourth season, Victor correctly stated "Next year is a critical one for *U.N.C.L.E.*"

Chapter 24

The Girl from U.N.C.L.E.

When you're hot, you're hot. And when *The Man from U.N.C.L.E.* was hot in the spring of 1965, from a business standpoint it was imperative that the popularity of the show be exploited as much as possible to maximize profits. NBC wanted to use the success of the show as a springboard for a spinoff, a separate series based on a character introduced on the established show, in the hope that some of the audience would carry over to the new show.

As early as May 31, 1965, Felton received a letter suggesting a spinoff series based on a female U.N.C.L.E. agent. Martha Wilkerson, the wife of an NBC executive in Scarsdale, New York, who was also a writer, sent him a two-page "thumbnail sketch" of a character named Misty Fortune, later called Caroline "Cookie" Fortune, accompanied by a seventeen-page script outline titled "The Gilded Cage Affair."

Three months later, in August 1965, discussions were taking place between Felton and Robert Weitman for a *Lady from U.N.C.L.E.* series. The character would be introduced on an episode of *The Man from U.N.C.L.E.*, and would then have a half-hour series of her own. It was felt that a half-hour series would be easier to fill with stories fitting a female agent, and that with a half-hour format the show would not "cannibalize" its predecessor show as much.

Shortly after this, Dean Hargrove was assigned to write a pilot spinoff script for *The Girl from U.N.C.L.E.* At this point consideration was given to dropping the title *The Man from U.N.C.L.E.* and providing a back-to-back two-hour presentation—one *Man from U.N.C.L.E.* story followed by a *Girl from U.N.C.L.E* story—to be called *The U.N.C.L.E. Show.*

Hargrove retained little, if anything, from Wilkerson's initial work. The first thing he rejected was the central character's name. He says that Cookie Fortune was "a name I was more than reluctant to use. The name April Dancer was something I found on Ian Fleming's Western Union blanks, as a name of a character. I liked the name so I used it." His story, "The Moonglow Affair," begins with Solo and Illya being rendered helpless and facing death in forty-eight hours after being exposed to a THRUSH beam. Waverly decides to assign a new trainee, twenty-four-year-old April Dancer, to take over their mission, assisted by Mark Slate, an older agent technically beyond the age of retirement from field service who resents working with someone so young and inexperienced.

Stefanie Powers as April Dancer—The Girl from U.N.C.L.E. © 1964–1967 Metro-Goldwyn-Mayer, Inc.

The episode was to air as an episode of *The Man from U.N.C.L.E.* in its second season, and the following fall the *Girl from U.N.C.L.E.* series itself would debut. (At one point it was planned that "The Concrete Overcoat Affair" would be a joint *Man* and *Girl* two-part episode, with Part 1 on *Man* and the conclusion on *Girl*, to force a carryover of

the audience, but this plan was abandoned.)

The hardest task in launching the spinoff series was casting the role of April Dancer. Consideration was given to several actresses. Dorothy Provine, who had guest-starred in "The Alexander the Greater Affair," was given consideration. Stefanie Powers was also considered, but the decision was finally made to have the role of April Dancer played by Mary Ann Mobley. Mobley had been Miss America of 1959. She had appeared in two Elvis Presley films, then moved into television with several guest appearances.

For the role of Mark Slate, Felton and Victor chose Norman Fell. Fell had previously costarred on NBC's *87th Precinct.*

"The Moonglow Affair" was met with high ratings. But, although this meant that *The Girl from U.N.C.L.E.* would appear on NBC's fall lineup in 1966, neither Mary Ann Mobley nor Norman Fell were retained. April Dancer was to be played by Stefanie Powers, and Mark Slate by Noel Harrison. *Girl from U.N.C.L.E.* producer Douglas Benton recalls that both actresses were considered to be good in the role: "They were originally asking for Stefanie Powers when they made the pilot. And she was in a motion picture at the time and wasn't available. And they said they would go with Mary Ann Mobley. And they looked at it and decided it would be a good thing, and would get an audience. But they still wanted Stefanie Powers, and by this time she had finished her picture and was available." Mary Ann Mobley accepted the network decision with grace: "You always know, in this business, that that can happen. You

179

really have to be very fatalistic. I didn't take it personally."

David Victor, who produced "The Moonglow Affair" and would later serve as supervising producer for *The Girl from U.N.C.L.E.*, thinks that this change had a profound effect on how the series eventually emerged. "I think essentially at that time it was a decision of the network and they felt Stefanie Powers was better known and better suited," he says. "I always liked Mary Ann Mobley, and I thought that in order for *Girl from U.N.C.L.E.* to have a life of it's own, it should have a more vulnerable, neophyte kind of a lady who was supported

in the beginning of her career. When Stefanie came in, she was so strong and so powerful in her own right, she became sort of an equal of the other agents, rather than being a neophyte and the new girl on the team. I love Stefanie very much, and we are very good friends, but that was a change in concept from the pilot to the series."

Robert Vaughn also feels that Mary Ann Mobley would have made a very different April Dancer than Stefanie Powers did: "I always thought she would have been better in some ways. I'm not taking anything away from Stefanie. Stefanie was the obvious choice for the

The original Girl from U.N.C.L.E., Mary Ann Mobley, receives instructions from director Joseph Sargent for "The Moonglow Affair." © *1964–1967 Metro-Goldwyn-Mayer, Inc.*

Girl from U.N.C.L.E. Mary Ann would have been the unusual choice—she was a Southerner, very vulnerable, very sweet, nonathletic, not a strong personality like Stefanie had."

Stefanie Powers was born Stefanie Zofja Federkievicz in Hollywood, California, on November 2, 1943 (her Polish father's name was Pawer, or Paul, which formed the basis of her stage name, Powers). At age eight, she took dance and ballet lessons, and graduated from Hollywood High School in 1960. She adopted the stage name of Taffy Paul, and obtained her first small role in the film *Tammy Tell Me True*. After two more films, Blake Edwards signed her to a seven-year contract with Columbia Pictures. She played roles in *The Interns* and *Die! Die! My Darling,* and in the Westerns *Stagecoach* and *McLintock*. She began to travel, and developed an interest in bullfighting. Her television credits were limited, although she had appeared in an episode of *Route 66*.

Girl from U.N.C.L.E. producer Douglas Benton had met Stefanie Powers when she was working as a child actress at Universal, and saw her as an actress on her way up. She chose to undertake a television series lead role even though it meant giving up what was a growing career in films. One of the reasons for her decision was the perceived certainty that *The Girl from U.N.C.L.E.* would be a hit like *The Man from U.N.C.L.E.,* and would make her a star on television as well. Since her Columbia contract was limiting her television career, she bought up the two years remaining on it and accepted the role of April Dancer.

Robert Vaughn had known Stefanie Powers before she was cast as April Dancer. When she was chosen for the role, Vaughn called her up, saying "Hi, Girl, this is Man."

By this time the role of April Dancer had undergone a change since the pilot episode on *The Man from U.N.C.L.E.* the year before. April was no longer a vulnerable female who needed protecting. In one episode, "The Mother Muffin Affair," April was a rather defenseless female who must rely on Napoleon Solo to help her escape a THRUSH trap. But for the remainder of the series, April Dancer would hold her own and more. Whereas Mary Ann Mobley's April Dancer had dressed in conservative clothes and evening gowns, Stefanie Powers's April would be seen in the latest fashions. The five-foot seven-inch actress weighed only 117 pounds, and her figure allowed the use of the latest mod clothes from England, such as miniskirts and go-go boots.

But April Dancer was not to operate alone. Since the concept of a team of U.N.C.L.E. agents had evolved so successfully on *The Man from U.N.C.L.E.,* it was decided from the start that April would have a fellow agent, and that that agent would be male. The new Slate was young, the same generation as April. He was no longer sour or disdainful of April, but rather admired her, flirted with her, saw himself as her big brother. He was to be British instead of American, a ski champion and former member of the RAF who would do the physical work on their assignments.

For the role of Mark Slate, producer Douglas Benton chose Noel Harrison. Born in London on January 29, 1936, the son of actor Rex Harrison, Noel had been a member of the British Olympic skiing teams in both 1952 and 1956, and was British champion at age nineteen.

From there he turned to singing in coffeehouses. "I actually never was a folksinger, although some people put me in that category," he says. "I was a nightclub entertainer. I played guitar, and that is what made people think I was a folksinger." During one of his nightclub performances, early in his career, the lighting was done by a stage hand he would later come to work with—David McCallum. Harrison also began acting on the stage, and eventually appeared on BBC television.

He emigrated to the United States in September of 1965. "I came over as sort of a last-ditch attempt," he recalls. "I was very bored with how my career was going in England. I thought, 'Well, I'll go to the States and if I don't make a go of it, I'm going to go into the restaurant business.' But then I opened in a club in New York called the Living Room and was very successful." This was followed by appearances on television on *The Ed Sullivan Show*, *The Merv Griffin Show*, *The Mike Douglas Show*, and *Hullabaloo*.

One of his songs, "A Young Girl," became a hit and he performed it on Johnny Carson's *Tonight Show*. Producer Douglas Benton was in the process of casting the role of Mark Slate at the time. He had fallen asleep in front of the television, and when his wife woke him Harrison was singing. Benton asked his wife's opinion, and decided that Harrison would be good for the role of Mark Slate. Benton recalls, "I saw Noel Harrison on a variety show singing, and I got a copy of it and rushed over and showed it to Norman. And since he was an English actor, and Noel was a big hit with his record he had out at the time, he just grabbed him. He was one of the most charming, intelligent, cooperative,

Noel Harrison as Mark Slate. © *1964–1967 Metro-Goldwyn-Mayer, Inc.*

and pleasant fellows that anyone could ever meet."

Noel Harrison flew out to Los Angeles and tested for the role. Harrison recalls, "My job in the screen test was to run down a set of stairs with a gun, and there was a girl standing at the bottom, and I had to kiss her. Then I had to turn around and shoot the gun twice up the stairs. That was the whole thing." He decided at that point to show Benton a little more: "So I thought, well, this is really silly. I know how to shoot a gun, I know how to kiss a girl, and I can more or less run downstairs." So Harrison slid down the banister, leaped across the room and jumped through an open window, and then kissed the girl.

After his screen test, his agent called

him and said he had the part. But instead of accepting immediately, he wanted two weeks to think it over. "I had no idea what being in a television series would do to me here. I was making records, and I was making music, and interested in acting and movies. But it never occurred to me to do a television series." But he decided that the role would benefit his career: "I thought to myself, there are two extremes that can happen to me if I accept this. One is that the series will be a success, and run for five years and I will be permanently typecast in this role. The other extreme is it will be a total failure and come off after three weeks and nobody will ever employ me again. And the ideal situation would be, if it ran for a year, and I make a personal success out of it. Which as it turned out was how it happened."

There was a quiet hope, or even expectation, that Noel Harrison might develop a fan following like McCallum had. He was chosen for the role in part because of his British accent, at a time when the Beatles and other English rock groups were causing a worldwide stir. In addition, he was a pop singer with a hit record that would appeal to a teenage audience. He even took to wearing a brown corduroy hat on the series, akin to McCallum's black turtleneck sweater, although he states he stopped wearing it when he started to become identified with it.

The only other role to cast for *The Girl from U.N.C.L.E.* was that of Randy Kovacs. Originally conceived as a teenage girl, this role was to be a teenage student hanging around headquarters, a "Boy from U.N.C.L.E." who would assist Mr. Waverly and even on occasion help April Dancer and Mark Slate.

For this role, Felton and Benton cast Randy Kirby, the son of Durward Kirby, of *The Garry Moore Show* and *Candid Camera*. Although he was twenty-three years old at the time, his boyish features made him a believable seventeen-year-old, and he was signed to appear in thirteen episodes.

Of course, Leo G. Carroll played the role of Mr. Waverly on *The Girl from U.N.C.L.E.* This gave him the distinction of being the only actor to be appearing on two prime-time television series at the same time. Because of his age, all his scenes were shot at once so as to require only one ten-hour day at the studio.

For the production staff of *The Girl from U.N.C.L.E.*, Felton effected a mass migration of *Man* personnel, such as David Victor, Arnold Goode, George Lehr, and others, in order to retain the *Man* flavor on the new show as well. For producer, Felton chose Douglas Benton,

Norman Felton with his two new U.N.C.L.E. stars. *Courtesy of the Norman Felton collection.*

"Girl from U.N.C.L.E." producer Douglas Benton in 1985. *Photo by Jon Heitland.*

Boris Karloff guest-starred as the female Mother Muffin: "We were shooting down at the Venice beach, and he was in his makeup trailer. And he was sitting there, and he had put his skirt on but he hadn't put the top of the outfit on, but he had put the wig on, and he and the makeup man were working on his makeup. And these two little boys walked up, and Boris turned around and looked at the door of the trailer and the two kids, one was about eight and the other about six. Boris swore to me that the older boy turned to the younger and said, 'Jeez, that's the ugliest old bag I ever saw in my life.'"

Sam Rolfe again had difficulty being who had worked for Felton on *Dr. Kildare,* first as story editor, then as associate producer, then as producer.

The Girl from U.N.C.L.E. had two associate producers. Besides George Lehr, who had been so instrumental in the success of *Man,* Max Hodge was brought on board. The same department heads appeared in the *Girl* credits, with the exception of music supervision, which was done by Al Mack. Director of photography was Harkness "Harky" Smith, another carryover from *Dr. Kildare.* Writers such as Dean Hargrove, Robert Hill, and Jerry McNeely carried over from *Man.* Joseph Calvelli returned, and even wrote "The Mother Muffin Affair" and "The Little John Doe Affair," as well as appearing in the latter episode.

Makeup was handled by Jack Dusick. The unusual guest stars on the show presented some real challenges in this area. For example, Doug Benton recalls when

Boris Karloff made an unusual guest appearance in "The Mother Muffin Affair." © *1964–1967 Metro-Goldwyn-Mayer, Inc.*

recognized in the credits. *Girl* was treated as completely separate from *Man,* and thus Rolfe was not to be credited at all. But Rolfe pointed out that the show used his U.N.C.L.E., his Waverly, his headquarters, etc., and his work was acknowledged this way: "U.N.C.L.E. format developed by Sam Rolfe."

Although *The Girl from U.N.C.L.E.* is sometimes seen as inferior to *The Man from U.N.C.L.E.,* Benton points out that "The same writers were writing both shows. I had the same thing happen on *Police Woman.* We were right down the hall from *Police Story* at Columbia. We had absolutely interchangeable directors, actors, and writers. But even critics said *Police Story* is a serious police social drama, and *Police Woman* is a formula,

trite, hackneyed police show."

For the music, two composers were used, Richard Shores (who would work on the fourth season of *Man)* and Dave Grusin. Grusin would later compose for *It Takes a Thief,* as well as the more recent *St. Elsewhere* and the feature *The Goonies.* One episode, "The Drublegratz Affair," contained an original number performed by the Daily Flash, a group produced by Noel Harrison's producers.

The Girl from U.N.C.L.E. premiered with "The Dog Gone Affair" on Tuesday, September 13, 1966, at 7:30 P.M. EST, scheduled against *Daktari* on CBS and *Combat* on ABC, with *Man* on Friday nights that season. The episode, which guest-starred Luciana Paluzzi, was favorably reviewed.

Randy Kirby, left, joins Leo G. Carroll and Stefanie Powers in watching Noel Harrison play a scene in Waverly's office. © *1964–1967 Metro-Goldwyn-Mayer, Inc.*

In one of two crossover episodes, Robert Vaughn guest-starred on "Girl from U.N.C.L.E." in "The Mother Muffin Affair." © 1964–1967 Metro-Goldwyn-Mayer, Inc.

It was determined early on that the four stars of the two shows would appear on each other's series to help get the new show off to a good start. Robert Vaughn appeared in "The Mother Muffin Affair" as Solo, and Noel Harrison appeared on *Man* in "The Galatea Affair." The original script for "The Montori Device Affair" was written for Illya and April to operate together, but McCallum never appeared on *Girl* and Powers never appeared on *Man*.

In spite of all this help from the big brother series, the show began to slip in the ratings as the stories began to rely more and more on comedy, parallelling what was occurring on *Man* at the same time. Noel Harrison recalls, "When we

started getting the scripts, both Stefanie and I thought they were really silly. Norman Felton used to come down during the first few episodes, almost every day, saying 'You've got to take this seriously.' And I would say, 'How can you take this seriously?' And so, in the end, it became a parody of its own weight in a way." Felton was not the only one to point this out to Harrison: "David McCallum said to me very early on, 'You really must take this seriously. You are going to bring both shows off the air by your attitude.' I didn't know what to say. You know, Stefanie is very much like me, we're both very irreverent."

Because the scripts were so outlandish, Powers and Harrison had a hard time playing their roles straight-faced: "The thing that sticks out in my mind," Harrison recalls, "is the day that Stefanie and I got so absolutely out of control with the giggles that we had to go home. And we were shooting this scene in some bushes, and every time I would look at Stefanie, I'd giggle. So finally, the director said, 'Alright, Stefie and Noel, go home, see you tomorrow.' So off we went, giggling to ourselves."

The series did give Harrison a new-found affluence: "I remember buying this used Cadillac for three thousand dollars. And I used to sit out in the MGM parking lot, listening to the radio and putting the hood up and down. I thought I'd died and gone to heaven."

Partway through the series, the Randy Kovacs character was dropped. Benton states, "He was a nice kid, but never made any impression on anybody, so he was dropped after the first thirteen shows. He didn't get any fan mail, and it was difficult to find things for him to do."

Another attempt to help the ratings

Noel Harrison brought Mark Slate to "The Man from U.N.C.L.E." in the crossover episode "The Galatea Affair." *Courtesy of the Norman Felton collection.*

involved Stefanie Powers making a walk-on cameo appearance as April Dancer in an episode of *Please Don't Eat the Daisies,* as Vaughn and McCallum had previously done, in the "Farewell to Lake Serene" episode.

Felton considered other changes to help the show as well. If a second season had been authorized, a possible second female agent, April's twin, might have been added. More importantly, the scripts would have contained less comedy, and the show would have been titled *The New Girl from U.N.C.L.E.*

But the ratings continued to slip. Benton states, "In those days, if you had a 30 share you were safe. And *Girl* was always averaging about 28 or 30." The premier episode in September was rated 19.7, with a 34-percent share. By De-

cember, however, that had dropped to a 16.3 rating, and a 26-percent share. By March, when reruns were set to begin and a decision on renewal was to be made, the show was rated at 15.0 with a 24 share. "What they really decided," Benton says, "was that there was too much *U.N.C.L.E.* on, and if they took *Girl* off, all of the *U.N.C.L.E.* fans would watch *Man,* which really wasn't doing much better than we were but they were in their third year."

Felton readily acknowledges that *"Girl from U.N.C.L.E.* began to step over the line and use too much comedy to replace some of the physical combat, and some episodes became too silly and totally overbalanced." The program was canceled at the end of its first season, ranking fifty-seventh among sixty shows.

187

Chapter 25

The Fourth Season and Cancellation

For the fourth season, Felton hired another new producer, Anthony Spinner. Spinner knew the series was in trouble. Going into the season, the show was ranked forty-sixth, with anything under thirtieth place subject to cancellation. *The Girl from U.N.C.L.E.* had been canceled, and the reason was clearly that the series was too far out and too ridiculous. *The Man from U.N.C.L.E.* had followed the same path in the third season, but had survived—barely—for a fourth season, probably just by the strength of viewer loyalty. *The Man from U.N.C.L.E.* needed to get back to basics, and fast.

On a superficial level, changes were made in the sets of U.N.C.L.E. headquarters to give the show a new look, such as the new NASA computers in the "computer alley" off Waverly's office. In addition, a new cast member was added. The idea of a recurring U.N.C.L.E. secretary had not been used since the first season, so Barbara Moore was hired to play Lisa Rogers. Tall and dark-haired, Moore became a girl Friday to Waverly and even went out into the field on at least one occasion. All of the female U.N.C.L.E. personnel seen in the fourth season were to wear a standard uniform—yellow turtleneck sweaters and black skirts.

But more importantly, Felton and Spinner knew the series would need to recapture those elements that had made it a success in the first two seasons. They instructed the writers to move away from comedy in the third season, to write more serious and more palatable plots. The writer's guide reflected the "new" approach: "In the fourth season, we intend to tip the balance back to . . . high adventure with built-in elements of humor." In a revealing self-examination that encapsulates the history of the entire show, the guide acknowledged "*The Man from U.N.C.L.E.* began as an almost entirely straight adventure, became high adventure with humor, and ultimately became broad comedy with satiric overtones." For the fourth season, the role of humor was set forth in no uncertain terms: *"it should be clearly understood that at no point can the humor stand in the way of the adventure or negate the suspense"* (emphasis in original). For the fourth season, writers were also told that *U.N.C.L.E.* would be "much, much closer to James Bond than *Get Smart*."

Thus, for the fourth season, the writers were told to get back to basics. The old formula would still be flexible: Waverly could appear other than in the first act, Solo and Illya could operate independently or together, etc. But, the stories still had to be "credible, important, glamorous, sophisticated, fast-moving, and laden with surprise and laced with humor." Solo and Illya could exchange banter, "but never joke during periods of jeopardy." For the most part, the fourth season episodes followed these guidelines, resembling the first season much more than the third. If anything, the fourth season episodes suffered from too *little* humor.

November 1, 1967, was the "pickup date" when the network would decide if it wanted to order the rest of the episodes for the season. The show had undergone another time-slot change for the fourth season, and was now seen on Monday nights again, at eight P.M. EST, opposite *Gunsmoke* and *The Lucy Show* on CBS, and *Cowboy in Africa* and *The Rat Patrol* on ABC. Felton tried to get the show moved to Saturday night, so it would be opposite *The Jackie Gleason Show* and *The Dating Game,* but was unsuccessful. The season before, CBS had

For the fourth season, U.N.C.L.E. headquarters added computers discarded by NASA. © *1964–1967 Metro-Goldwyn-Mayer, Inc.*

almost canceled its long-running *Gun-smoke,* which was airing on Saturdays at ten P.M. EST, a time when many younger viewers were out of the home. Sponsors were reluctant to finance a show that held mainly an older audience, so for the 1967–68 season CBS decided to give *Gunsmoke* one more chance, and moved it to Monday nights at seven-thirty. *The Man from U.N.C.L.E.* would start half an hour later at eight, which meant that viewers already watching *Gunsmoke* were unlikely to switch over to *U.N.C.L.E.* in the middle. Similarly, when *The Lucy Show* came on, they would be unlikely to switch over for the second half of an *U.N.C.L.E.* story.

Concern over the ratings caused a reshuffling of the air dates of the completed episodes. The show slot for November 25, 1967, occurring near the Thanksgiving holiday, was considered an important one for ratings. Felton asked Spinner to try and arrange to air "one of the very best" of the episodes available. Spinner responded by saying that he would schedule "The Deep Six Affair" for that slot, not because it was the best but because it was the best of three weak shows available, the other two being "The Armaggedon Affair" (later renamed "The Man from THRUSH Affair") and "The Maze Affair."

Spinner looked ahead to another important air date, Christmas 1967. He planned to shoot Dean Hargrove's script titled "The Frozen Time Affair" immediately following the filming of the two-part episode "The Seven Wonders of the World Affair," and air Hargrove's script on December 25.

But plans changed. *Gunsmoke,* in its new time slot, placed fourth in the

Nielsens and *Lucy* was number one. *The Man from U.N.C.L.E.,* one of the most popular shows on TV only two seasons before, came up in sixty-fourth place. The show was immediately canceled in midseason, a very embarrassing demise for an established show.

There was no warning. Normally the scripts for the next week's shooting were delivered to McCallum and Vaughn on each Friday, for them to study over the weekend. But one Friday no script arrived. David McCallum recalls, "We would go home, and they would say 'Come back.' And we would go home, and they would say 'Come back.' And one day we went home, and they never said to come back." McCallum had to call the studio to find out that what he read in the papers about the show's cancellation was true.

Traditionally, when a show comes to an end, the cast and crew get together for a "wrap" party. But with the suddenness and unexpectedness of *The Man from U.N.C.L.E.*'s cancellation, McCallum recalls, "There never was a gathering where they said 'This is it, fellas.'" Vaughn remembers "We simply got a notice that this would be our last show, and it surprised a few people." Even though end-of-year parties were common on the show, this was different. George Lehr recalls "In this business, you like to keep the good memories. It's like having to go to the funeral of a loved one. You'd like to remember it the way it was, rather than the way it is."

The cancellation occurred in November of 1967, at a point when sixteen episodes had been filmed. "The Seven Wonders of the World Affair" (parts 1 and 2), was the last episode to be aired, on January 8 and 15, 1968. Ironically, the final

U.N.C.L.E.'s new secretary Barbara Moore helps Robert Vaughn announce yet another time slot change for the fourth season. *Courtesy of the Norman Felton collection.*

scene of the episode shows a casket being loaded onto a plane and observed by Solo, Illya, and Waverly. A voice-over ends the episode, and the series: "The seemingly endless battle against evil . . . the battle ends once and for all in favor of good." It requires only a small stretch of the imagination to see the coffin as a symbolic burial of the show itself as it signed off of prime-time television.

Although only sixteen episodes were filmed for the fourth season, scripts had been written for twenty-four episodes by September 1967; "The Kamikaze Af-

fair," "The Mallinson Affair," "The Crown of Our Lady Affair," and others were left unproduced.

Neither Vaughn nor McCallum were particularly disturbed by the show's cancellation. McCallum stated at the time that the show's success had actually started to typecast him, and had hindered his obtaining other types of roles. Vaughn recalls, "By the time that started happening, my mind was focused on the war in Southeast Asia. I wasn't paying any attention to ratings. The day they told us we were canceled I don't think I even blinked." Vaughn states that he was ready to move on to more feature-film work, which from a financial view offered much more compensation with a much less hectic shooting schedule.

The Man from U.N.C.L.E.'s rapid downfall generated much speculation on what had gone wrong. Some people tried to put the blame on *The Girl from U.N.C.L.E.,* saying that too much U.N.C.L.E. the season before had worn out the concept, and that the comedy approach of *The Girl from U.N.C.L.E.* had hurt both shows. Robert Vaughn stated that without *The Girl from U.N.C.L.E.,* *The Man from U.N.C.L.E.* probably would have at least finished out the fourth season. However, he also feels that if that was a factor, it was only one of many. "I think it had more to do with the change in emphasis from action and adventure to farce." In the end, he felt the show had become "hokey" and "far out."

Douglas Benton agrees that both shows suffered from the shift in approach during the third season. "The year that we did *Girl from U.N.C.L.E.,* *Man from U.N.C.L.E.* had Kuryakin riding a two-thousand-pound bomb full of essence of skunk, and if you think that is serious adventure I'll eat it."

Robert Vaughn feels that the problems leading to the cancellation of the show can be traced to losing sight of the original appeal of the series. "I think because we changed producers so often, each producer wanted to put his signature on it and contribute something rather than letting something stand, and it went the way of farce instead of action and adventure and tongue-in-cheek James Bond."

David McCallum feels that what happened was inevitable. "You can save the world in one hour only so many times. And I think that a country lives upon the latest fad. It's extraordinary to me that now the fads come and go much faster than they used to. I think the latest novel idea in television becomes the big hit. You think of *The A Team* and *Miami Vice,* and you go back over the years, and there's always one that becomes intensely popular. The novel element wears thin, and the ratings begin to drop off. Then you hear the producer's injecting new talent, rewriting the basic premise, trying to come up with ideas to inject new life—that wonderful expression, inject new life—into a series. The fact is the public has had it. I think in the case of *U.N.C.L.E.* because the ideas were very extreme and very bold, the curve dropped off much faster because it went up much quicker."

Norman Felton feels that the show had had a "good run for the money." He points out that most shows only last one or two years, so four years toward the top of the ratings was nothing to sneeze at. He blamed the downfall mostly on the many imitation shows during *U.N.C.L.E.*'s second season. With audiences being deluged with spies on both their movie and television screens, it was not surprising to him that interest flagged. What was important and a source of pride to Felton was the fact that *The Man from U.N.C.L.E.* was the first of the genre, a correct prediction of what the audience was ready for.

The Man from U.N.C.L.E. was replaced with *Rowan and Martin's Laugh-In.* In the very first episode, various quips are being exchanged at a party. A busboy pushing a cart of dishes stops and turns out to be Leo G. Carroll. He pulls out an U.N.C.L.E. communicator and states "Mr. Solo, Mr. Kuryakin, come quick. I think I've found THRUSH headquarters at last!" It was safely assumed that the audience would recognize Waverly, the pen communicator, and the references to Solo, Kuryakin, and THRUSH—a testimonial to the impact the show had on American television in the 1960s.

The Show That Wouldn't Say U.N.C.L.E.

Chapter 26

U.N.C.L.E. Returns

It should not be surprising that a television show as popular as *The Man from U.N.C.L.E.* would not be forgotten by its audience. While the anti–TV violence campaign of the 1970s kept the show from even being seen in reruns in many markets, in Hollywood, behind the scenes, there were various attempts being made to revive the series in the form of a movie. As early as 1969, Norman Felton tried to evoke interest in a "return" movie, but MGM, an equal partner with Arena, was not interested.

In 1977, Sam Rolfe decided it was time to bring *U.N.C.L.E.* back also. After obtaining a go-ahead from producers Ivan Goff and Ben Roberts of *Charlie's Angels,* he wrote a two-hour made-for-TV *U.N.C.L.E.* movie titled "The Malthusian Affair," about a rampaging mechanical monster. But again MGM was not interested. Rolfe says, "By that time Metro had sold all the backlots, and they looked at this and they got the budget numbers, and they said 'There's no way we can do it.' Had we brought it back even five years earlier, I think we could have done it."

Shortly after Rolfe's attempt, two *U.N.C.L.E.* fans picked up the ball and ran with it. Danny Beiderman, an independent filmmaker who had made the documentary on the making of the Bond movie *Diamonds Are Forever,* titled *A Spy for All Seasons,* and the author of *The Book of Kisses,* teamed up with Bob Short, well known in the film industry for his special-effects work on *Star Trek: The Motion Picture* and *Close Encounters of the Third Kind.* Short would later work on *1941* (along with another *U.N.C.L.E.* fan, Dave Heilman), and would develop the glowing heart for *E.T.,* the mermaid skin for *Splash,* and the cocoons for *Cocoon.* Beiderman and Short, longtime avid *U.N.C.L.E.* fans, decided to try and launch their own *U.N.C.L.E.* project.

They came up with a treatment for an *U.N.C.L.E.* adventure that involved one last grand confrontation with THRUSH, which has already gained control of the world by buying out multinational corporations. The promotional materials promised a "confrontation with a magical wizard, a computerized killer tank and a deadly self-destructing pretzel vendor, and a high speed car chase on a subterranean super-highway stretching across all of Europe." According to Beiderman, "The basic thrust of the plot was the economic angle, because we thought we really wanted it updated and changed. It seemed much more contemporary, at least in 1978."

Beiderman and Short contemplated replacing Leo G. Carroll with Cloris

Leachman, and other stars who expressed an interest in the project included Jane Seymour and Klaus Kinski. Ringo Starr was written in as a cameo, and Stefanie Powers and Noel Harrison were also to reprise their *U.N.C.L.E.* roles briefly in the story. Laura Antonelli would play Serena, a character brought back from "The Double Affair." The action would take place in New York, London, and Berlin as well as the polar ice cap.

Beiderman and Short first went to Norman Felton with their idea, but found that approval would have to come from MGM. "When we went to the studio, people were constantly coming up and saying it was their favorite show," Beiderman recalls. "But the answer we got numerous times was that James Bond has the market covered, why do a spy thing."

An additional problem was the lack of understanding of the original show's appeal by the executives at MGM some twelve years later. One MGM official who read the script commented that it was "more of the same, tired stuff" that "depended on gimmicks, nick-of-time escapes, and wisecracks." He concluded by saying *Star Trek* yes, *U.N.C.L.E.* no."

Some interest was expressed, however, for a TV movie, which required a much lower financial investment than a feature film. Beiderman recalls, "It was not the ideal, but we decided we'd go for it. And then he came back and said there are three elements that are necessary to go forward: Robert Vaughn, David McCallum, and a network. We avoided [contacting Vaughn and McCallum] all through the feature thing because we always had this fear that, what if they just

don't want to do it? It will kill everything. We just didn't want to know. But both of them were very willing to reprise the roles."

Beiderman and Short started to work on finding a director. After first contacting Richard Donner, who was busy doing *Ladyhawke*, they approached another director with experience on the original series, Boris Sagal, and found he was interested. But, tragically, a week later, Sagal was killed by a helicopter's tail rotor while scouting locations for a film. They then talked to Peter Hyams. "He suggested Tom Selleck as Napoleon Solo," Beiderman says. "And Bob and I looked at each other. Now, I think maybe if we had pushed it maybe the movie would have been made with Tom Selleck and Peter Hyams, but we sure didn't want that. That wouldn't be *U.N.C.L.E.*"

For production designer, their first choice was Ken Adams, the production designer for many of the James Bond films. Adams was also enthusiastic about the project. For music and photography, they lined up *U.N.C.L.E.* alumni Gerald Fried and Fred Koenekamp.

But then a strange turn of events took place. "We kept running into this brick wall, when we suddenly heard on the lot these rumblings that somebody had screened *Karate Killers*. When we checked into it, we were told that Michael Sloan already had his project on the books." Sloan, who had produced *B.J. and the Bear, Quincy,* and *McCloud,* had been able to convince MGM to "lease" the property to him temporarily at no risk, thus insuring his project would go ahead, instead of Beiderman and Short's.

For his *Return of the Man from*

U.N.C.L.E.: The Fifteen Years Later Affair TV movie, Michael Sloan served not only as executive producer, but as writer as well. Sloan reversed the route followed by Beiderman and Short, going to Vaughn and McCallum first. Meeting with McCallum in the Russian Tea Room in New York, a location later simulated in the remake movie, Sloan found that he was willing to reprise his Illya role, and later found out that Vaughn was also interested.

Both Vaughn and McCallum hinted that a movie was in the works during a joint appearance on *Good Morning America,* which was the first time the two had seen each other since the series had been canceled fifteen years earlier. McCallum saw Vaughn signing autographs outside the ABC building before their appearance, and asked him for an autograph also. Their deal with Sloan for a remake movie was celebrated in Vaughn's backyard with a toast, and this scene appears in the closing credits of the movie. They also kicked off the movie with a press conference at the Overseas Press Club on Forty-first street—"somewhere in the East Forties"—complete with toy U.N.C.L.E. guns provided by *U.N.C.L.E.* fans Ron Plesniarski and Lee Pfeiffer.

Sloan also found that Vaughn and McCallum did not look substantially older than they had on the original series fifteen years earlier. When Sloan and McCallum walked along the sidewalk in New York, several people called the actor Illya and asked for autographs. In the role of Sir John Raleigh, the new head of U.N.C.L.E., Sloan cast Patrick Macnee, whose British air of authority would replace Leo G. Carroll's. Other cast members included Gayle Hunnicut, Keenan Wynn, Geoffrey Lewis, and Anthony Zerbe.

Although Sloan was able to get the project off the ground, his script lacked the flavor of the original series, playing more like James Bond. In preparing for the show, Sloan screened episodes from the third season, and declined to view the black-and-white episodes from the first season. He did use Bob Short as technical advisor, and Short was able to keep many aspects of the new movie true to the original format, although many of his suggestions were to be rejected with "This is the new *U.N.C.L.E.*"

The *Return* script revolved around a THRUSH blackmail threat after the organization hijacks a nuclear device—exactly the same plot as the Bond film *Thunderball.* But the similarity to James Bond does not end there. James Bond's armorer is a man called Q. At U.N.C.L.E. headquarters in *Return,* the armorer is known as Z. THRUSH is aided by a large, seemingly unbeatable strongarm man known as Guido, a heavy very reminiscent of Oddjob and Jaws of the Bond series. At the beginning of *Return,* we see Solo playing poker and looking up to introduce himself—"Solo, Napoleon Solo"—an exact duplicate of Sean Connery's introduction as Bond in *Doctor No.*

One scene was *intended* to be reminiscent of James Bond. The appearance of George Lazenby, who had played 007 in *On Her Majesties Secret Service,* as "JB," in an Aston Martin DB5 (owned by Bob Short) similar to that used by Bond in *Goldfinger* and *Thunderball,* was obviously an intentional tip of the hat to the brother in the genre, in spite of a warning by the MGM legal department. Originally, it was hoped that Sean Conn-

McCallum and Vaughn at the press conference for "The Return of the Man from U.N.C.L.E.: The Fifteen Years Later Affair." *Courtesy of Lee Pfeiffer and Ron Plesniarski.*

ery and Roger Moore, the other two James Bond film actors as of 1982, would make cameos as well. However, both men were filming Bond movies—Moore in *Octopussy* and Connery in *Never Say Never Again*—resulting in all three movie Bonds playing the role at the same time.

The script also errs by spending half the movie reuniting the two agents, then sending them off in opposite directions to defeat THRUSH at separate locations, robbing us of an essential element of the show's appeal—their interaction with each other.

Sloan did make some wise decisions in preparing his script. One was the acknowledgment that at least fifteen years had passed since *U.N.C.L.E.* had gone off the air, and that trying to put Solo and Kuryakin back into their roles at exactly the point where the series left off would have been ludicrous. Although the physical appearance of the two men had changed very little in that time, they were now in their fifties. Sloan's script posited that Solo was now in computers, and Illya held the surprising occupation of fashion designer, having resigned from U.N.C.L.E. several years after the series' end over the death of a girl in Yugoslavia. (A flashback scene showing this, as well as a resignation scene reminiscent of *The Prisoner,* were filmed but deleted from the movie for running-time considerations.) McCallum also took this time lapse into account, saying, "I figured that after living in the U.S. so long, Illya would have lost his accent, so I used very little accent in the movie."

Another clever element of the *Return* script was the recognition that U.N.C.L.E. itself would have changed over the past fifteen years. There is a humorous sequence where Solo returns to Del Floria's tailor shop in New York to resume his duties; he attempts to enter headquarters through the dressing booth, but finds that headquarters has been moved and the puzzled tailor thinks he is a mental case. Solo then goes back out onto the street, where a taxi pulls up and the driver tells him where to go—to a novelty store (another deleted sequence). Incredibly, however, the tailor shop sequence was taken almost verbatim from "The Foxes and Hounds Affair" in the second season of the original series!

The script did have some humor, in the form of inside jokes. When Solo and Illya meet again for the first time, Solo says, "What have you been doing the last fifteen years?"—a question posed to Vaughn and McCallum hundreds of times in press conferences and interviews for the movie. In references to their age, Solo also says at one point, "This all seemed a lot easier fifteen years ago"; and when asked by a THRUSH agent how he stays looking so young, he replies "Good makeup man," another line Vaughn often used in interviews.

Some of the original format was retained. The logo was modernized by Bob

David McCallum on the set of "The Return of the Man from U.N.C.L.E." *Photo by Jon Heitland.*

Short, and the theme was modernized by *U.N.C.L.E.* veteran Gerald Fried. Another alumnus, Fred Koenekamp, was used as director of photography, and he brought back the red cavern walls and the familiar whip pans between scenes, accomplished by fast-panning the cameras across Las Vegas video slot machines. But Sam Rolfe was nearly cut out of the credits, as nearly happened on *The Girl from U.N.C.L.E.* Ultimately, he was again listed as developer of the series.

But the gadgets suffered in the remake. It would naturally be difficult for Sloan to come up with eye-catching devices in the 1980s. The automatic sliding doors of U.N.C.L.E. headquarters in the original series were unique in 1964, but as common as your neighborhood grocery in 1982. The pen communicators were brought back in identical form, but with satellite TV in the backyard, it wasn't impressive. The new gadgets that were used, however, would not have been impressive even in 1964. The huge belt-buckle cutting torch would have attracted the attention of the most thick-headed THRUSH agent, and Illya's concealed bomb in the shoe heel was already a tired gimmick in the sixties.

But the U.N.C.L.E. Special did successfully make the transition to the eighties. Short, as a special-effects expert and an aficionado of the original series, was given the go-ahead by Sloan to develop a new U.N.C.L.E. gun. He chose a Heckler and Koch P-7, using 9-mm ammunition, for the basic pistol. He decided to retain the basic look of the Special in it's assembled carbine form, with a shoulder stock, extended barrel, silencer, telescopic sight, and extended magazine all added to the basic pistol.

The immediate problem was that

McCallum has his makeup adjusted for the cave sequence in "The Return of the Man from U.N.C.L.E.". *Photo by Jon Heitland.*

Short was given only two weeks to complete the gun before production was to start. A second problem was that only one gun was budgeted for, which meant that if the completed gun was lost, stolen, or broken, the production schedule would be interrupted. Short sought the aid of Dave Heilman, another special-effects man and *U.N.C.L.E.* fan, who had done work on *1941,* and would later work on *Deal of the Century* and *Baby.* They took the gun to San Diego for work by Bruce Wegman.

The finished product featured an Aimpoint sight. Instead of a shoulder stock, an aluminum stock with a wrist support was used. For the extended magazine, two magazines were welded together in dogleg fashion, but would not have been functional in real life. The special holsters for the movie were also designed by Short and made of Codura nylon instead of leather, utilizing Velcro fasteners.

Bob Short was instrumental in helping keep *Return* as close to the original format as it was. Thus, Solo's apartment in New York was left to him by his aunt in *Return,* and was decorated with nautical items—both entirely accurate according to the original series. Short also made the new U.N.C.L.E. badges, again triangular but black with a yellow logo and numeral. But the U.N.C.L.E. agents wear them outside of headquarters, evidencing a lack of understanding of their function.

Two additional props were simply photographs. One was a still of Leo G. Carroll as Alexander Waverly, which sat on a desk in the new U.N.C.L.E. headquarters—a nice touch, along with several references in the script to how Waverly was missed. Another was the photo of Vaughn and McCallum from the end credits of the original show, showing them firing their guns side by side against a background of red smoke. This photo, seen in Solo's apartment, was provided by Vaughn himself—his only souvenir from the series.

In addition to a professional cast, Sloan lined up a veteran crew as well. Sloan served as executive producer, with the actual production done by Nigel Watts. For director, he chose Ray Austin, a British director who had worked on *The Avengers.*

Shooting began in Las Vegas on November 19, 1982. The production crew was headquartered at Caesar's Palace Hotel and Casino. In addition to the availability of the casino and the famous Las Vegas Strip for backgrounds, within a short distance of the city were three useful locations: Hoover Dam, which would serve as THRUSH headquarters; the Southern Nevada Correctional Facility at Jean, Nevada, which would be used for the prison sequence; and, in the desert, the Blue Diamond Gypsum mine, which would be used for the interior cavern scenes for the story's climax. In addition to using the casino at Caesar's for the poker game scene, the crew used the deluxe Ann-Margret Suite for the fight between Solo and Guido. The inmates at the prison were allowed to appear as extras in the escape scene, with their pay consisting of a souvenir T-shirt.

Robert Vaughn stated numerous times that he enjoyed returning to the role, and although he had misgivings at first, once he donned Napoleon Solo's famil-

iar tuxedo, he felt at ease in the character. Bob Short states that when Vaughn was handed the old pen communicator prop from the original series on the set of *Return,* he had to be shown how to remove the cap and extend the antenna. But once he had done so, he instinctively knew to twist the antenna before stating "Open Channel D."

Shooting at the cave was briefly interrupted when a minor rockslide crushed the ankle of camera assistant Richard Barth. When McCallum was required to briefly hang from the overhead steam pipe in the cave sequence (prior to his stunt double taking over), he noticed a large, sharp rock directly underneath, and knew that if he or co-star Simon Williams would fall on it, an injury would result. But instead of asking one of many nearby crewmen to move the rock, he lugged the heavy rock out of the way himself.

Shooting in Las Vegas was completed by December 11, 1982, and the cast and crew flew back to Los Angeles to finish the film there. Before departing from McCarran airport, they filmed the scene where Illya bluffs his way onto Janus's plane.

Back in LA, production offices were set up at the Biltmore Hotel. Chuck Painter visited the set unannounced, and although he enjoyed a "big reunion, laughing and reminiscing" with Vaughn and McCallum, he noticed a difference between the old *U.N.C.L.E.* crew and the new: "We didn't have our family there. On a TV series, it becomes very laidback and very family. It was a very intimate thing on *The Man from U.N.C.L.E.* But this was a three- or four-week shoot, it was all pretty much strangers. There was no hanging around the set like on the old *U.N.C.L.E.*, people went back to their dressing rooms. That was the main difference."

On December 14, a long sequence where Solo and Illya discuss the case and why Illya left U.N.C.L.E. (supposedly in New York—but the scene was shot in Los Angeles, as evidenced by the reflection of palm trees in the store windows) was shot in one take, a tribute to the professionalism of the actors. After twenty-two days of shooting, the film was completed except for postproduction.

Once the film was done and the publicity about it mounted, Vaughn and McCallum found themselves once again the subjects of news conferences and interviews. The most common question was whether either or both of them would consider returning to a new *U.N.C.L.E.* series if the ratings brought that about. Both men expressed a preference for additional *U.N.C.L.E.* TV movies as opposed to a weekly series, because of both the time demands and the enhanced quality in a TV movie.

The Return of the Man from U.N.C.L.E.: The Fifteen Years Later Affair, aired as a CBS Tuesday Night Movie on Tuesday, April 5, 1983. The ninety-minute movie was aired in the usual two-hour time slot, beginning at nine P.M. eastern time, eight P.M. central. It competed against *Remington Steele*, *St. Elsewhere*, *Three's Company*, and *Ryan's Four* on the other networks.

In terms of ratings, *Return* swept the night, and placed twenty-second for the week's programming. The Nielsen weekly ratings showed it at 17.4, with an audience share of 28. For the whole season, *Return* was ranked eighty-fourth among 234 TV movies by Variety.

But CBS indicated that, although the ratings were good, they were not interested in doing a new *U.N.C.L.E.* series. *Return* was rerun in the worst of all possible time slots, on New Year's Eve 1983–84, where its ratings placed it behind reruns of *Love Boat* and *Fantasy Island* at fifty-third among sixty-two shows for the week, beating out *Manimal* and *Diff'rent Strokes*.

Clearly, the limited budget of a TV movie and the slant of the script hurt the remake effort. Norman Felton thought that "*Return* seemed to be written by an *U.N.C.L.E.* fan who remembered certain things, and gave them a twist. There was a lot of freshness." Sam Rolfe, however, felt that it was "silly putty . . . and had no concept of what the series was about." *Return* cost $2,259,246 to make, and as of December 31, 1984, was still operating at a loss. With the only successful remake effort deviating so far from the original series and failing to generate a profit, the chances are remote that another *U.N.C.L.E.* movie or series will emerge. However, both Vaughn and McCallum have indicated a willingness to again play the roles, and, considering the faltering start for the *Star Trek* movies, we may yet see the real return of Napoleon Solo and Illya Kuryakin on a regular basis.

Chapter 27

The *U.N.C.L.E.* Cast and Crew Today

After *The Man from U.N.C.L.E.* was canceled, the sets were torn down, and the cast and crew, who had been like family since 1963, went their separate ways.

The guns were stored in MGM's prop rooms until the company experienced financial problems and auctioned off all its props in May of 1970. Only one of the eight U.N.C.L.E. Special pistols was bought at the auction by a fan, but the others have now been located by fans. The Mausers sold at the auction for around $45 each, the Walthers for $150 each. The attachments were not even sold, but were found in a garbage dumpster afterward. As for the THRUSH guns, at least six, either real or resin mockups, existed, as evidenced by "The Children's Day Affair." One was bought by a man at the auction for rabbit hunt-

George Lehr, the author, and Norman Felton in Los Angeles, 1986. *Photo provided by Jon Heitland.*

ing; two are in the hands of U.N.C.L.E collectors, and the rest are unaccounted for.

Norman Felton continued as a television producer after the cancellation, with both series and TV movies, such as *Strange Report, Baffled, Hawkins on Murder, Babe,* and *And Your Name is Jonah.* Sam Rolfe went on to write numerous TV pilots, such as *Hardcase, Elisha Cooper,* and *The Delphi Bureau,* the latter of which retained many *U.N.C.L.E.* features and even emulated the plot of "The Iowa Scuba Affair." E. Darrell Hallenbeck served with Rolfe on that pilot. Rolfe has produced or written literally hundreds of TV and movie projects, and most recently has worked on *The New Mike Hammer.*

Douglas Benton went on to produce *Name of the Game, Ironside, The Rookies,* and *Columbo,* as well as *Hec Ramsey, Police Woman,* and the recent *Blacke's Magic.* Dean Hargrove worked with Benton on *Columbo,* and is currently producing the *Matlock* series as well as the Perry Mason TV movies.

Robert Vaughn appeared in the movie *Bullitt* shortly after the cancellation of *U.N.C.L.E.,* and received his PhD in the philosophy of communications in 1970. His thesis, dealing with McCarthy-era blacklisting of entertainers, was published as *Only Victims.* He married actress Linda Staab in 1974. He starred in the British series *The Protectors,* then made several appearances on U.S. television in various miniseries, such as *Washington: Behind Closed Doors* (with Stefanie Powers), *Centennial, Evergreen,* and *The Blue and the Gray.* He also appeared on Broadway in *That Man, FDR.* Other film appearances included *The Towering Inferno, Superman III,* and *Black Moon Rising.* He played short-lived

roles on the series *Emerald Point N.A.S.* and *The A Team.* On the latter series, David McCallum made a special guest appearance in the "Say U.N.C.L.E. Affair" episode as a secret agent, and the *U.N.C.L.E.* act-title format and other features of the old show were used in a special homage to their reunion. Today Vaughn lives with his wife and children, Cassidy and Caitlin, in Connecticut.

While *U.N.C.L.E.* was on the air, both Vaughn and McCallum made films during the periods between seasons, Vaughn appearing in *The Venetian Affair* and McCallum making his first starring role in a film in *Three Bites of the Apple,* and later appearing in *Sol Madrid.* Even before cancellation, he and his wife were divorced, and Jill later married their mutual friend, actor Charles Bronson. McCallum also produced three music albums during this period.

During an *U.N.C.L.E.* publicity photo session for *Glamour* magazine, McCallum met model Kathy Carpenter, whom he married in 1967. They moved to New York City, and eventually had two children, Peter and Sophie. McCallum appeared on television in the TV-Movie *Teacher, Teacher,* for which he was nominated for an Emmy, and a 1975 series, *The Invisible Man.* His films through the 1970s included *Escape from Colditz, Dogs, King Solomon's Treasure,* and *Watcher in the Woods.* He also starred in the British TV series *Sapphire and Steel.* He continued to appear on the stage in several touring productions, and he was the lead in the first cable miniseries, *Kidnapped.* He also played a role for a time on the daytime drama *As the World Turns.*

Stefanie Powers returned to TV guest appearances after *Girl* was canceled, as well as another starring role in *The*

Feather and Father Gang. She became a big hit in her costarring role in *Hart to Hart.* She now does fashion ads and markets a fitness program, and runs the African wildlife preservation organization started by the late William Holden.

Noel Harrison went back to music after his *Girl from U.N.C.L.E.* role, and his song for the film *The Thomas Crown Affair,* "Windmills of Your Mind," won him an Academy Award. He would later guest star on Stefanie Powers's *Hart to Hart,* but currently does mostly stage work. As for him and Stefanie Powers, he states, "We still stay in touch, although on a very irregular basis. Whenever we get together we bubble, bubble, because we have so much to tell each other."

George Lehr alternates his time between film projects and teaching film classes at the university level. Both Arnold Goode and Bob Murdock are retired, as is Til Gabbani. Murdock went

U.N.C.L.E. cameraman Til Gabbani in 1986. *Photo by Jon Heitland.*

from *U.N.C.L.E.* to work on features, such as *Apocalypse Now* and *Enigma.* Marcel Vercoutere later did work on *Exorcist II: The Heretic* and other features. Fred Koenekamp is still active as a director of photography. Peter Allan Fields later went on to write for such shows as *McCloud* and *The Six Million Dollar Man,* and is currently working on a novel. Alan Caillou is currently writing adventure novels as well.

The cast and crew, without exception, speak of Leo G. Carroll in the most glowing terms. David McCallum remembers, "When my first son was born, Leo loaned me his manuscript of Brahms's Lullaby. When we went on hiatus, I asked him if he was going on vacation, and he said no, there were too many classics he hadn't read." Richard Donner recalls Carroll as a "great man who always had a story about any actor you could mention." Chuck Painter remembers him as "a super, super man who performed like a pro, and had a heart of gold." Robert Vaughn recalls that Carroll once told him, "They wouldn't have hired me if they knew how old I was." Vaughn frequently described Carroll as "The real Man from U.N.C.L.E." Bill Finnegan describes Carroll's professionalism on the set: "He was getting along in years, and everyone went out of their way to be considerate. One time, we worked on a two-part episode until two or three in the morning, and we were all very concerned that he would be way too tired to do the work. But we woke him up, he came in, did what he was supposed to do, and went home. We were all very impressed." Carroll died October 16, 1972, at the age of eighty, and is interred at Grandview Cemetery in Glendale, California.

Several members of the crew and staff are no longer with us. E. Darrell Hallenbeck passed away shortly after his interview for this book. Joseph Calvelli, Boris Ingster, Barry Shear, and Bill Graham are all deceased.

Chapter 28

An *U.N.C.L.E.* Retrospective

Looking back on *The Man from U.N.C.L.E.,* several factors come to mind to explain why it became so popular, and why it met the fate it did. Perhaps no other show, with the exception of *Star Trek,* has created so profound an influence, extending far beyond the years it was broadcast. Certainly its uniqueness was an important factor. There simply were no spy shows on television in 1964, and certainly none that offered the sophisticated adventure that *U.N.C.L.E.* did. It was a refreshing change of pace compared to other TV fare of the time, and reflected the changing thinking of the sixties—fast-paced, daring, different, irreverent, "cool."

Undoubtedly another major factor was the professionalism of the production crew, which was nearly all drawn from prior successful series. Norman Felton was a brilliant administrator who put together a team able to surmount formidable production problems and turn out a quality series week after week.

The rapid rise to popularity the series experienced was based on the factors outlined earlier, but an additional factor that sustained the series was the on-screen relationship between the two main characters. We as viewers liked these two, and we looked forward to seeing them.

Writer Harlan Ellison feels that *U.N.C.L.E.* was popular because it "was riding the crest of the James Bond madness at the time. It was high style, which was unlike anything else on television at the time. It was slick, it was fast-moving, it was a precursor for all of the shows on now that look like rock videos. It had fast music, it had beautiful women, it had fast movement. And it was complete fantasy that made fun of one of the big fears of the time, since we were coming out of the fifties. People were still worried about international tensions, the Cold War and that kind of thing. And here was a Russian and an American working for the greater good. Sam Rolfe put all the elements together right, and with great imagination and verve."

Robert Vaughn feels that the setting of the show is responsible for its popularity even today: "It had a survivability that well transcends the time it was on the air," he says. "It seems to be remembered as a happy period, in what was otherwise a chaotic decade. This is probably because it was totally escapist fare."

David McCallum agrees: "I think the chemistry, the discipline, and the fact that it was purely escapism made for its success. At that time, there was enough serious political news going on overseas, that people needed an escape."

McCallum also feels that no one individual is responsible for the success of the series: "I don't think you can separate Robert and myself and Leo G. Carroll, and everything the writers did. It's all very well to say that so-and-so is terrific. Even today, Don Johnson is a product of *Miami Vice,* and *Miami Vice* is a product of Don Johnson. I think these things all play upon each other, and I think the chemistry the three of us had, along with Dean Hargrove, Peter Allan Fields, and Norman Felton and Sam Rolfe, is the reason why. It's an interplay of one upon the other."

Courtesy of the Norman Felton collection.

These observations are, to be sure, accurate. But it is impossible to thoroughly define the reasons why this show continues to occupy the place it does in the hearts and minds of so many adults today. The show appealed to its audience on many different levels: for children, it was a straight action-adventure show; for teens, it was an expression of nonconformity and rebellion; for the college crowd, it was glamorous entertainment appealing to the mind as well as the libido; for adults, it was a sophisticated, romantic series that offered escape from the doldrums of everyday life in an attractive setting.

Although much lip service was given to the tongue-in-cheek nature of the series, the show was not a spoof. It did not strive to poke fun at anything. It started out as an adventure show that vicariously involved real people in high intrigue. The show learned—almost too late—that humor, handled correctly and in moderate doses, could enhance that adventure. But it was not a spoof in the sense that *Get Smart* was a spoof—ironically, a spoof of *U.N.C.L.E.* itself. It is likely that the producers were the victims of their own press coverage. After reading so many reviews calling the show a spoof, the tendency was to move toward parody all the more.

Douglas Benton says, "At the time, we really didn't know what we had. Now I realize, and a lot of other people do, that a lot of people sitting there in my hometown in Texas really believed that U.N.C.L.E. existed, and that it was out to fight worldwide crime, and holy cow, it was hard to accept that. It was just a lot of fun to watch." No doubt, the end tag thanking U.N.C.L.E. contributed to this, but then again, U.N.C.L.E. was a very believable organization. Somehow, it seemed there should have been a real U.N.C.L.E.

U.N.C.L.E. also taught us to admire a new kind of hero. Solo and Illya taught us that David might defeat Goliath with his brains instead of brawn. Illya appealed to women to a large degree because he clearly didn't care if he appealed to them or not. Such heroes were totally new and unique—and are still fresh today.

The cast and crew of the show enjoyed making the show, and their enthusiasm carried over onto the screen. Darrell Hallenbeck called *U.N.C.L.E.* "my best experience in show business." David McCallum says he "enjoyed it enormously." Harlan Ellison calls it "one of my most pleasant television experiences . . . it was serious, but it was also great fun." David Victor recalls, "We had a lot of fun doing it," and Peter Allan Fields states, "It was a marvelous time . . . it was a family. It was the greatest."

As much as the cast and crew respected the show, they respected each other. George Lehr says "The secret to *U.N.C.L.E.* was, it really was a committee effort. It was a unique film family because everybody, including the prop man, the special-effects man, the director of photography, the editors, everybody was excited about it. The secret was, we had a can-do attitude. If someone said, 'You want me to build the Taj-Mahal?' we'd say sure. You never heard anyone say, 'Are you crazy?' Instead they'd say, 'We'll figure out a way to do it.' That went from the directors right on down to the craft servicemen."

Lehr himself was the epitome of that attitude. He was the jack-of-all-trades on the staff, performing an incredible assortment of duties. As Arnold Goode says, "When it comes down to all the people who worked on the show, my personal opinion is that George Lehr was in more things and helped more people on the show than all the rest combined. He's one of a kind, the guy that never received anywhere near the credit that was due him."

Lehr, Felton, Til Gabbani, Vaughn, and McCallum were the only cast and crew members who were with the show from start to finish. McCallum remembers each member of the crew fondly. He recalls particularly a special morning when the crew was on location in the Hollywood hills to film the jeep-and-motorcycle battle for "The Indian Affairs Affair": "I had my super-8 camera along that day. I was there early, and the bus with the crew arrived. I was just standing by the coffee with the camera pointing at the door of the bus, and every single member of the crew gets off there, and they all make faces and grin, in one continuous shot, and then they are all standing around drinking coffee. That piece of film is one of my favorites."

The two guiding lights of the series were, of course, Norman Felton and Sam Rolfe. Norman Felton was the pinnacle of the entire production staff. Alan Caillou remarks that Felton was "a very, very bright man." Felton was the administrator, the man who coordinated all the departments and kept the show on the air.

Sam Rolfe was, for the first, crucial season, the helmsman who gave the show its unique approach. Fred Koenekamp says of Rolfe, "He was just the nicest producer you'd ever want to run across. He was terribly interested in what we were doing, and he encouraged us to do different things and have fun with the show. That's what I think made this show popular at the time, it was just a little bit different from anything else on the air." Bob Murdock recalls that Rolfe was "great, he's a great innovator." David McCallum calls Rolfe "greatly talented," and Norman Felton states, "The work Sam Rolfe did in writing the extensive background for *U.N.C.L.E.* and in producing the first season was superb. Without it, we would never have made the series."

Felton himself says of the show, "I went on the set of *U.N.C.L.E.* more than any of my other shows. Every series has problems and on *U.N.C.L.E.* we had tremendous production problems, more than any other series because of the complexity of the production. Yet, somehow, on *U.N.C.L.E.*, when we would sit around the table to discuss a problem, we were always laughing. That made it endurable, and also created an *esprit.*"

The attitude of the cast was also a major factor. Mort Abrahams recalls that "Vaughn and McCallum were very professional, and always there when you needed them. They never fussed or fumed over unworthy matters, and they were always where they should be with their scripts. They were delightful to work with."

Doug Benton feels that *U.N.C.L.E.* was "ahead of its time. I think it was certainly much, much wittier than garbage you see on television today. It makes some of them look like graffiti on a subway wall." Benton adds that he's "very pleased that people remember the two shows as fondly as obviously they do. I guess we didn't waste our time after all." Sam Rolfe states simply: "It was the most fun of any series I have worked on." He also remarks on his "endless surprise at the continuing popularity of the series and its characters after so many years off the air—and in consideration of changing times and trends. I guess there's some wondrous escapist nerve it still strikes in people."

Those who tried to analyze the show in the 1960s used various adjectives—adventurous, humorous, sophisticated, ultramodern, futuristic, fast-paced, or "hip" or "cool." But if one word can sum up the appeal of this incredible show, it is perhaps a word favored by Norman Felton himself: *The Man from U.N.C.L.E.* had "dash." And it still does.

An Episode and Production Credit Guide to *The Man from U.N.C.L.E.* and *The Girl from U.N.C.L.E.*

Credits: *The Man from U.N.C.L.E.*

Continuous credits for all four seasons:

Executive Producer: Norman Felton
Series Developed by: Sam Rolfe
Theme by: Jerry Goldsmith
Supervising Producer (episode 40 on):
  David Victor
Supervising Film Editor: John Dunning
Recording Supervisor: Franklin Milton
Music Supervision: Frank Anderson
(Supervising) Set Decorator: Henry
  Grace

(Supervising) Art Director: George Davis
Art Director: Merrill Pye (episodes 1–
  35), James Sullivan (episodes 36–105)
Director of Photography:
  Fred Koenekamp, with the following
  exceptions: Joseph Biroc (episode 1),
  Kenneth Peach (episodes 52, 53), Dale
  Deverman (episodes 89, 91, 97), Ray
  Flin (episode 98), Robert Hauser
  (episodes 100, 101, 104–5),
  Koenekamp and Harold Wellman
  (episode 45)

The First Season: 1964–65

8:30 P.M. EST Tuesdays (episodes 1–14)
8:00 P.M. EST Mondays (episodes 15–29)

For the entire season:

Producer: Sam Rolfe (with exception of the pilot, which was produced by Norman Felton)
Associate Producer:
Joseph Gantman (pilot)
Joseph Calvelli (episodes 2–19)
Robert Foshko (episodes 20–29)
Assistant to the Producer: George Lehr

Entire season broadcast in black-and-white.

#1. The Vulcan Affair. After a THRUSH attempt to kill Waverly is thwarted, Solo is assigned to prevent the assassination of a visiting African premier (William Marshall) at the hands of Andrew Vulcan (Fritz Weaver), and with the help of a housewife (Patricia Crowley) he learns that the premier himself is allied with THRUSH and plans to kill his two top aides (Ivan Dixon and Rupert Crosse) in a fake accident.

Prod. #1059 (feature version, *To Trap a Spy,* #6006)
Airdate: September 22, 1964
Filmed: November 20–22, 26–27, 29, 1963; additional footage March 31, April 1–2, 1964
Former Title: "The Vulcan Files"
Producer: Norman Felton
Writer: Sam Rolfe
Director: Don Medford
Assistant Director: Maurice Vaccarino
Editor: Henry Berman
Music: Jerry Goldsmith
Set Decorator: Frank McEveety
Rerun Date: April 26, 1965

#2. The Iowa Scuba Affair. Solo investigates the curious death of an air force man in Iowa with scuba gear, and with the help of Jill Denison (Katherine Crawford) uncovers a plan by Clint Spinner (Slim Pickens) to steal a missile-plane from a secret base under a farm.

Prod. #7415
Airdate: September 29, 1964
Filmed: June 1–5, 8, 1964
Former titles: "The Kansas Scuba Affair," "The Silo Affair"

Writer: Harold J. Bloom
Director: Richard Donner
Assistant Director: Maurice Vaccarino
Editor: Fred Maguire
Music: Morton Stevens
Set Decorator: Jerry Wunderlich
Rerun Date: July 12, 1965

#3. The Quadripartite Affair. In Yugoslavia, Solo and Illya are aided by Marion Raven (Jill Ireland) in stopping Gervaise Ravel (Anne Francis) and her partners from using a fear gas to overthrow various governments.

Prod. #7414
Airdate: October 6, 1964
Filmed: August 3–7, 12–14, 17–18, 1964
Writer: Alan Caillou
Director: Richard Donner
Assistant Director: E. Darrell Hallenbeck
Editor: Henry Berman
Music: Walter Scharf
Set Decorator: Robert Benton
Rerun Date: May 3, 1965

#4. The Shark Affair. Solo and Illya investigate a series of kidnappings that lead to a modern-day pirate ship run by Captain Shark (Robert Culp), who is filling his Noah's Ark with craftsmen from all walks of life to repopulate the world after the nuclear holocaust he feels is imminent. With the help of Harry Barnman (Herbert Anderson) and his wife Elsa (Sue Anne Langdon), Solo and Illya pose as shipwrecked sailors to in turn wreck his plans.

Prod. #7408
Airdate: October 13, 1964
Filmed: June 26, 29–30, July 1–3, 1964
Former titles: "The Corsair Affair," "The Private Affair," "The Pirate Affair"
Writer: Alvin Sapinsley

Director: Marc Daniels
Assistant Director: E. Darrell Hallenbeck
Editor: Fred Maguire
Music: Walter Scharf
Set Decorator: Jerry Wunderlich
Rerun Date: May 10, 1965

#5. The Deadly Games Affair. When a rare postage stamp at an auction reveals that a former SS scientist, Professor Amadeus, is still alive and experimenting with the secret of "suspended animation," Solo and Illya enlist the aid of college students Terry Brent (Brooke Bundy) and Chuck Boskirk (Burt Brinckerhoff) to beat THRUSH agent Angelique (Janine Gray) to Amadeus's lab, where Solo is captured so his blood can be used to revive the suspended body of the Führer.

Prod. #7416
Airdate: October 20, 1964
Filmed: July 23–24, 27–30, 1964
Former title: "The Stamp Affair"
Writer: Dick Nelson
Director: Alvin Ganzer
Assistant Director: Tom McCrory
Editor: Joseph Dervin
Music: Jerry Goldsmith
Set Decorator: Robert Benton
Rerun Date: May 17, 1965

#6. The Green Opal Affair. In the Yucatan, THRUSH agent Walter Brach (Carroll O'Connor) brainwashes important people from many nations to be "time bombs" who will return to their jobs and do THRUSH's bidding. After eluding Brach's henchman Chuke (Shuji J. Nozawa) and his leopards, Solo and housewife Chris Linnel (Joan O'Brien) enlist the aid of Mrs. Karda (Dovima), Brach's numerologist, to help them escape.

Prod. #7419
Airdate: October 27, 1964
Filmed: July 15–17, 20–22, 1964
Former title: "The Missing Persons
  Affair"
Writer: Robert E. Thompson
Director: John Peyser
Assistant Director: E. Darrell Hallenbeck
Editor: Henry Berman
Music: Jerry Goldsmith
Set Decorator: Robert Benton
Rerun Date: August 16, 1965

#7. The Giuoco Piano Affair.
Gervaise Ravel (Anne Francis) returns
and Solo and Illya again enlist Marion
Raven (Jill Ireland) to help them pursue
her through the Andes, where the
treachery of police Lieutenant Manuera
(James Frawley) impedes their efforts to
capture Ravel.

Prod, #7422
Airdate: November 10, 1964
Filmed: August 6–7, 10–14, 18, 1964
Writer: Alan Caillou
Director: Richard Donner
Assistant Director: E. Darrell Hallenbeck
Editor: Joseph Dervin
Music: Walter Scharf
Set Decorator: Robert Benton
Rerun Date: May 24, 1965

#8. The Double Affair.
THRUSH creates a double for Solo, and with the seductive aid of Serena (Senta Berger),
Darius Two (Michael Evans) kidnaps
Solo and substitutes the phony into
U.N.C.L.E.'s efforts to transport the
code to a secret new weapon. Illya and
stewardess Sandy Wister (Sharon Farrell) eventually realize a switch has been
made, and the real Solo escapes and in a
climactic scene battles "himself."

Prod. #7417 (feature version, *The Spy
  with My Face,* #6011)
Airdate: November 17, 1964
Filmed: August 28, 31, September 1–4,
  8, 1964; additional footage for feature
  September 9–11, 1964
Writer: Joseph Calvelli, Clyde Ware
Director: John Newland
Assistant Director: E. Darrell Hallenbeck
Editor: Joseph Dervin
Music: Mort Stevens
Set Decorator: Robert Benton
Rerun Date: May 31, 1965

#9. The Project Strigas Affair.
Solo and Illya devise a clever scheme to discredit a Balkan intelligence chief
(Werner Klemperer) with a bogus secret
gas. With the help of a bankrupt exterminator (William Shatner) and his wife,
Illya poses as a fellow countryman and
exploits the paranoia of the chief and his
bumbling assistant (Leonard Nimoy).

Prod. #7426
Airdate: November 24, 1964
Filmed: September 29–30, October 1–2,
  5–6, 1964
Writer: Henry Misrock
Director: Joseph Sargent
Assistant Director: E. Darrell Hallenbeck
Editor: Bill Gulick
Music: Walter Scharf
Set Decorator: Robert Benton
Rerun Date: August 30, 1965

#10. The Finny Foot Affair.
Solo gets an unwelcome young companion (Kurt
Russell), a ten-year-old who wants Solo
to marry his widowed mother, in his efforts to find the source of a deadly chemical that killed an entire Scottish village.
In a race to find the source with General
Yokura (Leonard Strong), Solo eventually uses a ring on the finger of a statue

to pinpoint a cave where the deadly chemical has leaked from, but has to use his wits to escape when he is trapped there by Yokura and his men.

> Prod. #7426
> Airdate: November 24, 1964
> Filmed: September 29–30, October 1–2, 5–6, 1964
> Writers: Jack Turley, Jay Sims
> Director: Marc Daniels
> Assistant Director: Tom McCrory
> Editor: Joseph Dervin
> Music: Morton Stevens
> Set Decorator: Robert Benton
> Rerun Date: August 9, 1965

#11. The Neptune Affair. Solo races to avert a U.S.–Soviet war and finds the source of rockets spreading a fungus deadly to the Soviet wheat crop. Posing as a country bumpkin, he infiltrates a secret underwater rocket site run by Vincent Lockridge (Henry Jones). Assisted by Felicia Lavimore (Marta Kristen) and her boyfriend Gabe Melcroft (Jeremy Slate), Solo infiltrates the base and tries to stop the next launch.

> Prod. #7405
> Airdate: December 8, 1964
> Filmed: June 18–19, 22–25, 1964
> Writers: Henry Sharp (teleplay), John W. Block (story)
> Director: Vincent McEveety
> Assistant Director: Wilbur Mosier
> Editor: Henry Berman
> Music: Jerry Goldsmith, Walter Scharf
> Set Decorator: Jerry Wunderlich
> Rerun Date: None

#12. The Dove Affair. When a minor European leader is assassinated, Solo steals a medallion from his body containing a microdot listing the THRUSH agents in the country, but must elude the secret police and outwit intelligence agent Satine (Ricardo Montalban), who also wants the medal. Teacher and tour guide Sarah Taub (June Lockhart) and her high school students are used by Solo to try and sneak the medal over the border.

> Prod. #7410
> Airdate: December 15, 1964
> Filmed: August 19–21, 24–26, 1964
> Former title: "The Butterfly Affair"
> Writer: Robert Towne
> Director: John Peyser
> Assistant Director: Tom McCrory
> Editor: Bill Gulick
> Music: Jerry Goldsmith
> Set Decorator: Robert Benton
> Rerun Date: None

#13. The King of Knaves Affair. Solo and Illya investigate the disappearance of several crime figures, and the trail leads to Fasik el Pasad (Paul Stevens), a deposed ruler who is building an army of criminals to regain power. Solo poses as a black-market arms dealer and infiltrates the operation, but is hampered by well-meaning Ernestine Pepper (Diana Millay), a notary public trying to find one of Fasik's men, Angel Galley (Jan Merlin).

> Prod. #7418
> Airdate: December 22, 1964
> Filmed: July 7–10, 13–14, 1964
> Former titles: "The Notary Public Affair," "The Crimeless Wave Affair"
> Writer: Ellis Marcus
> Director: Michael O'Herlihy
> Assistant Director: Wilbur Mosier
> Editor: Joseph Dervin
> Music: Jerry Goldsmith
> Set Decorator: Robert Benton
> Rerun Date: None
> The First Season: 1964—65

#14. The Terbuf Affair. On vacation, Solo is asked by an old love interest, Clara Valdar (Madlyn Rhue) to help her smuggle gypsy leader Emil (Jacques Aubuchon) out of Terbuf with evidence that the corrupt head of the secret police, Colonel Morisco (Alan Caillou), has been embezzling foreign aid money with the aid of the repulsive Major Vicek (Albert Paulsen).

> Prod. #7435
> Airdate: December 29, 1964
> Filmed: October 27–30, November 2–3, 1964
> Former title: "The Lethal Ladies Affair"
> Writer: Alan Caillou
> Director: Richard Donner
> Assistant Director: Tom McCrory
> Editor: Bill Gulick
> Music: Jerry Goldsmith, Walter Scharf
> Set Decorator: Robert Benton
> Rerun Date: August 2, 1965

#15. The Deadly Decoy Affair. U.N.C.L.E. must transport captured THRUSH official Egon Stryker (Ralph Taeger) from New York to Washington without THRUSH rescuing him. While Waverly takes a decoy alone one route, Solo and Illya take the real Stryker—or is it the real one?—with them. But in a mixup, Fran Parsons (Joanna Moore), a secretary on her lunch hour, gets handcuffed to Stryker and has to go along.

> Prod. #7438
> Airdate: January 11, 1965
> Filmed: November 30, December 1–4, 7, 1964
> Former title: "The Decoy Affair"
> Writer: Albert Aley
> Director: Alvin Ganzer
> Assistant Director: E. Darrell Hallenbeck
> Editor: Bill Gulick
> Music: Walter Scharf

> Set Decorator: Budd Friend
> Rerun Date: June 7, 1965

Note: A new time slot and new introductory sequence began with this episode. Series was preempted by a special NBC White Paper on January 5, 1965.

#16. The Fiddlesticks Affair. THRUSH agent Anton Korbel (Ken Murray) guards THRUSH's fifty-million-dollar-treasury in a vault beneath his casino, and Solo and Illya recruit a naïve girl from Minneapolis, Susan Callaway (Marlyn Mason), and shady safecracker Marcel Rudolph (Dan O'Herlihy) to break in and destroy the cash.

> Prod. #7433
> Airdate: January 18, 1965
> Filmed: November 18–20, 23–25, 1964
> Former title: "The Jack and Jill Affair"
> Writers: Aben Kandel, Peter Allan Fields
> Director: Theodore Flicker
> Assistant Director: E. Darrell Hallenbeck
> Editor: Henry Berman
> Music: Lalo Schifrin
> Set Decorator: Budd Friend
> Rerun Date: June 14, 1965

#17. The Yellow Scarf Affair. Solo goes to India to investigate the death of a fellow U.N.C.L.E. agent in an airline crash, and discovers that a cult of Thuggees headed by a maharajah (Murray Matheson) is causing the crashes in order to loot the passengers. But Solo and THRUSH agent Tom Simpson (Linden Chiles) are looking to recover one item in particular—U.N.C.L.E.'s new polygraph device.

> Prod. #7424
> Airdate: January 25, 1965
> Filmed: October 19–23, 26, 1964

Writers: Robert Yale Lippincott
(teleplay), Boris Ingster (story)
Director: Ron Winston
Assistant Director: E. Darrell Hallenbeck
Editor: Henry Berman
Music: Morton Stevens
Set Decorator: Robert Benton
Rerun Date: None

#18. The Mad *Mad* Tea Party Affair.
Prior to an important conference at
U.N.C.L.E. headquarters, a bizarre series of events occurs revolving around a
strange man, Mr. Hemingway (Richard
Haydn), who keeps appearing and disap-
pearing at will in the building. Solo and
Illya learn that he has been placed there
by Waverly to test the security system,
but THRUSH also has an inside agent,
Riley (Peter Haskell), who plants an exploding false tabletop on the conference
table at the direction of Dr. Egret (Lee
Meriwether). Solo has only a few minutes, before the conference is to begin,
to try and find out who the infiltrator is.

Prod. #7421
Airdate: February 1, 1965
Filmed: December 16–18, 21–23, 1964
Former title: "The Hemingway Affair"
Writer: Dick Nelson
Director: Seymour Robbie
Assistant Director: Eric Von Stroheim,
Jr.
Editor: Bill Gulick
Music: Jerry Goldsmith, Morton Stevens
Set Decorator: Budd Friend
Rerun Date: June 21, 1965

#19. The Secret Sceptre Affair. Solo
and Illya agree to help Major Morgan
(Gene Raymond), Solo's old command-
ing officer, steal a national symbol
sceptre for his people from a dictator.
Morgan is killed, and Solo and Illya and
Zia (Ziva Rodann), Morgan's female

aide, are captured and sentenced to
death. After they escape, they find that
Morgan is still alive—and has duped
them into stealing the sceptre for him
because of the precious gems it contains.

Prod. #7437
Airdate: February 8, 1965
Filmed: December 8–11, 14, 1964
Former title: "The Pythias Affair"
Writer: Anthony Spinner
Director: Marc Daniels
Assistant Director: E. Darrell Hallenbeck
Editor: Joseph Dervin
Music: Jerry Goldsmith, Morton Stevens
Set Decorator: Budd Friend
Rerun Date: None

#20. The Bow Wow Affair. Waverly's
cousin is killed by his own dog when he
refuses to sell his stock to a gypsy named
Delgrovia (Paul Lambert), so Illya investigates and, with the help of Ursula
(Susan Oliver) and dog expert Guido
Panzini (Pat Harrington, Jr.), traces two
of the dogs to Delgrovia's estate, where
he and Ursula are soon cornered by a
pack of deadly Doberman pinschers.

Prod. #7411
Airdate: February 15, 1965
Filmed: December 28–31, 1964, January
1–4, 5, 1965
Former title: "The Pyrenees Affair"
Writer: Alan Caillou
Director: Sherman Marks
Assistant Director: E. Darrell Hallenbeck
Editor: Joseph Dervin
Music: Jerry Goldsmith, Morton Stevens
Set Decorator: Budd Friend
Rerun Date: July 26, 1965

#21. The Four Steps Affair. Solo and
Illya protect a young Himalayan prince
(Michel Petit) and his nurse (Susan Sea-
forth) from THRUSH agents who want

to kidnap him—one of whom turns out to be his bodyguard.

> Prod. #7445
> Airdate: February 22, 1965
> Filmed: January 1–8, 11–12, 1965
> Former title: "The Himalayan Affair"
> Writers: Peter Allan Fields, Joseph Calvelli
> Director: Alvin Ganzer
> Assistant Director: E. Darrell Hallenbeck
> Editor: Henry Berman
> Music: Jerry Goldsmith, Morton Stevens
> Set Decorator: Budd Friend
> Rerun Date: None

> *Note:* This episode consisted in large part of extra footage shot for feature versions of episodes 1 and 8.

Vaughn and McCallum with some of U.N.C.L.E.'s futuristic gadgetry. *Courtesy of the Norman Felton collection.*

#22. The See Paris and Die Affair.

Solo uses the former girlfriend (Kathryn Hays) of 2 brothers, Joseph and Max Van Schreetan (Gerald Mohr, Lloyd Bochner), to thwart their plan to control the diamond market, while at the same time THRUSH agent Corio (Alfred Ryder) tries to steal their cache of gems.

> Prod. #7442
> Airdate: March 1, 1965
> Filmed: January 13–15, 18–21, 1965
> Former title: "The Glittering Affair"
> Writers: Peter Allan Fields (story, teleplay), Sheldon Stark (story)
> Director: Alf Kjellin
> Assistant Director: Eddie Saeta
> Editor: Bill Gulick
> Music: Walter Scharf, Morton Stevens
> Set Decorator: Budd Friend
> Rerun Date: June 28, 1965

> Note: Episode 22 contained a special credit: "The Man from U.N.C.L.E. Theme Performed by The Gallants."

#23. The Brain Killer Affair. Waverly

is poisoned, and taken to a hospital where he is subjected to the rays of a brain-altering machine by THRUSH agent Dr. Dabree (Elsa Lanchester), designed to make him ineffective without killing him. While investigating others who have suffered the same fate, Solo finds Cecille Bergstrom (Yvonne Craig) and together they try to unravel the mystery and save Waverly.

> Prod. #7406
> Airdate: March 8, 1965
> Filmed: June 10–12, 15–17, 1964
> Writer: Archie Tegland
> Director: James Goldstone
> Assistant Director: E. Darrell Hallenbeck
> Editor: Joseph Dervin
> Music: Jerry Goldsmith
> Set Decorator: Jerry Wunderlich
> Rerun Date: August 23, 1965

#24. The Hong Kong Shilling Affair.

Solo is aided by tourist Bernie Oren (Glenn Corbett) in finding a black-market auction in Hong Kong run by Mr. Cleveland (Gavin MacLeod) that sells military secrets, including a microfilm in a rare coin. Oren is infatuated with Heavenly Cortello (Karen Sharpe), and hinders more than he helps Solo, while Illya tries to infiltrate the auction disguised as a Mongolian warlord.

Prod. #7453
Airdate: March 15, 1965
Filmed: January 25–29, February 1, 1965
Former title: "The Dragon's Tooth Affair"
Writer: Alan Caillou
Director: Alvin Ganzer
Assistant Director: E. Darrell Hallenbeck
Editor: Joseph Dervin
Music: Morton Stevens
Set Decorator: Budd Friend
Rerun Date: None

Note: Episode 24 contained a special credit: "Special Makeup by William Tuttle."

#25. The Never Never Affair.

U.N.C.L.E. Portuguese translator Mandy Stevenson (Barbara Feldon) hungers for more excitement, so Solo sends her on a fake mission to get Waverly's tobacco—not realizing she has taken an important microfilm that THRUSH is after. Solo, Illya, and THRUSH pursue her through the streets of Manhattan, and eventually she and Solo are captured by the THRUSH leader, Victor Gervais (Cesar Romero), and Solo has to use his skills as a marksman to escape.

Prod. #7451

Airdate: March 22, 1965
Filmed: February 2–5, 8–9, 1965
Writer: Dean Hargrove
Director: Joseph Sargent
Assistant Director: Bill Finnegan
Editor: Henry Berman
Music: Jerry Goldsmith, Morton Stevens
Set Decorator: Budd Friend
Rerun Date: September 6, 1965

#26. The Love Affair.

Solo attends a revival meeting conducted by evangelist Brother Love (Eddie Albert), who is actually a THRUSH leader constructing a nuclear spaceship with the aid of a kidnapped scientist, Dr. Hradny (Robert H. Harris). College student Pearl Rolfe (Maggie Pierce) is kidnapped by Love's followers, and Solo must rescue both victims and destroy Love's plan at the same time.

Prod. #7403
Airdate: March 29, 1965
Filmed: September 21–25, 28, 1964
Writer: Albert Aley
Director: Marc Daniels
Assistant Director: Tom McCrory
Editor: Henry Berman
Music: Walter Scharf
Set Decorator: Robert Benton
Rerun Date: None

#27. The Gazebo in the Maze Affair.

Squire G. Emory Partridge (George Sanders) kidnaps Illya and lures Solo to his manor in order to kill them off in his dungeon torture chamber in revenge for a past encounter. But Peggy Durance (Bonnie Franklin) helps them escape, with the unintended aid of Partridge's bumbling wife Edith (Jeanette Nolan).

Prod. #7450
Airdate: April 5, 1965
Filmed: February 19, 22–26, 1965

Former title: "The Old Fashioned
 Affair"
Writers: Dean Hargrove (story, teleplay),
 Anthony Ellis (story)
Director: Alf Kjellin
Assistant Director: Bill Finnegan
Editor: Joseph Dervin
Music: Walter Scharf
Set Decorator: Budd Friend
Rerun Date: July 5, 1965

#28. The Girls of Nazarone Affair.

Solo and Illya travel to the Riviera, where they search for a serum that supposedly provides great strength and even brings the dead back to life. There they meet Madame Streigau (Marian Moses), who is actually Dr. Egret of THRUSH, as well as Lucia Nazarone (Danica d'Hondt) and her bevy of beautiful blonde helpers. With the help of teacher Lavinia Brown (Kipp Hamilton), they trick Nazarone into thinking they have the serum also, and become the targets of her "superwomen."

Prod. #7449
Airdate: April 12, 1965
Filmed: February 11–12, 15–18, 1965
Former titles: "The Beware of Blondes
 Affair," "The Skin Deep Affair"
Writers: Peter Allan Fields (teleplay),
 Peter Barry (story)

Director: Alvin Ganzer
Assistant Director: E. Darrell Hallenbeck
 (also second-unit director)
Editor: Bill Gulick
Music: Jerry Goldsmith, Morton Stevens
Set Decorator: Budd Friend
Rerun Date: None

#29. The Odd Man Affair.

Retired U.N.C.L.E. agent Albert Sully (Martin Balsam) is brought back to impersonate a crime syndicate leader, and insists on leaving Solo and Illya behind and running the operation himself. He reunites with wartime fellow agent and old flame Bryn Watson (Barbara Shelly) and tracks down a secret crime conference, with the exasperated Solo and Illya trying to keep him from being killed in the process.

Prod. #7434
Airdate: April 19, 1965
Filmed: March 1–5, 8, 1965
Former titles: "The Odd Man Out
 Affair," "The Has Been Affair," "The
 86th Floor Affair"
Writer: Dick Nelson
Director: Joseph Sargent
Assistant Director: E. Darrell Hallenbeck
Editor: Henry Berman
Music: Morton Stevens
Set Decorator: Budd Friend
Rerun Date: July 19, 1965

The Second Season: 1965–66

10:00 P.M. EST Fridays

For the entire season:

Producers: David Victor (episodes 30–38), Mort Abrahams (episodes 39–48), Boris Ingster (Episodes 49–59)
Assistant to the Producer: George Lehr

#30 & #31. The Alexander the Greater Affair, parts 1 and 2.

Alexander (Rip Torn), a megalomaniac industrialist, plans to conquer the world like his namesake, Alexander the Great, by breaking each of the ten commandments along the way. He has his henchman Parviz (David Sheiner) steal the army's "will gas" to help him do so, and Solo investigates. Solo encounters Tracey Alexander (Dorothy Provine), Alexander's ex-wife, who wants to tag along with Solo to get the money Alexander owes her. The trail leads Solo, Illya, and Tracey to a posh party at Alexander's, where Solo defeats him in a human chess game; to a tomb, where Alexander and his aide Dr. Kavon (David Opatoshu) leave Solo tied under a descending scimitar while Illya and Tracey

are hanging over a bottomless pit with a candle burning their rope; to Alexander's farm in Virginia, where Illya is nearly cut in two by various farm implements.

Prod. #7458, 7459 (feature version, *One Spy Too Many*, #6014)
Airdate: September 17, 24, 1965
Filmed: July 15–16, 19–23, 26–30, August 2–5, 1965
Former title: "The Alexander Affair"
Producer: David Victor
Writer: Dean Hargrove
Director: Joseph Sargent
Assistant Director: E. Darrell Hallenbeck
Production Executive: Mort Abrahams
Editor: Henry Berman
Music: Gerald Fried
Set Decorator: Charles Thompson
Rerun Date: None

#32. The Ultimate Computer Affair.

Illya gets himself thrown into a Latin American penal colony to try and find THRUSH's Ultimate Computer, a supermachine which runs the entire organization. Solo poses as the husband of social worker Salty Oliver (Judy Carne) to get inside also, but Governor Callahan (Charlie Ruggles) and his Captain of the guards Cervantes (Roger C. Carmel) see through his cover, and trick Illya into blowing up a phony computer.

Prod. #7462
Airdate: October 1, 1965
Filmed: June 16–18, 21–23, 1965
Former titles: "The Ultimate Affair,"
  "The Calculated Risk Affair"
Producer: David Victor
Writer: Peter Allan Fields
Director: Joseph Sargent
Assistant Director: E. Darrell Hallenbeck
Production Executive: Mort Abrahams
Editor: Bill Gulick
Music: Lalo Schifrin
Set Decorator: Charles Thompson
Rerun Date: April 22, 1966

#33. The Foxes and Hounds Affair.

Illya tries to obtain a thought-reading device from a magician, but THRUSH agents Victor Marton (Vincent Price) and Lucia Belmont (Patricia Medina) are also after it. Mimi Doolittle (Julie Sommars), the magician's assistant, is drawn into the chase, and Solo is sent on a wild goose chase to distract Marton, complete with an exploding handkerchief and an untimely sneeze.

Prod. #7461
Airdate: October 8, 1965
Filmed: July 6–9, 12–13, 1965
Former title: "The Elba Affair"
Producer: David Victor
Writers: Peter Allan Fields, Eric
  Bercovicci
Director: Alf Kjellin
Assistant Director: Tom McCrory
Production Executive: Mort Abrahams
Editor: Bill Gulick
Music: Robert Drasnin
Set Decorator: Charles Thompson

Rerun Date: April 29, 1966

#34. The Discotheque Affair.

While U.N.C.L.E. tries to find a cache of THRUSH records hidden under a discotheque, THRUSH plants a sophisticated listening device in an apartment next to Waverly's office. Solo's arm is broken and in a cast, so he is assigned to take care of a rent dispute with tenant Sandy Wyler (Judi West); he turns up the device, while Illya infiltrates the discotheque, run by THRUSH agent Vincent Carver (Ray Danton), as a musician. Carver tells Tiger Ed (Harvey Lembeck) to kill Carver's girlfriend, Farina (Evelyn Ward), but she escapes and helps Solo, before making up with Carver, who sets fire to the discotheque with Solo, Illya, and Sandy locked in a cell inside.

Prod. #7476
Airdate: October 15, 1965
Filmed: August 6, 9–13, 16, 1965
Former titles: "The Finnian Affair,"
  "The Old Chameleon Affair"
Producer: David Victor
Writers: Leonard Stadd (story), Dean
  Hargrove (teleplay)
Director: Tom Gries
Assistant Director: Wilbur Mosier
Production Executive: Mort Abrahams
Editor: Bill Gulick
Music: Gerald Fried
Set Decorator: Charles Thompson
Rerun Date: May 6, 1966

#35. The Recollectors Affair.

Solo and Illya investigate the Recollectors, a group headed by Demos (George Macready) that hunts down and kills ex-Nazis in order to steal their looted art collections and resell them to the original owners. Gregori Valetti (Theodore Marcuse),

Solo, and Illya all vie to find the store-house of art treasures.

Prod. #7455
Airdate: October 22, 1965
Filmed: June 24–25, 28–30, July 1, 1965
Producer: David Victor
Writer: Alan Caillou
Director: Alvin Ganzer
Assistant Director: Tom McCrory
Production Executive: Mort Abrahams
Editor: Henry Berman
Music: Robert Drasnin
Set Decorator: Charles Thompson
Rerun Date: None

#36. The Arabian Affair.
Illya goes to the Arabian desert to find THRUSH's vaporizing machine, but is captured by Sophie (Phyllis Newman), the head-strong daughter of the local tribal chief, Sulador (Michael Ansara). In New York, Solo convinces retiring THRUSH agent David Lewin (Robert Ellenstein) that THRUSH intends to kill him, and elicits his help. Lewin and Solo are taken to the base in the desert, just as Illya leads the band of nomads, whose confidence he has gained, in an attack on the base.

Prod. #7484
Airdate: October 29, 1965
Filmed: September 14–17, 20–21, 1965
Producer: David Victor
Writer: Peter Allan Fields
Director: E. Darrell Hallenbeck
Assistant Director: Wilbur Mosier
Production Executive: Mort Abrahams
Editor: Joseph Dervin
Music: Gerald Fried
Set Decorator: Charles Thompson
Rerun Date: May 13, 1966

#37. The Tigers Are Coming Affair.
Solo and Illya go to India to help Suzanne de Serre (Jill Ireland), a French botanist trying to find out why the jungle is dying and local natives are dis-appearing. Prince Panat (Lee Bergere) and Drusilla Davina (Florence Marly), along with Colonel Quillon (Alan Caillou), are systematically using a chemical to destroy the jungle and kid-napping natives to work in the jewel mines for the prince.

Prod. #7456
Airdate: November 5, 1965
Filmed: September 3, 7–10, 13, 1965
Producer: David Victor
Writers: Alan Caillou (teleplay), Paul Tuckahoe (story)
Director: Herschel Daugherty
Assistant Directors: E. Darrell Hallenbeck, Robert M. Webb
Production Executive: Mort Abrahams
Editor: Bill Gulick
Music: Robert Drasnin
Set Decorator: Francisco Lombardo
Rerun Date: None

#38. The Deadly Toys Affair.
THRUSH has plans to exploit boy genius Bartlett Warshowsky (Jay North) for its own purposes. Solo, posing as a toy sales-man, and Illya, disguised as a hair-dresser, try to rescue the boy from the clutches of THRUSH agent Noubar Tal-emakian (Arnold Moss). But Bartlett's aunt Elfie Von Donck (Angela Lans-bury), an eccentric movie star, comes to assume his custody. Eventually she, her companion Joanna Lydecker (Diane Mc-Bain), and Solo and Illya must try to help Bartlett escape the THRUSH guards at the school.

Prod. #8401
Airdate: November 12, 1965
Filmed: August 25–27, 30–31, September 1–2, 1965

Former title: "The Most Deadly Game Affair"
Producer: David Victor
Writer: Robert Hill
Director: John Brahm
Assistant Director: Wilbur Mosier
Production Executive: Mort Abrahams
Editor: Henry Berman
Music: Gerald Fried
Set Decorator: Charles Thompson
Rerun Date: June 10, 1966

#39. The Cherry Blossom Affair.

THRUSH Eastern in Japan acquires a volcano-activating device, and Solo and Illya, along with Cricket Okasada (France Nuyen), a film student, infiltrate a toy store and a karate school to find it. THRUSH leader Mr. Kutuzov (Woodrow Parfrey) oversees local THRUSH head Harada (Jerry H. Fujikawa) in the operation, and Solo finds himself fighting for his life against a life-size sword-wielding puppet.

Prod. #7487
Airdate: November 19, 1965
Filmed: September 22–24, 27–29, 1965
Former titles: "The Tokyo Affair," "The War Games Affair"
Producer: Mort Abrahams
Writers: Mark Weingart (teleplay), Sherman Yellen (story)
Director: Joseph Sargent
Assistant Director: Donald C. Klune
Production Executive: Boris Ingster
Editor: Henry Berman
Music: Gerald Fried
Set Decorator: Charles Thompson
Rerun Date: June 3, 1966

#40. The Virtue Affair.

French fanatic Robespierre (Ronald Long) seeks to destroy France's vineyards in his quest for virtue, and Solo enlists the aid of scientist Raoul Dubois (Marcel Hillaire) and his daughter Albert (Mala Powers) in combating the plan. Illya is captured by THRUSH agent Carl Voegler (Frank Marth) and, with a target painted on his back, is hunted through the woods by Voegler's archers.

Prod. #8402
Airdate: December 3, 1965
Filmed: September 30, October 1, 4–7, 1965
Former title: "The L.E.F. Affair"
Producer: Mort Abrahams
Writer: Henry Slesar
Director: Jud Taylor
Assistant Director: E. Darrell Hallenbeck
Production Executive: Boris Ingster
Editor: Bill Gulick
Music: Robert Drasnin
Set Decorator: Francisco Lombardo
Rerun Date: August 5, 1966

#41. The Children's Day Affair.

A top-level U.N.C.L.E. conference is to be held in Switzerland, but a nearby boys' school is actually a THRUSH front run by Mother Fear (Jeanne Cooper) and Dennis Jenks (Warren Stevens) that is training its students to be assassins. Solo is captured by the boys, and, when he refuses to reveal the conference location, is forced to operate the controls of two electric trains so they do not collide—with each carrying a vial of deadly nerve gas. Illya and Anna Paola (Susan Silo), a social worker who resents children, are also captured. They escape, and arrive at the conference just as the boy's choir is ready to kill Waverly and the others with THRUSH rifles from under their robes.

Prod. #7460
Airdate: December 10, 1965
Filmed: October 11–15, 18, 1965

Former title: "The Most Dangerous
Affair"
Producer: Mort Abrahams
Writer: Dean Hargrove
Director: Sherman Marks
Assistant Director: Bill Finnegan
Production Executive: Boris Ingster
Editor: Joseph Dervin
Music: Gerald Fried, Robert Drasnin
Set Decorator: Charles Thompson
Rerun Date: May 27, 1966

#42. The Adriatic Express Affair.
Solo and Illya board the Adriatic Express
train on New Year's Eve to intercept
Madame Nemirovitch (Jessie Royce
Landis), a THRUSH agent who is carrying a chemical that is capable of stopping
the reproductive process. Eva (Juliet
Mills), a young girl who delivers a message to Madame Nemirovitch as the
train leaves, is caught on board.
Throughout the evening, the THRUSH
agent and Solo and Illya engage in a battle of wits as the train speeds along its
route.

Prod. #8406
Airdate: December 17, 1965
Filmed: October 20–22, 25–28, 1965
Former title: "The Vienna-Venice Affair"
Producer: Mort Abrahams
Writer: Robert Hill
Director: Seymour Robbie
Assistant Director: E. Darrell Hallenbeck
Production Executive: Boris Ingster
Editor: Bill Gulick
Music: Gerald Fried, Robert Drasnin
Set Decorator: Francisco Lombardo
Rerun: June 17, 1966

#43. The Yukon Affair. Squire G.
Emory Partridge (George Sanders) returns, having acquired in Alaska a large
quantity of Quadrillenium X, a very

heavy metal with high magnetic powers
which THRUSH wants to use to disrupt
world communications. Solo and Illya
are nearly killed by the local Eskimos,
but are saved by the chief's daughter,
Murphy (Tianne Gabrielle). Partridge
and his niece Victoria (Marion
Thompson) capture them, but they escape only to end up in a tavern brawl.

Prod. #7477
Airdate: December 24, 1965
Filmed: August 17–20, 23–24, 1965
Producer: David Victor
Writer: Marc Siegel
Director: Alf Kjellin
Assistant Director: E. Darrell Hallenbeck
Production Executive: Mort Abrahams
Editor: Joseph Dervin
Music: Gerald Fried, Robert Drasnin
Set Decorator: Francisco Lombardo
Rerun Date: None

#44. The Very Important Zombie Af-
fair. Solo and Illya travel to the Carib-
bean to help Dr. Delgado (Ken Renard),
who is under a voodoo curse and in a
zombielike trance thanks to the local dictator, El Supremo (Claude Akins), and
his chief of police, Captain Ramirez
(Rodolfo Acosta). The U.N.C.L.E. agents
are assisted by Suzy (Linda Gaye Scott),
an American hairdresser whom El Supremo will not let leave the island. They
eventually turn to voodoo queen Mama
Lou (Maidie Norman) to turn the tables
on him.

Prod. #8404
Airdate: December 31, 1965
Filmed: October 29, November 1–5,
1965
Producer: Mort Abrahams
Writer: Boris Ingster
Director: David Alexander

Assistant Director: Donald C. Klune
Production Executive: Boris Ingster
Editor: Joseph Dervin
Music: Gerald Fried
Set Decorator: Charles Thompson
Rerun Date: May 20, 1966

#45. The Dippy Blonde Affair.

THRUSH agent Harry Pendleton (Fabrizio Mioni) is captured and commits "suicide" with a reversible chemical, but his superior, Simon Baldinado (Robert Strauss), refuses to revive him because he is attracted to Pendleton's girlfriend, Jojo Tyler (Joyce Jameson). Solo gets Jojo to help U.N.C.L.E. retrieve the ion-projection machine Badinado has hidden at the mortuary front for THRUSH by feigning affection for Baldinado, who allows his personal plans for Jojo to affect his judgment.

Prod. #7485
Airdate: January 7, 1966
Filmed: November 9–12, 15–17, 1965
Former title: "The Very Grave Affair"
Producer: Mort Abrahams
Writer: Peter Allan Fields
Director: E. Darrell Hallenbeck
Assistant Director: Bill Finnegan
Production Executive: Boris Ingster
Editor: Bill Gulick
Music: Robert Drasnin
Set Decorator: Francisco Lombardo
Rerun Date: None

#46. The Deadly Goddess Affair.

Solo and Illya travel to Circe to intercept a drone plane carrying a load of THRUSH cash. There, they encounter THRUSH agent Colonel Hubris (Victor Buono), as well as two local girls who are looking for husbands.

Prod. #8412

Airdate: January 14, 1966
Filmed: November 18–19, 22–24, 26, 1965
Producer: Mort Abrahams
Writer: Robert Hill
Director: Seymour Robbie
Assistant Director: Wilbur Mosier
Production Executive: Boris Ingster
Editor: Ray Williford
Music: Gerald Fried
Set Decorator: Charles Thompson
Rerun Date: July 15, 1966

#47. The Birds and the Bees Affair.

THRUSH has developed, with the aid of Dr. Elias Swan (John Abbott), a strain of minute, deadly bees. THRUSH agent Mr. Mozart (John McGiver) captures Illya and Tavia Sandor (Anna Capri) and uses a high-frequency sound machine that threatens to shatter their eardrums to force Illya to take him to U.N.C.L.E. headquarters so he can release the bees. Illya does so, but Mozart is intercepted, and in a battle on a rooftop Mozart is shot and the bees get loose.

Prod. #8411
Airdate: January 21, 1966
Filmed: December 8–10, 13–15, 1965
Former title: "The Pygmalion Affair"
Producer: Mort Abrahams
Writer: Mark Weingart
Director: Alvin Ganzer
Assistant Director: Wilbur Mosier
Production Executive: Boris Ingster
Editor: Bill Gulick
Music: Robert Drasnin
Set Decorator: Jack Mills
Rerun Date: July 1, 1966

#48. The Waverly Ring Affair.

When secret "File 40" documents turn up outside headquarters, Waverly assigns Solo and Illya to find out if George Donnell

(Larry Blyden) is a double agent. Carla Drosten (Elizabeth Allen) is too anxious to accuse Donnell—and Solo must use special "Waverly rings" to try and expose the real double agent.

Prod. #8409
Airdate: January 28, 1966
Filmed: December 16–17, 20–23, 1965
Producer: Mort Abrahams
Writer: Jerry McNeely
Director: John Brahm
Assistant Director: Bill Finnegan
Production Executive: Boris Ingster
Editor: Joseph Dervin
Music: Robert Drasnin
Set Decorator: Charles Thompson
Rerun Date: July 8, 1966

#49 & #50. The Bridge of Lions Affair, parts 1 and 2. Illya investigates the mysterious disappearance of cats in

© 1964–1967 Metro-Goldwyn-Mayer, Inc.

Soho, and he and Solo discover that a salon run by Madame De Sala (Vera Miles) is a front for her plan to develop a rejuvenation process, which De Sala plans to use on the now-elderly target of her romantic desires, Sir Norman Swickert (Maurice Evans). Assisted by Joanna Sweet (Ann Elder), a nurse, they end up in the bottom of a wine press. Meanwhile, THRUSH agent Jordin (Bernard Fox) plots to obtain the process for THRUSH.

Prod. #7481, 7482 (feature version, *One of Our Spies Is Missing,* #6013)
Airdate: February 4, 11, 1966
Filmed: December 28–31, 1965, January 3–7, 10–12, 1966
Former title: "The Wounded Time Affair"
Producer: Boris Ingster
Writers: Howard Rodman (teleplay), Henry Slesar (story)
Director: E. Darrell Hallenbeck
Assistant Director: Wilbur Mosier
Production Executive: None credited
Editors: Henry Berman (Part 1), Bill Gulick (Part 2)
Music: Robert Drasnin, Gerald Fried
Set Decorator: Charles Thompson (Part 1 and feature), Jack Mills (Part 2)
Rerun Date: None

#51. The Foreign Legion Affair. Illya parachutes out of a plane carrying THRUSH code documents, but lands in the desert at an abandoned Foreign Legion post run by Captain Basil Calhoun (Howard Da Silva). Illya is accompanied by a stewardess, Barbara (Danielle DeMetz) while Solo races to find them before THRUSH does.

Prod. #8415
Airdate: February 18, 1966

Filmed: January 13–14, 17–20, 1966
Former titles: "The Beau Jest Affair,"
    "The Beau Geste Affair"
Producer: Boris Ingster
Writer: Bernie Giler
Director: John Brahm
Assistant Directors: Richard Bennett, Bill
    Finnegan
Production Executive: None credited
Editor: Joseph Dervin
Music: Gerald Fried
Set Decorator: Jack Mills
Rerun Date: September 9, 1966 (first
    half preempted by football)

#52. The Moonglow Affair.

While investigating a THRUSH plot to sabotage space shots, Solo and Illya are incapacitated by a quartzite radiation projector. Waverly assigns new trainee April Dancer (Mary Ann Mobley) along with over-the-age-of-retirement agent Mark Slate (Norman Fell) to find the antidote and destroy the plan. April infiltrates the cosmetics company of THRUSH agent Arthur Caresse (Kevin McCarthy) as a model, but she is uncovered by Caresse's sister Jean (Mary Carver).

Prod. #7490
Airdate: February 25, 1966
Filmed: November 30, December 1–3,
    6–8, 1965
Former title: "The Girl from U.N.C.L.E.
    Affair"
Producer: David Victor
Writer: Dean Hargrove
Director: Joseph Sargent
Assistant Director: Bill Finnegan
Production Executive: Boris Ingster
Editor: Henry Berman
Music: Gerald Fried
Set Decorator: Charles Thompson
Rerun Date: None

#53. The Nowhere Affair.

Solo, while searching for a secret map in Nevada, swallows an amnesia capsule just before being captured. THRUSH agents Arum Tertunian (Lou Jacobi) and Longolius (David Sheiner) try to revive his memory with a seductive female agent, Mara (Diana Hyland), while Illya races to find him before he starts to remember.

Prod. #8414
Airdate: March 4, 1966
Filmed: January 17–21, 24, 1966
Former titles: "The Contained Affair,"
    "The Corsican Affair"
Producer: Boris Ingster
Writer: Robert Hill
Director: Michael Ritchie
Assistant Director: Eddie Saeta
Production Executive: None credited
Editor: Henry Berman
Music: Robert Drasnin
Set Decorator: Charles Thompson
Rerun Date: June 24, 1966

#54. The King of Diamonds Affair.

Solo and Illya discover that the world diamond market is being affected by a gang of English criminals headed by Blodgett (Larry D. Mann), who smuggle diamonds inside pudding sold unwittingly by Victoria Pogue (Nancy Kovack). They enlist the aid of a master diamond thief, Rafael Delgado (Ricardo Montalban). Solo and Victoria end up in Brazil, with Solo tied to the front of a cannon and about to be executed.

Prod. #8410
Airdate: March 11, 1966
Filmed: January 24–28, 31, 1966
Producer: Boris Ingster
Writers: Ed Blum (story and teleplay),
    Leo Townsend (teleplay)
Director: Joseph Sargent

Assistant Director: Wilbur Mosier
Production Executive: None credited
Editor: Bill Gulick
Music: Robert Drasnin
Set Decorator: Jack Mills
Rerun Date: September 2, 1966

#55. The Project Deephole Affair.

THRUSH agent Elom (Leon Askin) tries to kidnap a geologist who has developed an earthquake-activating machine, but mistakes debt-ridden salesman Buzz Conway (Jack Weston) for the scientist. Solo and Illya let THRUSH go on thinking Conway is the scientist, while Elom lets his attraction for THRUSH agent Narcissus Darling (Barbara Bouchet) interfere with his judgment. Conway is captured, and Solo and Illya must rescue him and find the machine.

Prod. #7491
Airdate: March 18, 1966
Filmed: February 1–4, 7–8, 1966
Producer: Boris Ingster
Writer: Dean Hargrove
Director: Alex March
Assistant Director: James Sullivan
Production Executive: None credited
Editor: Joseph Dervin
Music: Gerald Fried, Robert Drasnin
Set Decorator: Charles Thompson
Rerun Date: July 22, 1966

#56. The Roundtable Affair.

Lucho Nostra (Bruce Gordon) and a group of criminals take over a tiny European country, Ingolstein, because it has no extradition treaty. Prince Frederick (Reginald Gardiner) is afraid to kick them out, so Solo convinces princess Vicky (Valora Nolan) to return and do so, only to find that she cannot because the treasury has been replaced with IOUs to Nostra for the prince's gambling debts.

Nostra arranges for permanent protection by forcing a marriage between Vicky and one of his henchmen, Artie King (Don Francks), but the two actually do fall in love. King duels Nostra, with the fate of the country riding on the outcome.

Prod. #8403
Airdate: March 25, 1966
Filmed: February 9–11, 14–16, 1966
Former titles: "The Future Affair," "The Animal Fare Affair"
Producer: Boris Ingster
Writer: Robert Hill
Director: E. Darrell Hallenbeck
Assistant Director: Wilbur Mosier
Production Executive: None credited
Editor: Henry Berman
Music: Robert Drasnin
Set Decorator: Jack Mills
Rerun Date: August 26, 1966

#57. The Bat Cave Affair.

Solo uses hillbilly clairvoyant Clemency McGill (Joan Freeman) to counter the efforts of Count Zark (Martin Landau), a vampirish THRUSH agent who plans to use radioactive bats to jam the world's radar systems from his castle. Solo and Clemency make their way to the castle with Illya, but Zark manages to release the bats.

Prod. #8418
Airdate: April 1, 1966
Filmed: February 17–18, 21–24, 1966
Former title: "The Night Flight Affair"
Producer: Boris Ingster
Writer: Jerry McNeeley
Director: Alf Kjellin
Assistant Director: Eddie Saeta
Production Executive: None credited
Editor: Bill Gulick
Music: Gerald Fried
Set Decorator: Charles Thompson

Rerun Date: August 12, 1966

Rerun Date: July 29, 1966

#58. The Minus X Affair. Solo and Illya try to protect Professor Lillian Stemmler (Eve Arden) from THRUSH after she invents a drug called Plus X, which heightens all the human senses. Unbeknownst to them, she is a THRUSH agent herself who at first co-operates willingly, then has second thoughts. But THRUSH agent Rollo (Theodore Marcuse) kidnaps her daughter Leslie (Sharon Farrell) and forces her to cooperate. The drug is given to three THRUSH agents who will attack a U.S. government plutonium plant using their superior senses, while at the same time the guards will be given a dose of Minus X, which dulls the senses.

Prod. #8419
Airdate: April 8, 1966
Filmed: February 25, 28, March 1–4, 10, 1966
Producer: Boris Ingster
Writer: Peter Allan Fields
Director: Barry Shear
Assistant Director: E. Darrell Hallenbeck
Production Executive: None credited
Editor: Joseph Dervin
Music: Gerald Fried
Set Decorator: Jack Mills

#59. The Indian Affairs Affair. THRUSH agent L. C. Carson (Joe Mantell) uses an Indian reservation as a front for his plan to assemble a hydrogen bomb, and kidnaps the tribe's chief, High Cloud (Ted DeCorsia), to ensure cooperation. Solo arranges for the chief's daughter Charisma (Angela Dorian) to return, but she ends up being kidnapped along with Solo and Illya, who is disguised as an Indian. Solo and Illya, along with a band of young Indian warriors on motorcycles, encircle Carson and his men and try to stop them before its too late.

Prod. #7492
Airdate: April 15, 1966
Filmed: March 4, 7–11, 14, 1966
Producer: Boris Ingster
Writer: Dean Hargrove
Director: Alf Kjellin
Assistant Director: Eddie Saeta
Production Executive: None credited
Editor: Henry Berman
Music: Gerald Fried
Set Decorator: Charles Thompson
Rerun Date: August 19, 1966

Note: This episode was preempted November 26, 1965, by *The Incredible World of James Bond.*

The Third Season: 1966–67

8:30 P.M. EST Fridays

For the entire season:

Producer: Boris Ingster
    Irv Pearlberg (episodes 85, 86 only)
Production Executive: None
Associate Producer: Irv Pearlberg
Assistant to the Producer: Norman
    Siegel

#60. The Her Master's Voice Affair.
Solo investigates a girl's school for the daughters of VIPs, including Miki Matsu (Victoria Young), who has valuable secret information from her father, a Japanese diplomat. THRUSH agent Jason Sutro (Joseph Ruskin) has gained the cooperation of the headmistress, Hester Partridge (Estelle Winwood). The assistant dean, Verity Burgoyne (Marianne Osborne), and all of the girl students have been brainwashed by Sutro to go into a trance upon hearing a recording of Brahms's lullaby, and are ordered to kill Solo.

Prod. #8426
Airdate: September 16, 1966

Filmed: June 23–24, 27–30, 1966
Former titles: "The Master's Voice
    Affair," "The Creme de la Creme
    Affair"
Writer: Bernie Giler
Director: Barry Shear
Assistant Director: Eddie Saeta
Editor: Ray Williford
Music: Gerald Fried
Set Decorator: Francisco Lombardo
Rerun Date: April 28, 1966

#61. The Sort-of-Do-It-Yourself-Dreadful Affair. Solo is nearly killed by a superhuman, robotlike girl, Margo Hayward (Pamela Curran), one of an army of such devices invented by Dr. Pertwee (Woodrow Parfrey) for THRUSH. Illya joins up with Margo's ex-roommate, Andy Francis (Jeannine Riley), and finds the laboratory, where a roomful of robots attack them.

Prod. #8413
Airdate: September 23, 1966
Filmed: July 13–15, 18–20, 1966
Former title: "The Dreadful Affair"
Writer: Harlan Ellison
Director: E. Darrell Hallenbeck
Assistant Director: Eddie Saeta

Editor: Bill Gulick
Music: Gerald Fried
Set Decorator: Francisco Lombardo
Rerun Date: None

#62. The Galatea Affair.

In a spoof of "My Fair Lady," Solo is recuperating from a fall into a Venice canal, Illya teams with Mark Slate to uncover Baroness Bibi de Chasseur (Joan Collins), a THRUSH money courier who has contact with the treasurer of THRUSH. They recruit a barroom entertainer, Rosy Shlagenheimer (also played by Collins), an exact double, to impersonate her. The switch is made, but in the confusion the Baroness makes another switch and poses as Rosy, then finds herself falling in love with Slate.

Prod. #8424
Airdate: September 30, 1966
Filmed: June 14–17, 20–21, 1966
Writer: Jackson Gillis
Director: E. Darrell Hallenbeck
Assistant Director: Bill Finnegan
Editor: Bill Gulick
Music: Robert Drasnin
Set Decorator: Francisco Lombardo
Rerun Date: August 4, 1967

#63. The Super-Colossal Affair.

Frank Cariago (Bernard Fein), the U.S. head of a crime syndicate, is under pressure from Uncle Giuliano (J. Carrol Naish). Cariago decides to buy a movie production directed by Sheldon Veblan (Shelley Berman) so his girlfriend, Ginger Laveer (Carol Wayne) can have the starring role. But the picture is a disguised plan to drop a bomb on the family's biggest rival—Las Vegas.

Prod. #8438
Airdate: October 7, 1966

Filmed: July 21–22, 25–28, 1966
Former title: "The Sodom and Gomorrah Affair"
Writer: Stanford Sherman
Director: Barry Shear
Assistant Director: Bill Finnegan
Editor: Ray Williford
Music: Gerald Fried
Set Decorator: Richard Pefferle
Rerun Date: September 1, 1967

#64. The Monks of St. Thomas Affair.

THRUSH agent Abbot Simon (David J. Peter) takes over the monastery at St. Thomas to use the mountain location to aim a new laser gun at a long-distance target—the Louvre in Paris. Solo visits the area and meets Andrea Fouchet (Celeste Yarnall), and together they try to stop Simon before he destroys the world's greatest art treasures.

Prod. #8429
Airdate: October 14, 1966
Filmed: June 6–10, 13, 1966
Former title: "The Monastery Affair"
Writer: Sheldon Stark
Director: Alex March
Assistant Director: Eddie Saeta
Editor: Joseph Dervin
Music: Gerald Fried
Set Decorator: Francisco Lombardo
Rerun Date: None

#65. The Pop Art Affair.

A dissatisfied THRUSH collaborator tips U.N.C.L.E. off to a new deadly hiccup gas. A pendant he wears leads Illya to Greenwich Village and an art gallery run by Mark Ole (Robert H. Harris), a THRUSH agent. Starving artist Sylvia Harrison (Sherry Alberoni) joins Illya, who is nearly suffocated at the hands of a foam-producing machine.

Prod. #8423

235

Airdate: October 21, 1966
Filmed: July 29, August 1–5, 1966
Writers: John Shaner, Al Ramus
Director: George WaGGner
Assistant Director: Richard F. Landry
Editor: Joseph Dervin
Music: Robert Drasnin
Set Decorator: Francisco Lombardo
Rerun Date: April 21, 1967

#66. The Thor Affair. Solo and Illya are assigned to protect Dr. Fazie Nahdi (Harry Davis), a Gandhi-like peace advocate, during a conference. Nellie Canford (Linda Foster), a school teacher, becomes linked to their efforts when her dental work begins receiving radio transmissions. Nahdi stays at the home of Brutus Thor (Bernard Fox), who is actually a THRUSH leader who is trying to kill him and Illya is trapped in a room full of toys that begin firing real bullets.

Prod. #8428
Airdate: October 28, 1966
Filmed: August 9–12, 15, 1966
Former title: "The Second Banana
    Affair"
Writers: Don Richman, Stanley Ralph
    Ross
Director: Sherman Marks
Assistant Director: Bill Finnegan
Editor: Bill Gulick
Music: Gerald Fried, Robert Drasnin
Set Decorator: Richard Pefferle
Rerun Date: April 21, 1967

#67. The Candidate's Wife Affair. Solo and Illya protect Miranda Bryant (Diana Hyland), the wife of a presidential candidate, from a THRUSH plot to kidnap her, not realizing that she has already been kidnapped and replaced with a double, Irina (also played by Hyland), an unwitting dupe of THRUSH. When they do catch on, the candidate, Senator Bryant (Richard Anderson), and his aide, Fairbanks (Larry D. Mann), agree to play along—but Fairbanks is the one behind the plot to put a THRUSH agent in the White House.

Prod. #8420
Airdate: November 4, 1966
Filmed: July 5–8, 11–12, 1966
Former title: "The White House Affair"
Writer: Robert Hill
Director: George WaGGner
Assistant Director: Bill Finnegan
Editor: Joseph Dervin
Music: Gerald Fried, Robert Drasnin
Set Decorator: Richard Pefferle
Rerun Date: May 5, 1967

#68. The Come with Me to the Casbah Affair. Solo and Illya go to Algiers to obtain a rare old book containing a THRUSH code from Pierrot La Mouche (Pat Harrington, Jr.) who has stolen it from his boss, Colonel Hamid (Jacques Aubuchon). But La Mouche has a high price—he wants U.N.C.L.E. to help him obtain Janine (Danielle DeMetz) whom he is in love with.

Prod. #8436
Airdate: November 21, 1966
Filmed: September 7–9, 12–14, 1966
Writer: Robert Hill (teleplay and story),
    Danielle Branton and Norman Lenzer
    (story)
Director: E. Darrell Hallenbeck
Assistant Director: Bill Finnegan
Editor: Bill Gulick
Music: Gerald Fried
Set Decorator: Keough Gleason
Rerun Date: August 11, 1967

#69. The Off-Broadway Affair. An off-broadway actress is murdered during a phone call to U.N.C.L.E., and Solo and Illya investigate a connection between the show and a sudden malfunction in U.N.C.L.E.'s communications. The understudy, Janet Jarrod (Shari Lewis), takes over the lead role, and Illya joins the cast to find the jamming device.

> Prod. #8427
> Airdate: November 18, 1966
> Filmed: September 15–16, 19–22, 1966
> Former title: "The Legit Affair"
> Writer: Jerry McNeely
> Director: Sherman Marks
> Assistant Director: Eddie Saeta
> Editor: Elmo Veron
> Music: Gerald Fried
> Set Decorator: Richard Pefferle
> Rerun Date: August 25, 1967

#70 & #71. The Concrete Overcoat Affair, parts 1 and 2. While in Italy investigating a THRUSH plan to divert the Gulf Stream with heavy water, Solo finds himself eluding THRUSH guards, and ends up hiding under the bed of Pia Monteri (Letitia Roman). Solo escapes a shotgun wedding, the family feels Pia's honor has been compromised, and the girl's American uncles, retired Prohibition-era gangsters "Fingers" Stilletto (Eduardo Giannelli), Enzo "Pretty" Stilletto (Allen Jenkins), and Federico "Feet" Stilletto (Jack LaRue) are called. At the island headquarters of Louis Strago (Jack Palance), Illya is tortured by Strago's sadistic female assistant, Miss Diketon (Janet Leigh). Solo joins forces with the Stilletto brothers to try and rescue him.

> Prod. #8433, 8434 (feature version, *The Spy in the Green Hat*, #6021)
> Airdate: November 25, December 2, 1966

Courtesy of the Norman Felton collection.

> Filmed: August 18–19, 22–26, 29–31, September 1–2, 6–7 1966
> Former title: "The Hood Affair"
> Writers: Peter Allan Fields (teleplay), David Victor (story)
> Director: Joseph Sargent
> Assistant Directors: Robert Webb, Bill Finnegan
> Editors: Ray Williford (Part 1), Joseph Dervin (Part 2)
> Music: Nelson Riddle
> Set Decorators: Richard Pefferle, Francisco Lombardo
> Rerun Date: None

#72. The Abominable Snowman Affair. Illya goes to the Himalayan country of Chupat to protect the high lama, but is shot by "Calamity" Rogers (Anne Jeffreys), an American rodeo star. Solo is sent to find Illya, and learns that the

237

prime minister (David Sheiner) has kidnapped the real successor to the throne and intends to install his own son instead. An entranced girl, Amra Palli (Pilar Seurat) tries to kill Solo after being brainwashed by the prime minister.

Prod. #8430
Airdate: December 9, 1966
Filmed: September 23, 26–29, 1966
Former title: "The Nervous Elephant Affair"
Writer: Kirshna Shah
Director: Otto Lang
Assistant Director: Bill Finnegan
Editor: Joseph Dervin
Music: Gerald Fried
Set Decorator: Keough Gleason
Rerun Date: May 12, 1967

#73. The My Friend the Gorilla Affair.

In Africa, Professor Kenton (Arthur Malet) has developed a superman formula, which he has been using on the natives, hoping to build an army with which to conquer all of Africa. Premier Khufu (Percy Rodriguez) resists the use of the drug on his people. Illya meets up with Harry Blackburn (Alan Mowbray), a shady safari guide, and Marsha Woodhugh (Joyce Jillson), who is searching for her lost sister, a Tarzan-like woman named "Girl" (Vitina Marcus) who has captured Solo.

Prod. #8440
Airdate: December 16, 1966
Filmed: October 20–21, 24–27, 1966
Former titles: "The Not So Far Safari Affair," "The African Affair"
Writers: Don Richman, Joseph Sandy
Director: Alex Singer
Assistant Director: Eddie Saeta
Editor: Ray Williford

Music: Gerald Fried
Set Decorator: Richard Pefferle
Story Consultant: Milton S. Gelman
Rerun Date: None

#74. The Jingle Bells Affair.

Solo and Illya must protect Premier Georgi Koz (Akim Tamiroff), a Khrushchev-like European leader, on a visit to New York. Priscilla Worth (Ellen Willard) is befriended by Koz and she takes him to a school for Santa Clauses run by Francis X. O'Reilly (J. Pat O Malley) where just one of a series of assassination attempts against him must be thwarted by the two U.N.C.L.E. agents.

Prod. #8443
Airdate: December 23, 1966
Filmed: November 8–11, 14–15 1966
Writer: William Fay
Director: John Brahm
Assistant Director: Eddie Saeta
Editor: Elmo Veron
Music: Gerald Fried
Set Decorator: Richard Pefferle
Story Consultant: Milton S. Gelman
Rerun Date: August 18, 1967

#75. The Take Me to Your Leader Affair.

Scientist Adrian Cool (Woodrow Parfrey) spots a UFO approaching earth on his radar. His daughter, Coco (Nancy Sinatra) is kidnapped, and Illya follows and he's captured also. Simon Sparrow (Paul Lambert), a power-mad millionaire, has faked the approaching UFO to secure power for himself as the representative on earth of the "aliens." Sparrow captures Solo and puts him in an experimental wind tunnel to kill him, but he is saved by Corinne (Whitney Blake). Coco develops a crush on Illya; while they are trying to stop Sparrow, they end up aboard his "UFO."

Prod. #8437
Airdate: December 30, 1966
Filmed: October 12–14, 17–19, 1966
Former title: "The Flying Saucer Affair"
Writer: Bernie Giler
Director: George WaGGner
Assistant Director: Bill Finnegan
Editor: Elmo Veron
Music: Nelson Riddle, Gerald Fried
Set Decorator: Keough Gleason
Rerun Date: None

#76. The Suburbia Affair.
Dr. Rutter (Victor Borge), after inventing antimatter, hides out in Suburbia under the name Willoughby because he fears his creation will be used destructively. Solo and Illya take a house there to find him. But THRUSH agent Miss Witherspoon (Reta Shaw) also wants to find Rutter, and when Rutter sends his neighbor Betsy (Beth Brickell) after some rare medicine from the pharmacist, Fletcher (Herbert Anderson), the chase is literally on to find Rutter first.

Prod. #8439
Airdate: January 6, 1967
Filmed: October 28, 31, November 1–4, 1966
Writers: Stanford Sherman (teleplay), Sheldon Gibney (story)
Director: Charles Haas
Assistant Directors: Bill Finnegan, Dick Bennett
Editor: Bill Gulick
Music: Gerald Fried
Set Decorator: Keough Gleason
Rerun Date: May 19, 1967

#77. The Deadly Smorgasbord Affair.
Solo goes to Sweden to obtain a new suspended-animation device from Dr. A. C. Nillson (Peter Brocco), but the device and its inventor are taken by THRUSH. The doctor's daughter Neila (Lynn Loring) helps Solo find him, and the doctor's assistant, Inga Anderson (Pamela Curran) also feigns cooperation but is actually working for THRUSH agent Heinrich Beckmann (Robert Emhardt). Beckmann uses the device to invade U.N.C.L.E.'s Scandinavian headquarters, and only Solo has a chance to stop him.

Prod. #8441
Airdate: January 13, 1967
Filmed: November 16–18, 21–23, 1966
Former title: "The Sad Gun Affair"
Writers: Ralph Soos, Peter Bourne
Director: Barry Shear
Assistant Director: Bill Finnegan
Editor: Ray Williford
Music: Gerald Fried, Nelson Riddle
Set Decorator: Keough Gleason
Rerun Date: June 16, 1967

#78. The Yo-Ho-Ho and a Bottle of Rum Affair.
Investigating the shipment of a tidal-wave machine by THRUSH, Illya ends up aboard a merchant vessel run by Captain Morton (Dan O'Herlihy). Morton is obsessed with his past disgrace in a court-martial, and the crew is on the verge of a mutiny, which Illya leads—just as THRUSH arrives to take possession of the device.

Prod. #8450
Airdate: January 20, 1967
Filmed: November 28–30, December 1–2, 5, 1966
Former title: "The Bounding Main Affair"
Writer: Norman Hudis
Director: E. Darrell Hallenbeck
Assistant Director: Eddie Saeta
Editor: Joseph Dervin
Music: Gerald Fried
Set Decorator: Richard Pefferle

Story Consultant: Milton S. Gelman
Rerun Date: May 26, 1967

#79. The Napoleon's Tomb Affair.

President Nasasos Tunik (Kurt Kaznar) visits Paris. His assistant, Malanez (Joseph Sirola), is determined to persuade the president that the French are his enemy, and arranges for various embarrassing and insulting incidents to occur. Solo and Illya are assigned to see that the visit goes smoothly, but Tunik falls in love with Candyce (Mercedes Moliner), and Malanez plans to disgrace Tunik by framing him in a plot to steal the body of Napoleon from his tomb.

Prod. #8431
Airdate: January 27, 1967
Filmed: October 4–7, 10–11, 1966
Former Title: "The Napoleon
    Bonaparte's Tomb Affair"
Writer: James N. Whiton
Director: John Brahm
Assistant Director: Eddie Saeta
Editor: Bill Gulick
Music: Gerald Fried
Set Decorator: Keough Gleason
Rerun Date: None

#80. The It's All Greek to Me Affair.

In Greece, Illya tries to recover stolen U.N.C.L.E. documents, but they fall into the hands of Stavros (Harold J. Stone), a Greek bandit, who has ambushed Illya, thinking he is his daughter (Linda Marsh) Kira's convict husband, Manolakas (George Keymas) returning from prison. Kira is in love with Nico (Ted Roter) instead, and Solo and Illya must resolve the love triangle in order to retrieve the documents.

Prod. #8445
Airdate: February 3, 1967

Filmed: December 6–9, 12–13, 1966
Writers: Robert Hill (teleplay), Eric Faust
    (story)
Director: George WaGGner
Assistant Director: Bill Finnegan
Editor: Bill Gulick
Music: Gerald Fried
Set Decorator: Keough Gleason
Story Consultant: Milton S. Gelman
Rerun Date: None

Note: February 10, 1967, episode
    preempted by Danny Thomas special.

#81. The Hula Doll Affair.

Brothers Simon and Peter Sweet (Jan Murray, Pat Harrington, Jr.), both rival THRUSH leaders vying for promotion, do not realize that the toy hula doll they possess has an extremely powerful new U.N.C.L.E. explosive inside that is activated by heat. As the outside temperature rises, Illya and Solo try to recover it with the help of Wendy Thyme (Grace Gaynor). Solo poses as a representative of THRUSH Central, but Mama Sweet (Patsy Kelly)—a real member of THRUSH Central—appears on the scene.

Prod. #8442
Airdate: February 17, 1967
Filmed: December 14–16, 19–21, 1966
Former Titles: "The Executive Sweets
    Affair," "The Inside THRUSH Affair"
Writer: Stanford Sherman
Director: Eddie Saeta
Assistant Director: Al Sheinberg
Editor: Ray Williford
Music: Nelson Riddle, Gerald Fried
Set Decorator: Richard Pefferle
Rerun Date: July 28, 1967

Note: Rerun of #81 scheduled for June 9,
    1967, preempted by coverage of Arab-
    Israeli war and UN proceedings.

#82. The Pieces of Fate Affair.
Jacqueline Midcult (Sharon Farrell) writes a best-selling novel, *The Pieces of Fate,* which U.N.C.L.E. recognizes as being based on a series of missing THRUSH diaries. She loses her memory during a THRUSH attempt to kill her, and THRUSH agents Ellipsis Zark (Theodore Marcuse) and Jody Moore (Grayson Hall), a book critic, plot to kidnap her and find out where she found the diaries. Solo and Illya take Jacqueline to a small town where her Uncle Charly (Charles Seel) and Aunt Jessie (Opal Evard) live, to try and revive her memory, but Zark and Moore follow and they all converge on the attic where the diaries are hidden at the same time.

Prod. #8447
Airdate: February 24, 1967
Filmed: January 4–6, 9–11, 1967
Former titles: "The Missing Diaries Affair," "The Novel Affair"
Writers: Harlan Ellison, Yale Udoff
Director: John Brahm
Assistant Director: Bill Finnegan
Editor: Ray Williford
Music: Nelson Riddle, Gerald Fried
Set Decorator: Keough Gleason
Story Consultant: Milton S. Gelman
Rerun Date: None

#83. The Matterhorn Affair. A dying man carrying a partial film with the secret of Project Quasimodo, a miniature atomic bomb, gives only one clue to finding the rest of the film: the name of Marvin Klump (Bill Dana), inept car salesman. THRUSH agents Rodney Backstreet (Oscar Beregi) and Beirut (Vito Scotti) capture Klump. Solo and Illya, with the aid of Klump's sister Heather (Norma Chase), follow them first to the Alps, then back to the U.S.,

where the answer to the puzzle lies in a cemetery.

Prod. #8449
Airdate: March 3, 1967
Filmed: January 20, 23–27, 1967
Former title: "The Long Blonde Wig Affair"
Writers: David Giler, Boris Ingster
Director: Bill Finnegan
Assistant Director: Donald Verk
Editor: Bill Gulick
Music: Gerald Fried, Nelson Riddle
Set Decorator: Don Greenwood, Jr.
Rerun Date: None

#84. The Hot Number Affair. A THRUSH code is hidden in a dress pattern, and Solo and Illya go to the garment district and encounter the design shop of two down-on-their-luck designers (George Tobias, Ned Glass) and their model, Ramona (Cher Bono) and the cutter who has a crush on her, Jerry (Sonny Bono). THRUSH also tries to retrieve the garment, but Ramona keeps forgetting where she left it.

Prod. #8456
Airdate: March 10, 1967
Filmed: January 12–13, 16–19, 1967
Former title: "The Fashion House Affair"
Writers: Joseph and Carol Cavanaugh
Director: George WaGGner
Assistant Director: Al Sheinberg
Editor: Joseph Dervin
Music: Gerald Fried
Set Decorator: Richard Pefferle
Rerun Date: June 30, 1967

#85. The When in Roma Affair. In Rome, American tourist Darlene Sims (Julie Sommars) becomes the unwitting carrier of a perfume atomizer with a secret formula. THRUSH uses a suave ladies' man, Cesare Guardia (Cesare Danova) to charm Darlene, but he falls in love with her in the process.

> Prod. #8445
> Airdate: March 17, 1967
> Filmed: January 31, February 1–3, 6–7, 1967
> Writer: Gloria Elmore
> Director: George WaGGner
> Assistant Director: John Banse
> Editor: Ray Williford
> Music: Nelson Riddle, Gerald Fried, Robert Drasnin
> Set Decorator: Richard Pefferle
> Rerun Date: July 7, 1967

#86. The Apple a Day Affair. Solo and Illya find that THRUSH agent Colonel Picks (Robert Emhardt) has developed exploding apples, which will be used to trigger a nuclear stockpile. Nina Lillette (Jeanine Riley), a pretty hillbilly girl, latches onto them for excitement. Illya joins a picking crew at the farm, but he is buried alive in a tunnel with the volatile apples.

> Prod. #8453
> Airdate: March 24, 1967
> Filmed: February 8–10, 13–15, 1967
> Writers: Joseph Calvelli, Les Roberts
> Director: E. Darrell Hallenbeck
> Assistant Director: Bill Finnegan
> Editor: Joseph Dervin
> Music: Gerald Fried
> Set Decorator: Don Greenwood, Jr.
> Story Consultant: Milton S. Gelman
> Rerun Date: July 14, 1967

#87 & #88. The Five Daughters Affair, parts 1 and 2. Solo and Illya visit the laboratory of Dr. True (Jim Boles), who has discovered how to extract gold from seawater. But Dr. True dies from a poison given him by THRUSH agent

Randolph (Herbert Lom), and Randolph also kills his wife, Amanda (Joan Crawford). The gold-extraction formula was distributed in portions by True to his daughters, in inscriptions on a photo of himself. Solo and Illya meet Sandy True (Kim Darby), who accompanies them to: Rome, to find her half-sister Margo (Diane McBain), now unhappily married to the destitute Baron de Fanzini (Telly Savalas); London, to find the next sister, Imogen (Jill Ireland), who has been arrested by a Constable (Terry-Thomas) for indecent exposure; and finally the Alps, to find Yvonne (Danielle DeMetz), who is breaking off an unhappy relationship with Karl Von Kesser (Curt Jurgens). But after decoding the message in Japan, Solo, Illya, and Sandy

Napoleon Solo fights for his life. *Courtesy of the Norman Felton collection.*

are captured by Randolph and taken to THRUSH Central for execution.

> Prod. #8457, 8458 (feature version, *The Karate Killers,* #6025)
> Airdate: March 31, April 7, 1967
> Filmed: February 17, 20–24, 27–28, March 1–3, 6–9, 1967
> Former title: "The Five Women Affair"
> Writers: Boris Ingster, Norman Hudis
> Director: Barry Shear
> Assistant Director: Bill Finnegan
> Editors: Ray Williford (Part 1), Bill Gulick (Part 2)
> Music: Nelson Riddle, Gerald Fried, Robert Drasnin
> Set Decorators: Richard Pefferle, Don Greenwood, Jr.
> Story Consultant: Milton S. Gelman
> Rerun Date: None

#89. The Cap and Gown Affair. Solo and Illya are responsible for the security during Waverly's upcoming address to his alma mater, but the campus is seething with protest. Illya joins the demonstrators, and meets Minerva Dwight (Carole Shelyne), the daughter of the dean (Henry Jones). The head of the board of regents, Jonathan Trumble (Larry Mann), is a THRUSH agent, and he hires campus agitator Gregory Haymish (Zalman King) to try and kill Solo and Illya, while Trumbull's THRUSH superior, Number 24 (Tom Palmer), undergoes plastic surgery so he can impersonate the dean during the ceremony and kill Waverly himself.

> Prod. #8459
> Airdate: April 14, 1967
> Filmed: March 10, 13–17, 1967
> Writer: Stanford Sherman
> Director: George WaGGner
> Assistant Director: Eddie Saeta
> Editor: Joseph Dervin
> Music: Nelson Riddle, Gerald Fried
> Set Decorator: Don Greenwood, Jr.
> Story Consultant: Milton S. Gelman
> Rerun Date: July 21, 1967

Note: Rerun preempted June 2, 1967, by special, *Welcome to Japan, Mr. Bond.*

The Fourth Season: 1967–68

8:00 P.M. EST Mondays

For the entire season:

Producer: Anthony Spinner
Associate Producers: George Lehr, Irv Pearlberg

There was no production executive in the fourth season. Since the series was canceled, there were no reruns.

#90. The Summit Five Affair. Visiting Berlin headquarters in preparation for a high-level U.N.C.L.E. conference, "Summit Five," Solo finds agent Heinz Newman (Don Chastain) mysteriously murdered. Illya goes to Berlin, as does Harry Beldon (Albert Dekker), one of Waverly's counterparts in Section I. Beldon suspects that either Solo or Gerald Struthers (Lloyd Bochner) committed the murder, while Illya suspects Beldon's secretary Helga Deniken (Suzanne Cramer), but Beldon himself turns out to be the traitor, and he plans to kill Waverly at the conference.

Prod. #8483
Airdate: September 11, 1967

Filmed: July 21, 24–28, 1967
Former title: "The Heir Apparent Affair"
Writer: Robert E. Thompson
Director: Sutton Roley
Assistant Director: Donald Verk
Editor: Bill Gulick
Music: Richard Shores
Set Decorator: Richard Spero

#91. The Test Tube Killer Affair. In Mexico, Solo and Illya are nearly killed by an eighteen-year-old "superman," Greg Martin (Christopher Jones), trained by THRUSH agent Dr. Steller (Paul Lukas) to destroy a village to demonstrate what graduates of Steller's special school can do for THRUSH. After outwitting Solo and Illya's attempts to stop him, Martin starts to fall in love with Christine Hobson (Lynn Loring) and must decide between her and his mission for THRUSH.

Prod. #8468
Airdate: September 18, 1967
Filmed: June 15–16, 19–22, 1967
Writer: Jack Turley
Director: E. Darrell Hallenbeck

Assistant Director: Glenn N. Cook
Editor: John Rogers
Music: Gerald Fried
Set Decorator: Richard Pefferle

#92. The J for Judas Affair.
Solo and Illya are asked by Adam Tenza (Chad Everett) to protect his millionaire industrialist father Mark Tenza (Broderick Crawford) from assassination by THRUSH, much to the resentment of the elder Tenza. When Tenza is killed by a bomb, Solo and Illya must find out where J—Tenza's other son, James— is, to protect him also. But Adam Tenza is actually planning to kill J, in order to hand his father's empire over to THRUSH.

Prod. #8464
Airdate: September 25, 1967
Filmed: June 23, 26–30, 1967
Former title: "The J Affair"
Writer: Norman Hudis
Director: Alf Kjellin
Assistant Director: Maurice Vaccarino
Editor: Bill Gulick
Music: Richard Shores
Set Decorator: James I. Berkey

#93 & #94. The Prince of Darkness Affair, parts 1 and 2.
Solo and Illya are assigned to investigate a mysterious ray from the sky that killed the inhabitants of an African village. They find expert safecracker and fugitive from justice Luther Sebastian (Bradford Dillman), now a leader of a cult called the Third Way, and enlist his help in their plan to break into the safe of Parviz Kharmusi (John Dehner) and steal the thermal prism that powers that deadly ray. Solo runs into Annie Justin (Carol Lynley), who is also looking for Sebastian, who framed her boyfriend. Azalea (Lola Al-

bright) helps Solo escape from Annie, and takes him to Kharmusi. But Sebastian reveals he has stolen the prism for himself so he can put it into orbit and extort the world.

Prod. #8467, 8477 (feature version, *The Helicopter Spies*, #6026)
Airdates: October 2, 9, 1967
Filmed: August 9–11, 14–18, 21–25, 28–29, 1967
Former title: "The Search and Destroy Affair"
Writer: Dean Hargrove
Director: Boris Sagal
Assistant Director: Glen S. Cook
Editors: Joseph Dervin (Part 1), Jack Rogers (Part 2)
Music: Richard Shores
Set Decorators: James I. Berkey, Hugh Hunt

#95. The Master's Touch Affair.
In Portugal, Solo is taken prisoner by Pharos Mandor (Jack Lord), a THRUSH chief ready to defect if his archrival, THRUSH assassin Stepan Valandros (Nehemiah Persoff), does not kill him first. Solo meets Mandor's girlfriend, Cathy Welling (Leslie Parrish). Mandor tells Solo U.N.C.L.E. must kill Valandros or he will not defect, but his real aim is to eliminate Valandros and promote himself up the THRUSH ranks.

Prod. #8470
Airdate: October 16, 1967
Filmed: July 13–14, 17–20, 1967
Former title: "The Lisbon Affair"
Writer: Boris Sobelman
Director: John Brahm
Assistant Director: Maurice Vaccarino
Editor: John Rogers
Music: Richard Shores
Set Decorator: James I. Berkey

#96. The THRUSH Roulette Affair.

THRUSH agent Barnaby Partridge (Michael Rennie) uses his island gambling casino to brainwash VIPs into committing suicide by playing on their secret fears. U.N.C.L.E. sends Taggart Coleman (Charles Drake) to the island to help Solo and Illya uncover the process, and he encounters an old love interest there, Monica (Nobu McCarthy). But Partridge takes Illya prisoner and subjects him to the process—training him to kill Solo.

Prod. #8471
Airdate: October 23, 1967
Filmed: July 5–7, 10–12, 1967
Former title: "The Deadly Club Affair"
Writer: Arthur Weingarten
Director: Sherman Marks
Assistant Director: Glenn N. Cook
Editor: Joseph Dervin
Music: Richard Shores
Set Decorator: Richard Spero

#97. The Deadly Quest Affair.

Illya, recuperating in the hospital, is kidnapped by an old enemy, Viktor Karmak (Darrin McGavin), to lure Solo into a trap. Solo follows a clue to a twelve-block condemned area of Manhattan, and finds modern artist Sheila Van Tillson (Marlyn Mason). Karmak appears and announces that Solo has until dawn to find Illya before a deadly gas kills him, while Karmak and his pet jaguar will try to hunt Solo down at the same time.

Prod. #8467
Airdate: October 30, 1967
Filmed: June 7–9, 12–14, 1967
Former title: "The Manhattan Affair"
Writer: Robert E. Thompson
Director: Alf Kjellin
Assistant Director: Maurice Vaccarino

Editor: Joseph Dervin
Music: Jerry Goldsmith
Set Director: James I. Berkey

#98. The Fiery Angel Affair.

In a Latin American country, Illya and Solo try to help the popular national leader, Angela (Madlyn Rhue) protect her government from the Secret Three, a revolutionary group backed by THRUSH. Solo is captured by the Secret Three, but escapes after learning that Vinay (Victor Ludlin), a friend of Angela's, is plotting against her. He tells her husband, General Abaca (Joe Sirola), but the general is actually the one plotting to overthrow his wife's government and have her killed.

Prod. #8469
Airdate: November 6, 1967
Filmed: September 8, 11–15, 1967
Former titles: "The Boomerang Affair,"
    "The White Queen Affair"
Writer: John W. Bloch
Director: Richard Benedict
Assistant Director: Dick Bennett
Editor: Harry Knapp
Music: Richard Shores
Set Decorator: Joseph Stone

Note: November 13, 1967, episode preempted by Ice Follies special.

#99. The Survival School Affair.

Illya goes to U.N.C.L.E.'s secret island training academy, the Survival School, to help Jules Cutter (Richard Beymer) find a THRUSH infiltrator who has assassinated a trainee. Suspicion focuses on three trainees—Melissa Hargrove (Susan Odin), John Saimes (Chris Robinson), and Harry Williams (Charles McGraw), and Illya must find out who is the real double agent.

Prod. #8474
Airdate: November 20, 1967
Filmed: September 28–29, October 2–5,
  1967
Former title: "The Training School
  Affair"
Writers: Donald A. Brinkley (teleplay),
  Jack Turley (story and teleplay)
Director: Charles Rondeau
Assistant Director: Dick Bennett
Editor: Jack Rogers
Music: Richard Shores
Set Decorator: Joseph Stone

#100. The Gurnius Affair. Solo and
Illya go to visit a Nazi war criminal in
prison, Von Etske (Will Kulova), but find
he has escaped with the aid of a special
thought-controlling device. His escape
was observed by photographer Terry
Cook (Judy Carne). Von Etske is joining
forces with Zorgon Gurnius (George
Macready), a fellow former Nazi, and
Nexor (David McCallum), the son of another former Nazi, to reactivate their
wartime triumvirate. Illya intercept
Nexor, and finds that he is his exact double. He decides to impersonate Nexor to
foil the plan.

Prod. #8463
Airdate: November 27, 1967
Filmed: October 6, 9–13, 1967
Writer: Milton S. Gelman
Director: Barry Shear
Assistant Director: Maurice Vaccarino
Editor: Bill Gulick
Music: Richard Shores
Set Decorator: James I. Berkey

**#101. The Man from THRUSH Af-
fair.** Solo and agent Andreas Petros
(Robert Wolders) are sent to the island
of Irbos, where THRUSH has been
spending huge amounts of money on

Courtesy of the Norman Felton collection.

some unknown project. Solo, posing as a
visiting THRUSH official, meets Dr. Killman (John Larch), the head of the project, and Marnya (Barbara Luna), who
reveals that Killman is working on an
earthquake device, as the real THRUSH
emissary arrives.

Prod. #8485
Airdate: December 4, 1967
Filmed: September 18–22, 25, 1967
Former title: "The Armageddon Affair"
Writer: Robert I. Holt
Director: James Sheldon
Assistant Director: Maurice Vaccarino
Editor: Joseph Dervin
Music: Richard Shores
Set Decorator: Joseph Stone

Note: December 11, 1967, episode
  preempted by Nancy Sinatra special.

247

#102. The Maze Affair. Oliver Barnes (Lawrence Montaigne), a THRUSH agent, unsuccessfully tries to destroy U.N.C.L.E. headquarters with a bomb in a package. Solo and Illya suspect a connection between this and a new "molecutronic gun" developed by Dr. Fabray (William Marshall). Solo runs into Abbe Melton (Anna Capri). Fabray turns out to be a THRUSH collaborator. The entire scheme was a plan to get Illya to take the "gun," actually a bomb, into U.N.C.L.E. headquarters in Trojan Horse fashion.

Prod. #8480
Airdate: December 18, 1967
Filmed: July 31, August 1–4, 7, 1967
Writer: Leonard Stadd
Director: John Brahm
Assistant Director: Maurice Vaccarino
Editors: Albert Wilson, Joseph Dervin
Music: Richard Shores
Set Decorator: James I. Berkey

#103. The Deep Six Affair. In London, U.N.C.L.E. agent Brian Morton (Peter Bromilow) is planning on getting married, much to Waverly's disapproval. Solo and Illya help Morton on his current mission, stopping THRUSH agent Commander Kroler (Alfred Ryder) from stealing the plans for a new supersubmarine. Waverly tries to dissuade Laura Adams (Diana Van Der Vlis), Morton's fiancée, but to no avail. Morton and Laura are then kidnapped by Kroler, and Kroler threatens to kill Laura if Morton does not obtain the sub for him.

Prod. #8488
Airdate: December 25, 1967
Filmed: August 30–31, September 5–7, 1967
Former title: "The Judas Goat Affair"

Writer: Leonard Stadd
Director: E. Darrell Hallenbeck
Assistant Director: Maurice Vaccarino
Editor: Bill Gulick
Music: Richard Shores
Set Decorator: Joseph Stone

Note: January 1, 1968, episode preempted by Orange Bowl football game.

#104 & #105. The Seven Wonders of the World Affair, parts 1 and 2. Mr. Webb (Mark Richman), a THRUSH agent, and Margitta Kingsley (Eleanor Parker), the wife of U.N.C.L.E. agent Robert Kingsley (Barry Sullivan), plot to steal a docility gas from General Maximilian Harmon (Leslie Nielsen), who

Robert Vaughn poses for an U.N.C.L.E. holiday greeting. *Courtesy of the Norman Felton collection.*

has kidnapped Professor David Garrow (Dan O'Herlihy) and his son Steve (Tony Bill). Harmon and a group of scientists consider themselves the "Seven Intellectual Wonders of the World" and, with the gas and the troops, plan to take over control of the world and ensure peace.

Prod. #8465, 8484 (feature version, *How to Steal the World,* #6027)
Airdates: January 8, 15, 1968

Filmed: October 16–20, 23–27, 30–31, November 1–3, 6–8, 1967
Former titles: "The Three Eyes Affair," "The 72 Hours Affair," "The To Be or Not to Be Affair"
Writer: Norman Hudis
Director: Sutton Roley
Assistant Director: Maurice Vaccarino
Editors: Harry Knapp (Part 1), Joseph Dervin (Part 2)
Music: Richard Shores
Set Decorator: Joseph Stone

Credits: *The Girl from U.N.C.L.E. 1966–67*

7:30 P.M. EST Tuesdays

For the entire season:

Executive Producer: Norman Felton
U.N.C.L.E. Format Developed by: Sam Rolfe
Producer: Douglas Benton
Associate Producers: George Lehr, Max Hodge
Supervising Producer: David Victor
Supervising Film Editor: John Dunning
Recording Supervisor: Franklin Milton
Director of Photography: Harkness Smith
Music Supervisor: Al Mack *
(Supervising) Set Decorator: Henry Grace
(Supervising) Art Director: George Davis
Art Director: Charles K. Hagedon
U.N.C.L.E. theme by: Jerry Goldsmith

* All supervising positions for *Girl* were the same as on *Man* with this exception; Henry Lojewski supervised the music for the first episode.

#1. The Dog Gone Affair. Apollo

Zakinthios (Kurt Kaznar) plans to use Apathane, a slow-motion gas, for THRUSH. He tests it on a Greek island, and April Dancer jets to the island with a dachshund whose fleas carry the antidote. Mark makes friends with lovely Tuesday Hajadakis (Luciana Paluzzi). April loses the dog. She is captured by Apollo, and hung over a piranha pit.

Prod. #8622
Airdate: September 13, 1966
Writer: Tony Barrett
Director: Barry Shear
Assistant Director: Ray DeCamp
Editor: John Rogers
Music: Dave Grusin
Set Decorator: Richard Spero
Rerun: April 18, 1967

#2. The Prisoner of Zalamar Affair.

April masquerades as Princess Fatima when the vizier (Michael Ansara) of Zalamar murders the sheik to gain power for himself.

Prod. #8611
Airdate: September 20, 1966
Writer: Max Hodge
Director: Herschel Daugherty

Assistant Director: Ray DeCamp
Editor: Albert P. Wilson
Music: Richard Shores
Set Decorator: Richard Spero
Rerun: April 25, 1967

#3. The Mother Muffin Affair.

Mother Muffin (Boris Karloff) and Rodney (Bernard Fox) head a group of murderers who try to keep April and Solo from returning the daughter of Vito Pomade (Bruce Gordon) to the U.S., his price for testifying against a criminal organization. A haypenny for a fortune machine is the clue to the girl's location. Mother intends to make wax figures of Solo and April.

Prod. #8624
Airdate: September 27, 1966
Writer: Joseph Calvelli
Director: Sherman Marks
Assistant Director: Ray DeCamp
Editor: Jack Kampschroer
Music: Dave Grusin
Set Director: Richard Spero
Rerun: May 2, 1967

#4. The Mata Hari Affair.

April assumes the identity of Marta Hurens, an exotic dancer killed while carrying vital information for U.N.C.L.E., in a new play about Mata Hari. Mark bluffs that he has a photo of the killer and the director, Sir Terrance Keats (Edward Mulhare), panics and tries to kill both of them.

Prd. #8617
Airdate: October 4, 1966
Writer: Samuel Peeples
Director: Joseph Sargent
Assistant Director: Ray Decamp
Editor: John Rogers
Music: Dave Grusin

Set Decorator: Richard Spero
Rerun: May 9, 1967

#5. The Montori Device Affair.

April poses as a buyer to get next to fashion model Chu-Chu (Dee Hartford), who April suspects knows something of a new THRUSH device that is destroying U.N.C.L.E.'s communications. Mark disguises himself as a policeman guarding fashion designer Conrad Brassano (Edward Andrews), a THRUSH agent. Brassano arranges a special showing for a VIP and his wife, at which Professor Budge (John Carradine) uses a special tuning fork to hypnotize him into helping plot the assassination of several world leaders at an upcoming meeting.

Prod. #8601
Airdate: October 11, 1966
Writer: Boris Sobelman
Director: John Brahm
Assistant Director: Dick Bennett
Editor: John Rogers
Music: Richard Shores
Set Decorator: James Berkey
Rerun: None

#6. The Horns of the Dilemma Affair.

THRUSH kidnaps three scientists who have developed a high-speed rocket. April goes to the home of Alejandro DeSada (Fernando Lamas), a THRUSH agent in Mexico, and runs afoul of Sarita (Sandra Sullivan), DeSada's jealous girlfriend. Desada finds out April is a spy and tries to kill her in the bullring.

Prod. #8606
Airdate: October 18, 1966
Writer: Tony Barrett
Director: John Brahm
Assistant Director: Dick Bennett
Editor: Jack Kampschroer

Music: Jack Marshall
Set Decorator: James Berkey
Rerun: None

#7. The Danish Blue Affair.
Stanley Umlaut (Dom DeLuise), a master imposter, accidentally eats a Danish blue cheese dressing with a microdot for a Sonic Propulsion Underwater Demolition weapon developed by THRUSH to destroy a ship, the *Remos*. Ole Bergman (Lloyd Bochner), the THRUSH head of the operation, has Stanley kidnapped for surgical removal of the dot, and April must try to rescue Stanley before the surgery.

Prod. #8615
Airdate: October 25, 1966
Writer: Arthur Weingarten
Director: Mitchell Leisen
Assistant Director: Dick Bennett
Editor: Jack Kampschroer
Music: Richard Shores
Set Decorator: James Berkey
Rerun: August 22, 1967

#8. The Garden of Evil Affair.
An ancient cult plans to kidnap Greta Wolf (Sabrina Scharf), the only descendent of their founder, so they can reincarnate him into her body with a new serum that both THRUSH and U.N.C.L.E. want. April poses as Greta and is taken to a Middle East tomb, where she is about to become their doomed guinea pig.

Prod. #8607
Airdate: November 1, 1966
Writers: John O'Dea, Arthur Rowe
Director: Jud Taylor
Assistant Director: Dick Bennett
Editor: Albert R. Wilson
Music: Jeff Alexander, Dave Grusin, Richard Shores

Set Decorator: James Berkey
Rerun: None

Note: November 8, 1966, episode preempted by election coverage.

#9. The Atlantis Affair.
April and Mark encounter Professor Antrum (Sidney Blackmer), who maintains he has found the entrance to Atlantis, as well as some deadly laser crystals there that THRUSH wants, on the estate of Honore Le Gallows (Claude Woolman), an eccentric who pretends it's the seventeenth century. Vic Ryan (Denny Miller) takes them to Le Gallows, where April ends up in a sword duel with Le Gallows.

Prod. #8609
Airdate: November 15, 1966
Writer: Richard Matheson
Director: E. Darrell Hallenbeck
Assistant Director: Dick Bennett
Editor: John Rogers
Music: Dave Grusin, Richard Shores
Set Decorator: James Berkey
Rerun: August 15, 1967

#10. The Paradise Lost Affair.
April and Mark, investigating a THRUSH ship, become shipwrecked on Lost Paradise Island, inhabited by several eccentrics led by Genghis Gomez VIII (Monte Landis). April is forced to marry Liverpool 'Enry (Chips Rafferty), but THRUSH agents arrive and she finds herself in an even worse predicament.

Prod. #8621
Airdate: November 22, 1966
Former titles: None
Writers: John O'Dea and Arthur Rowe
Director: Alf Kjellin
Assistant Director: Ray DeCamp
Editor: Albert P. Wilson
Music: Dave Grusin, Richard Shores

Set Decorator: James Berkey
Rerun: May 16, 1967

#11. The Lethal Eagle Affair. Franz-Joseph (Michael Wilding) develops a molecular reorganizer for THRUSH agent Gita Volander (Margaret Leighton). Count Egon (Cesare Danova), another THRUSH agent, takes a liking to April, who poses as a lab assistant. Gita takes April to a local discotheque to find a human subject, Dieter (Brian Avery), for the device. But what none of them know is that the machine destroys matter instead of transporting it.

Prod. #8626
Airdate: November 29, 1966
Writer: Robert Hill
Director: John Brahm
Assistant Director: Ray DeCamp
Editor: Jack Kampschroer
Music: Dave Grusin, Richard Shores
Set Decorator: James Berkey
Rerun: May 23, 1967

#12. The Romany Lie Affair. Sadvaricci (Lloyd Bochner), a gypsy circus owner, murders several wealthy women after a fortune teller, Mama Rosha (Gladys Cooper), advises them to sell their stock. April joins the circus as an aerialist, but a jealous sharpshooter named Panthea (Anna Mizrahi) twice tries to kill her. Mark, as a clown, tries to help April, who ends up locked in a cage with an angry bear.

Prod. #8630
Airdate: December 6, 1966
Writer: Tony Barrett
Director: Richard Sarafian
Assistant Director: Dick Bennett
Editor: John Rogers
Music: Dave Grusin, Richard Shores

Set Decorator: Richard Spero
Rerun: May 30, 1967

#13. The Little John Doe Affair. April is assigned to protect Joey Celeste (Pernell Roberts), a witness in a rackets case. But Little John Doe (Wally Cox), a mild-mannered assassin, is hired to see that he does not testify. Celeste becomes attracted to April, who finds herself returning the feelings.

Prod. #8628
Airdate: December 13, 1966
Writer: Joseph Calvelli
Director: Leo Penn
Assistant Director: Dick Bennett
Editor: Jack Kampschroer
Music: Dave Grusin, Richard Shores
Set Decorator: Richard Spero
Rerun: None

#14. The Jewels of Topango Affair. April and Mark set off for Topango, a jewel-rich African nation, to help protect its treasury. But Natasha Brimstone (Leslie Uggams) poses as an U.N.C.L.E. agent in April's place. Prince Nicholas (Booker Bradshaw) takes a liking to Natasha, who is actually part of the plot to steal the jewels. Mark is sentenced to die when his cover is blown.

Prod. #8614
Airdate: December 20, 1966
Former title: "The Jewels of Ubango Affair"
Writer: Berne Giler
Director: John Brahm
Assistant Director: Arthur Jacobsen
Editor: Albert P. Wilson
Music: Dave Grusin, Richard Shores
Set Decorator: Richard Spero
Rerun: None

#15. The Faustus Affair. A satanic character named B. Elsie Bubb (Raymond Massey) offers to grant any wish in exchange for a color-extracting machine developed by Professor Quantum (Tom Bosley). Bubb intends to use the device to turn the world's art treasures white. Bosley falls in love with April, who is assigned to stop Bubb.

Prod. #8613
Airdate: December 27, 1966
Writer: Jerry McNeely
Director: Barry Shear
Assistant Director: Dick Bennett
Editor: Albert P. Wilson
Music: Dave Grusin, Richard Shores
Set Decorator: Richard Spero
Rerun: None

#16. The U.F.O. Affair. April is kidnapped because she knows the identity of a crime figure planning to loot the gold treasury of Kuwait, Salim ibn Hydari (Fernando Lamas). He takes her to his harem in Africa. Mark poses as a reporter and goes to the harem, and with the help of harem girl Nur (Janet MacLachlan) tries to rescue April.

Prod. #8623
Airdate: January 3, 1967
Writer: Warren Duff
Director: Barry Shear
Assistant Director: Ray DeCamp
Editor: Jack Kampschroer
Music: Dave Grusin, Richard Shores
Set Decorator: James Berkey
Rerun: None (June 6, 1967, rerun was preempted by All-Star baseball game)

#17. The Moulin Ruse Affair. Dr. Toulouse (Shelley Berman) has developed Vitamin Q, a super-strength pill, and blackmails U.N.C.L.E. after demonstrating its power. Mark visits Toulouse's friend Nadia Marcolescu (Yvonne DeCarlo), but Toulouse arrives and tries to use him as a guinea pig for the pill.

Prod. #8610
Airdate: January 17, 1967
Writers: Jay Sims, Fred Eggers
Director: Barry Shear
Assistant Director: Ray DeCamp
Editor: John Rogers
Music: Dave Grusin, Richard Shores
Set Decorator: James Berkey
Rerun: June 13, 1967

#18. The Catacomb and Dogma Affair. Prince Boriarsi (Eduardo Ciannelli) plans to loot the Vatican treasury, but captures April when she investigates. Mark frees April, but in the process a young girl who helped him, Adriana Rafaelli (Danielle DeMetz), is captured, and Mark and April return to rescue her.

Prod. #8629
Airdate: January 24, 1967
Former titles: "The Curia Affair"
Writer: Warren Duff
Director: E. Darrell Hallenbeck
Assistant Director: Dick Bennett
Editor: Jack Kampschroer
Music: Dave Grusin, Richard Shores
Set Decorator: Richard Sepro
Rerun: June 20, 1967

Note: This episode was preempted January 10, 1967, for President Johnson's State of the Union address.

#19. The Drublegratz Affair. In Drublegratz, Princess Rapunzel (Patricia Barry) pays Dr. Gork (Vito Scotti) to assassinate Prince Efram (Christopher Held) so she can take over the country. April, as a go-go dancer, and Mark, as a musician, discover that Gork has written a particular song that will cause a glacier to avalanche and kill the prince.

Prod. #8625
Airdate: January 31, 1967
Writer: Boris Sobelman
Director: Mitchell Leisen
Assistant Director: Ray DeCamp
Editor: Albert P. Wilson
Music: Dave Grusin, Richard Shores
Song: "My Bulgarian Baby," lyrics by
    Doug Benton and Boris Sobelman
Set Decorator: Richard Spero
Rerun: June 27, 1967

#20. The Fountain of Youth Affair.

Baroness Ingrid Blangsted (Gena Rowlands) uses a rejuvenation serum to get power over world leaders through their vain wives at her beauty spa. April and Mark follow Madame Dao (Miiko Taka), the wife of a head of state, to the spa and the baroness injects Mark with a serum that makes him eighty years old.

Prod. #8605
Airdate: February 7, 1967
Writers: Robert Bloch, Richard DeRoy
Director: E. Darrell Hallenbeck
Assistant Director: Dick Bennett
Editor: Jack Kampschroer
Music: Dave Grusin, Richard Shores
Set Decorator: Richard Spero
Rerun: July 4, 1967

#21. The Carpathian Caper Affair.

Mother Magda, a THRUSH agent operating as a soup canner, plans to replace world leaders with exact doubles. Mark obtains a tape of her plan, but newlywed Shirley Fummer (Joyce Jameson) thinks he is a spy for her father, who disapproves of her marriage to Herbert Fummer (Stan Freberg), and takes the tape.

Stefanie Powers and Arnold Goode pose with items from the propwagon.
© *1964–1967 Metro-Goldwyn-Mayer, Inc.*

April arrives to help Mark, and she and Herbert are put into a giant toaster.

Prod. #8631
Airdate: February 14, 1967
Writer: Arthur Weingarten
Director: Barry Shear
Assistant Director: Ray DeCamp
Editor: John Rogers
Music: Dave Grusin, Richard Shores
Set Decorator: James Berkey
Rerun: July 18, 1967

#22. The Furnace Flats Affair.
THRUSH wants to obtain laser crystals from a gold mine, which has been left by a prospector to whomever can reenact his mother's ride across Death Valley in the 1800s. Packer Jo (Peggy Lee) holds a race between April, THRUSH agent Dolly X (Ruth Roman), and Ladybug Byrd (Susan Browning) to determine the winner.

Prod. #8603
Airdate: February 21, 1967
Writer: Archie Tegland
Director: Barry Shear
Assistant Director: Ray DeCamp
Editor: John Rogers
Music: Dave Grusin
Set Decorator: James Berkey
Rerun: None

#23. The Low Blue C Affair.
Soyil Irosian (Broderick Crawford), a retired gangster in line for the throne of a small country, plans to kill Major Stella (Hermione Gingold), a charity worker and the only other heir ahead of him. Waverly convinces Stella to assume the throne, but Soyil appears and wants to duel her for the position—with a rigged roulette wheel.

Prod. #8632
Airdate: February 28, 1967
Former title: "The Beauty Is Truth Affair"
Writers: Berne and David Giler
Director: Barry Shear
Assistant Director: Ray DeCamp
Editor: Albert P. Wilson
Music: Dave Grusin, Richard Shores
Set Decorator: James Berkey
Rerun: July 25, 1967

#24. The Petit Prix Affair.
April and Mark go to the site of the Petit Prix race in France to intercept a planned hijacking of a truckload of U.S. money. April encounters Professor Pamplemousse (Marcel Hillaire) and Desiree d'Oeuf (Nanette Fabray), who head a group of commandos who are masterminding the heist as a training exercise. The money is put into a hot-air balloon for the getaway, and April, Mark, and several others pursue it in the go-carts of the Petit Prix.

Prod. #8634
Airdate: March 7, 1967
Writer: Robert Hill
Director: Mitchell Leisen
Assistant Director: Ray DeCamp
Editors: Jack Kampschroer, David Gill
Music: Dave Grusin, Richard Shores
Set Decorator: James Berkey
Rerun: August 1, 1967

#25. The Phi Beta Killer Affair.
When a crime syndicate leader is killed by his own bodyguard, Mark enlists in the bodyguard school run by Sir Cecil Seabrook (Victor Buono) and Miss Bessie Twickum (Lynn Bari). April learns from stripper Ida Marx (Barbara Nichols) that the slain man was setting up the world's richest poker game, where Seabrook and Twickum plan to kill the players with their bodyguards and steal the lucrative pot.

Prod. #8619
Airdate: March 14, 1967
Writer: Jackson Gillis
Director: Barry Shear
Assistant Director: Dick Bennett
Editor: John Rogers
Music: Dave Grusin, Richard Shores
Set Decorator: Richard Spero
Rerun: None

#26. The Double-O-Nothing Affair.

Mark secrets a tape of valuable THRUSH information in a car, but loses it when the car drives off. The owner of the car, Sydney Morgan (Sorrell Booke), places an ad in the paper, saying the tape is for sale. April finds Sydney, but they are both captured by THRUSH leader George Kramer (Ed Asner).

> Prod. #8638
> Airdate: March 21, 1967
> Writer: Dean Hargrove
> Director: John Brahm
> Assistant Director: Dick Bennett
> Editor: Albert P. Wilson
> Music: Dave Grusin, Richard Shores
> Set Decorator: Richard Sepro
> Rerun: August 8, 1967

#27. The U.N.C.L.E. Samurai Affair.

In Hawaii, April and Mark seek a Japanese war criminal by contacting his sister, Sumata (Signe Hasso). They discover a stolen submarine, and Mark ends up fighting a cleverly disguised Sumata in a sword duel.

> Prod. #8636
> Airdate: March 28, 1967
> Former title: "The Killer Wave Affair"
> Writer: Tony Barrett
> Director: Alf Kjellin
> Assistant Director: Ray DeCamp
> Editor: John Rogers
> Music: Dave Grusin, Richard Shores
> Set Decorator: James Berkey
> Rerun: August 29, 1967

#28. The High and Deadly Affair.

Dr. Merek (Murray Matheson) has invented a substance spread by birds that is capable of killing the human race. Dr. Hawkins has developed an antidote. Both men are on board a plane, and April, as a stewardess, must keep Merek from killing Hawkins during the flight—even though she does not know which passengers are the two scientists.

> Prod. #8620
> Airdate: April 4, 1967
> Writer: Jameson Brewer
> Director: Dick Bennett
> Music: Dave Grusin, Richard Shores
> Rerun: None

#29. The Kooky Spook Affair.

April is threatened when she is a witness in a case, so Waverly sends her to stay until the trial in an English manor Mark has inherited. At the manor, Mark and April encounter Lady Bramwich (Estelle Winwood) and her son Cecil (Harvey Jason), who want to kill Mark so they can inherit the manor, as does Heatchcliff (John Orchard) and Treacle, the butler (Arthur Malet).

> Prod. #8640
> Airdate: April 11, 1967
> Writers: John O'Dea, Arthur Rowe
> Director: Dick Bennett
> Assistant Director: Ray DeCamp
> Editor: Jack Kampschroer
> Music: Dave Grusin, Richard Shores
> Set Decorator: Richard Spero
> Rerun: None

> *Note:* July 11, 1967, rerun was preempted by All-Star baseball game.

The *U.N.C.L.E.* Literary Works

American Publications

Man from U.N.C.L.E. U.S. paperback books, by Ace:

(unnumbered) *The Man from U.N.C.L.E.,* by Michael Avallone (British #1)

#2. *The Doomsday Affair,* by Harry Whittington (British #2)

#3. *The Copenhagen Affair,* by John Oram (British #3)

#4. *The Dagger Affair,* by David McDaniel (British #6)

#5. *The Mad Scientist Affair,* by John T. Phillifent (British #8)

#6. *The Vampire Affair,* by David McDaniel (British #9)

#7. *The Radioactive Camel Affair,* by Peter Leslie (British #7)

#8. *The Monster Wheel Affair,* by David McDaniel (British #12)

#9. *The Diving Dames Affair,* by Peter Leslie (British #10)

#10. *The Assassination Affair,* by J. Hunter Holly

#11. *The Invisibility Affair,* by Thomas Stratton

#12. *The Mind Twisters Affair,* by Thomas Stratton

#13. *The Rainbow Affair,* by David McDaniel

#14. *The Cross of Gold Affair,* by Fredric Davies

#15. *The Utopia Affair,* by David McDaniel

#16. *The Splintered Sunglasses Affair,* by Peter Leslie (British #14)

#17. *The Hollow Crown Affair,* by David McDaniel

#18. *The Unfair Fare Affair,* by Peter Leslie (British #16)

#19. *The Power Cube Affair,* by John T. Phillifent (British #15)

#20. *The Corfu Affair,* by John T. Phillifent (British #13)

#21. *The Thinking Machine Affair,* by Joel Bernard (British #11)

#22. *The Stone Cold Dead in the Market Affair,* by John Oram (British #4)

#23. *The Finger in the Sky Affair,* by Peter Leslie (British #5)

Girl from U.N.C.L.E. U.S. paperback books, by Signet:

#1. *The Birds of a Feather Affair,* by Michael Avallone

#2. *The Blazing Affair,* by Michael Avallone

The Man from U.N.C.L.E. Magazine:

Vol. 1, no. 1, "The Howling Teenagers Affair," February 1966, written by Dennis Lynds

Vol. 1, No. 2, "The Beauty and the Beast Affair," March 1966, written by Harry Whittington

Vol. 1, No. 3, "The Unspeakable Affair," April 1966, written by Dennis Lynds

Vol. 1, No. 4, "The World's End Affair," May 1966, written by John Jakes

Vol. 1, No. 5, "The Vanishing Act Affair," June 1966, written by Dennis Lynds

Vol. 1, No. 6, "The Ghost Riders Affair," July 1966, written by Harry Whittington

Vol. 2, No. 1, "The Cat and Mouse Affair," August 1966, written by Dennis Lynds

Vol. 2, No. 2, "The Brainwash Affair," September 1966, written by Harry Whittington

Vol. 2, No. 3, "The Moby Dick Affair," October 1966, written by John Jakes

Vol. 2, No. 4, "The THRUSH from THRUSH Affair," November 1966, written by Dennis Lynds

Vol. 2, No. 5, "The Goliath Affair," December 1966, written by John Jakes

Vol. 2, No. 6, "The Light Kill Affair" January 1967, written by Harry Whittington

Vol. 3, No. 1, "The Deadly Dark Affair," February 1967, written by John Jakes

Vol. 3, No. 2, "The Hungry World Affair," March 1967, written by Talmage Powell.

Vol. 3, No. 3, "The Dolls of Death Affair," April 1967, written by John Jakes

Vol. 3, No. 4, "The Synthetic Storm Affair," May 1967, written by I. G. Edmonds

Vol. 3, No. 5, "The Ugly Man Affair," May 1967, written by John Jakes

Vol. 3, No. 6, "The Electronic Frankenstein Affair," July 1967, written by Frank Belknap Long

Vol. 4, No. 1, "The Genghis Khan Affair," August 1967, written by Dennis Lynds

Vol. 4, No. 2, "The Man from Yesterday Affair," September 1967, written by John Jakes

Vol. 4, No. 3, "The Mind Sweeper Affair," October, 1967, written by Dennis Lynds

Vol. 4, No. 4, "The Volcano Box Affair," November 1967, written by Richard Curtis

Vol. 4, No. 5, "The Pillars of Salt Affair," December 1967, written by Bill Pronzini (included article on the U.N.C.L.E. Special gun written by George H. Duckworth)

Vol. 4, No. 6, "The Million Monsters Affair," January 1968, written by I. G. Edmonds

The Girl from U.N.C.L.E. Magazine:

Vol. 1, No. 1, "The Sheik of Araby Affair," December 1966, written by Richard Deming

Vol. 1, No. 2, "The Velvet Voice Affair," February 1967, written by Richard Deming

Vol. 1, No. 3, "The Burning Air Affair," April 1967, written by I. G. Edmonds

Vol. 1, No. 4, "The Deadly Drug Affair," June 1967, written by Richard Deming

Vol. 1, No. 5, "The Mesmerizing Mist Affair," August 1967, written by Charles Ventura

Vol. 1, No. 6, "The Stolen Spaceman Affair," October 1967, written by I. G. Edmonds

Vol. 2, No. 1, "The Sinister Satellite Affair," December 1967, written by I. G. Edmonds.

Man from U.N.C.L.E. comic books (published by Gold Key Comics):

#1. "The Explosive Affair," May 1965

#2. "The Fortune Cookie Affair," October 1965

#3. "The Deadly Devices Affair," November 1965

#4. "The Rip Van Solo Affair," January 1966

#5. "The Ten Little U.N.C.L.E.s Affair," March 1966

#6. "The Three Blind Mice Affair," May 1966

#7. "The Pixilated Puzzle Affair," July 1966

#8. "The Floating People Affair," September 1966

#9. "The Spirit of St. Louis Affair," November 1966

#10. "The Trojan Horse Affair," January 1967

#11. "The Three Story Giant Affair," March 1967

#12. "The Dead Man's Diary Affair," May 1967

#13. "The Flying Clowns Affair," July 1967

#14. "The Brain Drain Affair," September 1967

#15. "The Animal Agents Affair," November 1967

#16. "The Instant Disaster Affair," January 1968

#17. "The Deadly Visions Affair," March 1968

#18. "The Alien Affair," May 1968

#19. "The Knight in Shining Armor Affair," July 1968

#20. "The Deep Freeze Affair," October 1968

#21. Reprint of #10

#22. Reprint of #7

Girl from U.N.C.L.E. comic books:

#1. "The Fatal Accidents Affair," February 1967

#1. "The Kid Commandos Caper," April 1967

#3. "The Captain Kidd Affair," June 1967

#4. "The One-Way Tourist Affair," August 1967

#5. "The Harem-Scarem Affair," October 1967

British Publications

British *Man from U.N.C.L.E.* paperbacks:

There were sixteen British *Man from U.N.C.L.E.* paperbacks published. All 16 titles for *The Man from U.N.C.L.E.* series were identical to the U.S. titles, although the order was different (see listing under "American Publications").

Girl from U.N.C.L.E. paperbacks, by Four Square Books:

#1. *The Global Globules Affair,* by Simon Latter

#2. *The Birds of a Feather Affair,* by Michael Avallone

#3. *The Golden Boats of Taradata Affair,* by Simon Latter

#4. *The Cornish Pixie Affair,* by Peter Leslie

British comic books:

There were fourteen *U.N.C.L.E.* comics put out by World Distributors as part of their World Adventure Library.

#1. "The Ten Little U.N.C.L.E.s Affair"
#2. "The Three Blind Mice Affair"
#3. "The Pixilated Puzzle Affair"
#4. "The Floating People Affair"
#5. "The Target Blue Affair"
#6. "The Hong Kong Affair"
#7. "The Shufti Peanuts Affair"
#8. "The Assassins Affair"
#9. "The Magic Carpet Affair"
#10. "The Mad, Mad, Mad Affair"
#11. "The Big Bazoom Affair"
#12. "The Hot Line Affair"
#13. "The Two Face Affair"
#14. "The Humpty Dumpty Affair"

Index

Index